Digital Defence

This book aims to provide a comprehensive overview of the applications of Artificial Intelligence (AI) in the area of Cybersecurity and Digital Forensics. The various chapters of this book are written to explore how cutting-edge technologies can be used to improve the detection, prevention, and investigation of cybercrime and help protect digital assets.

Digital Defence covers an overview of deep learning and AI techniques and their relevance to cybersecurity and digital forensics, discusses common cyber threats and vulnerabilities, and how deep learning and AI can detect and prevent them. It focuses on how deep learning/artificial learning techniques can be used for intrusion detection in networks and systems, analyze and classify malware, and identify potential sources of malware attacks. This book also explores AI's role in digital forensics investigations, including data recovery, incident response and management, real-time monitoring, automated response analysis, ethical and legal considerations, and visualization. By covering these topics, this book will provide a valuable resource for researchers, students, and cybersecurity and digital forensics professionals interested in learning about the latest advances in deep learning and AI techniques and their applications.

Digital Defence

Harnessing the Power of Artificial Intelligence for Cybersecurity and Digital Forensics

Edited by Ahlad Kumar, Naveen Kumar Chaudhary, Apoorva S. Shastri, Mangal Singh, and Anand J. Kulkarni

CRC Press
Taylor & Francis Group
Boca Raton London New York

CRC Press is an imprint of the
Taylor & Francis Group, an **informa** business

Designed cover image: Shutterstock Images

First edition published 2025
by CRC Press
2385 NW Executive Center Drive, Suite 320, Boca Raton FL 33431

and by CRC Press
4 Park Square, Milton Park, Abingdon, Oxon, OX14 4RN

CRC Press is an imprint of Taylor & Francis Group, LLC

ISBN: 9781032698113 (hbk)
ISBN: 9781032714837 (pbk)
ISBN: 9781032714813 (ebk)

DOI: 10.1201/9781032714813

Typeset in Minion
by codeMantra

Contents

Preface

In an age where the digital world increasingly shapes every aspect of our lives, the threats to our cyber landscape have grown exponentially. Cyber-attacks are no longer isolated incidents; they have evolved into sophisticated, coordinated efforts capable of disrupting entire industries and governments. As technology progresses, the methods used by malicious actors also increase. The emergence of Artificial Intelligence (AI) presents both new challenges and unprecedented opportunities in the field of cybersecurity and digital forensics. This book, *Digital Defence: Harnessing the Power of Artificial Intelligence for Cybersecurity and Digital Forensics*, explores how AI-driven technologies are redefining the ways we protect and investigate the digital world. By exploring the cutting-edge advancements in AI technology and strategies, we aim to provide readers with a deep understanding of how AI can be harnessed to secure systems, mitigate risks, and enhance investigative processes in the fight against cybercrime.

Throughout the pages of this book, we will explore the intersection of AI and cybersecurity from both theoretical and practical perspectives. We examine how machine learning algorithms can detect threats in real time, how deep learning models are being used to uncover hidden patterns in complex datasets, and how AI tools are assisting forensic investigators in identifying evidence of digital crime. Whether you are a cybersecurity professional, a student of digital forensics, or simply someone keen to understand the future of digital defense, this book offers valuable insights into the dynamic role that AI plays in safeguarding our digital infrastructure.

Chapter 1, "Artificial Intelligence for Cybersecurity—Fundamentals and Evaluation," lays the foundation by exploring the core concepts of AI and its transformative role in threat detection and response mechanisms. It discusses how AI, particularly machine learning algorithms, can analyze vast datasets to identify potential security breaches, providing a proactive defense against emerging threats. By automating incident response, AI-driven tools are also revolutionizing how organizations mitigate cyber risks, ensuring rapid, efficient reactions to incidents. This chapter sets the stage for deeper discussions on how AI technologies are reshaping the landscape of cybersecurity, enabling more adaptive and robust digital defenses. Each subsequent chapter builds on this knowledge, guiding readers through advanced AI applications in digital forensics, data protection, and future trends in the ever-evolving world of cyber defense.

Chapter 2, "Predicting Tomorrow's Threats: A Legal Framework for AI-Based Predictive Analytics in Cybersecurity," explores the delicate balance between the rapid advancements of AI in predicting cyber threats and the slower pace of legal regulation. Drawing on the metaphor of Zeno's paradox, this chapter illustrates the constant race between technological innovation and the legal system's efforts to regulate it. As AI becomes increasingly effective at identifying and mitigating future threats through predictive analytics, there is a growing need for legal frameworks to ensure the responsible use of such technologies. This chapter examines the pressing challenge of aligning AI's predictive capabilities with the protection of individuals' rights, proposing that an enhanced regulatory structure is essential to maintain privacy and uphold procedural fairness. By addressing the legal and ethical considerations tied to AI-based cybersecurity, this chapter provides a crucial discussion on how laws must evolve to keep pace with the emerging digital threat landscape.

Chapter 3, "The Invisible Defence: Detecting Zero-Day Threats with AI," tackles one of the most formidable challenges in cybersecurity—zero-day threats, which exploit unknown vulnerabilities. This chapter explores how AI provides an innovative and proactive defense against these hidden dangers, surpassing traditional methods that often struggle to detect them. By analyzing behavior patterns and identifying potential exploits, AI offers a dynamic approach to zero-day threat detection, adapting to unforeseen challenges in real time. Through real-world case studies, this chapter showcases successful implementations of AI in mitigating zero-day attacks, highlighting its evolving capabilities. It also contrasts AI-driven solutions with conventional security measures, such as signature-based detection, illustrating how AI fills crucial gaps by learning and improving continuously. Furthermore, this chapter delves into the technical foundations of AI in cybersecurity, from machine learning algorithms to neural networks, while emphasizing the critical role of large datasets in training these systems. This exploration provides readers with a thorough understanding of how AI is revolutionizing zero-day threat detection, offering a forward-thinking defense strategy that not only reacts but anticipates threats before they can cause harm.

Chapter 4, "Fusion of Deep Architectures in Intent-Driven Networks for Intrusion Detection" explores the cutting-edge integration of AI into Intent-Based Networking (IBN), a modern approach to network management designed to fulfill specific business objectives. This chapter delves into how IBN differs from traditional network management by ensuring networks operate reliably and efficiently, adhering to business policies and intent. It further examines the potential of leveraging AI—specifically machine learning and deep learning—to enhance security and manage network intrusions within these intent-driven environments. This chapter highlights the use of advanced AI models, including Random Forest Classifiers, ID-convolutional neural networks, and hybrid architectures combining convolutional layers with Long short-term memory (LSTM) networks, to detect and respond to security breaches. By presenting results from models trained on both imbalanced and balanced datasets, this chapter offers insight into how deep learning architectures can be utilized to create smarter, more secure networks. Through this fusion of AI and IBN, this chapter demonstrates the effectiveness of using deep architectures to improve intrusion detection, thereby laying the groundwork for more secure and adaptive business networks.

Chapter 5, "An In-depth Analysis of Intrusion Detection Systems with an Emphasis on Multi-Access Edge Computing and Machine Learning," addresses the growing complexity of network security in the age of the Internet of Things (IoT). As IoT applications expand, the volume of network data and computational demands increase, creating vulnerabilities in resource-constrained IoT devices. This chapter explores how Multi-Access Edge Computing (MEC) offers a solution by offloading tasks to the edge, enhancing network efficiency and security. It provides a comprehensive review of network intrusion detection systems (NIDSs) for IoT environments, with a particular focus on the integration of MEC and machine learning to improve detection capabilities. This chapter compares various datasets, performance metrics, and deployment strategies in NIDS design, proposing a MEC-based framework to address the security challenges posed by IoT networks. Special attention is given to the evolution of IoT and Industrial IoT (IIoT), the growing demand for specialized intrusion detection systems, and the application of anomaly-based Intrusion Detection System (IDS) methods. It also presents a critical analysis of security mechanisms, emerging tools, and the unique challenges of securing IoT/IIoT environments, offering insights into future trends and the role of machine learning in addressing these evolving threats.

Chapter 6, "The Legal and Ethical Crossroads of Artificial Intelligence in Cybersecurity and Digital Forensics," represents the complex intersection of AI technologies with legal and ethical frameworks in the digital security landscape. AI, with its broad applications in deep learning and machine learning, has become integral to securing cyberspace, yet its rapid evolution presents significant challenges in terms of accountability and ethical responsibility. This chapter begins by examining the current gaps in cybersecurity solutions, emphasizing the need for more advanced practices that align with both legal regulations and ethical standards. It provides a thorough review of existing legal frameworks governing AI's role in cybersecurity and digital forensics, addressing the critical issue of decision-making accountability when AI systems are involved. The latter half delves into the challenges posed by the use of automation in digital forensics, highlighting legal discrepancies and the urgent need for a standardized global approach to AI regulation. This chapter stresses the importance of developing legal infrastructures that protect human rights while enabling the continued advancement of AI in cybersecurity, underscoring the delicate balance between technological progress and ethical governance.

Chapter 7, "Multi-factor Authentication for Smart Internet Transactions," explores the growing need for enhanced security measures in online communication, particularly as internet usage continues to rise. As traditional text-based passwords become increasingly vulnerable to attacks, this chapter introduces multi-level graphical password authentication as a more secure and user-friendly alternative. By allowing users to select images, patterns, or gestures for authentication, graphical passwords address the limitations of text-based methods, offering better memorability and increased resistance to dictionary-based and brute-force attacks. This chapter discusses how this approach not only enhances security by expanding the search space but also provides a more inclusive experience, benefiting users who may struggle with alphanumeric passwords or have visual impairments. By integrating graphical and multi-factor authentication, this chapter highlights innovative solutions to safeguard sensitive information in smart internet transactions.

Chapter 8, "Adaptive Machine Learning Strategies for Next-Generation Botnet Host Detection" addresses the rising threat of botnet attacks in the expanding IoT ecosystem.

With IoT devices increasing the vulnerability of networks, this chapter introduces advanced machine learning and deep learning techniques to enhance the detection of botnet hosts. A novel detection framework is presented, leveraging balanced datasets and dimensionality reduction to improve anomaly detection accuracy. Experimental results demonstrate significant improvements over traditional detection methods, proving that the proposed solution is not only more effective but also adaptable to evolving threats. This chapter highlights the scalability of the method and its potential to reshape cybersecurity strategies for IoT networks. Additionally, it explores the integration of emerging technologies, such as anomaly detection techniques and blockchain, to bolster security. By urging interdisciplinary collaboration and innovation, this chapter envisions a more secure digital landscape, advocating for continued research and methodological advancements to address the sophisticated nature of modern botnet threats.

Chapter 9, "Artificial Intelligence-Based Cybercrime Prevention and Data Security," examines the critical role of legal frameworks in regulating online activities and protecting against cybercrime. This chapter begins by examining key legislation, such as India's Information Technology Act of 2000, designed to address and mitigate cyber threats. It contrasts this with China's stringent internet censorship and highlights the necessity for self-regulation in cyberspace given its unique geopolitical context. This chapter also explores the intersection of cyber forensics—where technology aids legal processes—and the global nature of cybercrime, including the use of credit cards and online bank accounts for illicit activities. By discussing real cases and the establishment of specialized units, such as the Cyber Crime Unit by the CBI, this chapter underscores the growing prevalence of cybercrime. It emphasizes the importance of cybersecurity education and awareness initiatives, particularly for women, and the need for law enforcement to be well-versed in cyber threats and safety. Additionally, this chapter highlights the significance of robust backup methods and archiving strategies to ensure business continuity and resilience against cyber incidents.

Chapter 10, "Insight into How Legal and Ethical Considerations Improve Artificial Intelligence Capabilities to Enhance the Performance of Cyber Forensic Accounting," illustrates the intricate relationship between legal and ethical considerations (LEC) and the performance of cyber forensic accounting (PCFA). This chapter investigates how artificial intelligence capabilities (AIC) mediate this relationship, using a proposed model supported by structural equation modeling and validated through statistical data from surveys conducted with accountants in small and medium-sized enterprises (SMEs). The analysis confirms significant interconnections between LEC, AIC, and PCFA, demonstrating how thoughtful legal and ethical frameworks can enhance the performance of AI in forensic accounting. By providing nuanced insights into these dynamics, this chapter not only offers a foundation for further research but also serves as a practical guide for practitioners and policymakers. It highlights how effective rules and policies regarding AI management can optimize cyber forensic accounting practices, ultimately leading to more robust and reliable financial investigations.

Editor Biographies

Ahlad Kumar is currently serving as Assistant Professor at the National Forensic Sciences University (Institute of National Importance) (under the Home Ministry), Gandhinagar. Dr. Kumar has several papers published in well-renowned journals, including those of IEEE. His areas of interest include machine learning, deep learning, reinforcement learning, and analog design.

Naveen Kumar Chaudhary is a Professor of Cyber Security and Campus Director of National Forensic Sciences University Goa Campus. He is also Courtesy Research Professor at Florida International University in Miami, USA. He has extensive experience spanning more than 27 years in engineering education, research, and government. He has worked extensively on the formulation and implementation of policies and techno-legal frameworks in the domain of cybersecurity, e-governance, and forensic science. He has been part of many high-level committees and inter-ministerial groups on education, cybersecurity, and emerging technologies. He is actively involved in promoting start-up ecosystems for developing low-cost indigenous cyber-forensic solutions and his area of interest includes cybersecurity, digital forensics, drones, advanced cyber range, next generation networks, artificial intelligence, and cyber-forensic investigations. Dr. Naveen Kumar Chaudhary is an IETE Fellow, IEEE Senior Member, and Honorary Life Member of the Soft Computing Research Society. He is the recipient of a letter of appreciation for his contribution toward the cause of literacy from Brent St. Denis, MP, Algoma Canada, in 1994, Dubai SEWA award for his contribution to cybersecurity education in 2022, and Suryadatta Cybertech Award 2024, for exemplary contribution in the field of cybersecurity and digital forensics.

Apoorva S. Shastri holds a PhD in Optimization Algorithms and Applications from Symbiosis International (Deemed University). Currently, she is Research Assistant Professor at Institute of Artificial Intelligence at the Dr. Vishwanath Karad MITWPU, Pune, India. Her research interests include optimization algorithms, VLSI design, multi-objective optimization, continuous, discrete, and combinatorial optimization, complex systems, manufacturing, and self-organizing systems.

Mangal Singh is working as Associate Professor, Electronics & Telecommunication Engineering at Symbiosis Institute of Technology, Symbiosis International (Deemed University), Pune. He has an experience of more than 23 years in the field of Teaching,

Research and Administration. He is Senior Member of IEEE and a life member of the IETE and ISTE, India.

Anand J. Kulkarni holds a PhD in Optimization from Nanyang Technological University, Singapore, MS in AI from University of Regina, Canada. He worked as Research Fellow at University of Windsor, Canada. Currently, he is working as Professor & Associate Director at Institute of Artificial Intelligence at the Dr. Vishwanath Karad MITWPU, Pune, India. He is the founder of OAT Research Lab and has published over 80 research papers along with 23 books.

Contributors

Basim Alhadidi
Department of Computer Information System
AI-Balqa Applied University, Jordan

Mangesh Bedekar
Department of Computer Engineering and Technology
Dr. Vishwanath Karad MIT World Peace University, Pune, Maharashtra

Panem Charanarur
Department of Cyber Security and Digital Forensics
National Forensic Sciences University (NFSU), Tripura, India

Manali Desai
Department of Computer Engineering and Technology
Dr. Vishwanath Karad MIT World Peace University, Pune, Maharashtra

Ndubuisi Godcares
Department of Artificial Intelligence & Machine Learning Symbiosis Institute of Technology
Symbiosis International (Deemed University), Pune, Maharashtra, India

Srinivasa Rao Gundu
Department of Digital Forensic Sciences, School of Sciences
Malla Reddy University, Hyderabad, India

Debojyoti Gupta
MSc. Digital Forensics and Information Security
National Forensic Sciences University, Gandhinagar, Gujarat, India

Aniket Jhariya
Symbiosis Institute of Technology
Symbiosis International (Deemed University), Pune, Maharashtra, India

Obinna Johnbosco Awoke
Department of Computer Science
African University of Science and Technology, Abuja, Nigeria

Manas Ranjan Kabat
Department of Computer Science and Engineering
Veer Surendra Sai University of Technology, Burla, India

Shubham Kumar Saras
Department of CSE Dr. Ambedkar Institute of Technology
Bengaluru

Joshua Lobo
Symbiosis Institute of Technology
Symbiosis International (Deemed University), Pune, India

B. Madhu
Department of CSE Dr. Ambedkar Institute of Technology
Bengaluru

Rasmita Kumari Mohanty
Department of (CyS, DS) and AI&DS, VNR Vignana Jyothi Institute of Engineering and Technology
Bachupally, Hyderabad, India

Anurag Mogal
Symbiosis Institute of Technology
Symbiosis International (Deemed University), Pune, India

Vinayak Musale
Department of Computer Engineering and Technology,
Dr. Vishwanath Karad MIT World Peace University, Pune, Maharashtra

Sarvesh Nimbulkar
Student, School of Law
CHRIST (Deemed to be University), Bengaluru

Khushi Pandey
Department of Computer Engineering and Technology,
Dr. Vishwanath Karad MIT World Peace University, Pune, Maharashtra

Dhvani Parekh
Symbiosis Institute of Technology
Symbiosis International (Deemed University), Pune, India

M.A. Vu Kien Phuc
University of Economics, Ho Chi Minh City, Vietnam

Satya Prakash Sahoo
Department of Computer Science and Engineering
Veer Surendra Sai University of Technology, Burla, India

Rajesh Prasad
Department of Computer Science
African University of Science and Technology, Abuja, Nigeria

Pham Quang Huy
University of Economics, Ho Chi Minh City, Vietnam

Souradeep Rakshit
Assistant Professor, School of Law
CHRIST (Deemed to be University), Bengaluru

Najeeb Saiyed
Department of Artificial Intelligence & Mac hine Learning Symbiosis Institute of Technology
Symbiosis International (Deemed University), Pune, Maharashtra, India

Shruti Saxena
School of Cyber Security and Digital Forensics
National Forensics Sciences University, Gujarat, India

B.N. Shubhada
Department of CSE Dr. Ambedkar Institute of Technology
Bengaluru

Mangal Singh
Symbiosis Institute of Technology
Symbiosis International (Deemed University), Pune, India

Nikunj Tahilramani
Department of Big Data Analytics, Adani Institute of Digital Technology Management
Gujarat, India

Gyanendra Tiwari
Department of Computer Engineering and Technology,
Dr. Vishwanath Karad MIT World Peace University, Pune, Maharashtra

J. Vijaylaxmi
PVKK Degree & PG College
Andhra Pradesh, India

Dhanashri Wategaonkar
Department of Computer Engineering and Technology
Dr. Vishwanath Karad MIT World Peace University, Pune, Maharashtra

CHAPTER 1

Artificial Intelligence for Cybersecurity—Fundamentals and Evaluation

Rasmita Kumari Mohanty, Satya Prakash Sahoo, Manas Ranjan Kabat, and Basim Alhadidi

1.1 INTRODUCTION

An overview of the field of artificial intelligence (AI) for cybersecurity is provided in this chapter.

This automation is particularly valuable in handling routine tasks, allowing human experts to focus on more complex and strategic aspects of cybersecurity [1]. AI's role extends to the prediction and prevention of cyberattacks. By leveraging predictive analytics and machine learning (ML), AI systems can anticipate potential vulnerabilities, weak points, or attack patterns, enabling organizations to preemptively fortify their defenses. This proactive stance is critical in the dynamic landscape of cyber threats, where swift adaptation to emerging risks is paramount. Furthermore, AI plays a pivotal role in user behavior analytics. By establishing baselines of normal behavior for users and systems, AI algorithms can identify deviations that may indicate unauthorized access or malicious activities [2]. This behavior-based approach enhances the accuracy of threat detection and reduces false positives, contributing to more effective cybersecurity strategies.

The deployment of AI in cybersecurity also addresses the challenge of handling the overwhelming volume of security data generated daily. AI-driven tools can sift through and analyze massive datasets, extracting actionable insights and trends that might go unnoticed using traditional methods. This data-centric approach allows organizations to make informed decisions and prioritize their response efforts based on the most significant threats [3].

DOI: 10.1201/9781032714813-1

Nevertheless, there are several difficulties with implementing AI in cybersecurity. It is concerning that adversarial assaults, in which malevolent parties control AI systems, are a possibility. Generative adversarial networks (GANs), an area of active research and development, are being used to ensure the security and resilience of AI systems against such attacks. We will begin with a brief theoretical overview of GANs, showing how they are the impartial equivalent of the more extensively researched discriminative networks. Next, we will develop a framework that outlines the ideal characteristics of a high-quality generative model. Additionally, we will outline the fundamental probabilistic ideas that are necessary to comprehend in order to completely understand how various strategies address the problem of GANs. GANs may be used to learn deep models without the requirement for extensively annotated training data [4]. They do this by deriving propagation signals from two networks in a competitive manner. The notions that GANs may learn are applicable to a wide range of applications, including image synthesis, semantic modification of pictures, style transfer, image super resolution, and categorization. The purpose of this chapter is to provide an overview of GANs to the signal engineering community by leveraging well-known concepts and analogies whenever possible [5]. Apart from distinguishing various techniques for training and building GANs, we also highlight unresolved issues in their theory and implementation.

As the digital landscape expands and evolves, cybersecurity has become a critical concern for individuals, organizations, and governments worldwide. Traditional security measures often struggle to keep pace with the rapidly changing threat environment, where new vulnerabilities and sophisticated attack methods emerge daily [6]. AI has emerged as a transformative technology in addressing these challenges, offering innovative solutions that enhance the effectiveness and efficiency of cybersecurity practices. AI's application in cybersecurity encompasses a range of techniques, from ML and deep learning to natural language processing (NLP) and anomaly detection. These technologies enable the automation of threat detection, the prediction of potential security breaches, and the intelligent response to incidents. By analyzing vast amounts of data and identifying patterns that may be indicative of malicious activities, AI systems can provide real-time insights and responses that traditional methods may not achieve [7].

The integration of AI into cybersecurity not only improves the accuracy and speed of threat identification but also enhances the ability to adapt to new and evolving threats. For instance, AI-driven systems can detect and classify malware with high precision, recognize unusual network behaviors, and automate incident response processes. This proactive approach helps organizations stay ahead of potential threats and reduce the impact of cyberattacks. AI encompasses a range of technologies that utilize algorithms to simulate human intelligence. In cybersecurity, the most relevant AI techniques include ML, deep learning, and NLP. ML algorithms, such as supervised, unsupervised, and reinforcement learning, are employed to analyze and interpret large volumes of security data. Deep learning, a subset of ML, involves neural networks with multiple layers that can detect complex patterns and anomalies. NLP helps in analyzing and understanding textual data from security logs and communications. AI algorithms can identify and classify potential threats by analyzing network traffic, system behaviors, and historical data. This includes detecting malware, phishing attacks, and unauthorized access attempts. By establishing a baseline of normal system behavior, AI can detect deviations that may indicate a security breach. This proactive approach helps in identifying previously unknown threats and zero-day attacks. AI-driven systems can automate responses to detected threats, such as isolating affected systems, blocking malicious activities, and initiating predefined security protocols. This reduces the response time and minimizes human intervention [8]. AI tools can predict and assess vulnerabilities in software and hardware systems, helping organizations to prioritize and address security weaknesses before they are exploited by attackers.

1.2 BACKGROUND DETAILS

1.2.1 The Surge of Artificial Intelligence

The rapid advancement of AI is evidence of humanity's continuous effort to imitate and surpass human cognitive capacities in computers. AI has undergone an unprecedented increase over the past few decades, moving from theoretical concepts to practical, impacting technologies that are present in almost every facet of modern life. A number of elements have come together to cause this increase, including previously unheard-of computer capacity, an abundance of data, and revolutionary developments in ML and algorithms [9]. These factors have sparked a renaissance in AI, pushing it to the forefront of innovation in a variety of sectors, including healthcare, finance, delivery, and entertainment. The spread of AI can be seen in many different ways, such as self-driving cars negotiating tricky terrain, consumer decisions being shaped by personalized recommendation systems, and smooth human-computer communication made possible by NLP. Furthermore, the automation and augmentation capabilities of AI have completely changed the way businesses run, redefining worker roles and boosting production. But there are several things to take into account with this spike. As AI integration grows, caution is required due to ethical quandaries, privacy issues, and the possibility of societal disruption. The rapid development of AI necessitates a methodical strategy that strikes a balance between innovation, moral standards, and government regulation. However, the explosion of AI offers countless prospects, with advancements in scientific research, environmental sustainability, and healthcare diagnostics all anticipated. This new era is characterized by the combination of human creativity with technical innovation, and it represents a significant turning point in our quest for machines that are more intelligent and adaptable than humans, enabling us to perform tasks beyond our current capacity [10].

1.2.2 Aggregation or Assembly of Generative Models

The combination or assemblage of generative models is a significant development in the field of AI, as the coming together of several models results in increased capacities and improved creative potential. With this method, various generative models—all of which are skilled at yielding distinctive results—are combined to form a single, integrated framework that can produce data that is richer, more varied, and more accurate. The goal of this strategic fusion is to leverage the unique architectures, training approaches, and specialized functionality of various generative models to combine their strengths. The resulting group overcomes the constraints of any one method by inheriting the collective wisdom and variety of viewpoints stored within each component model. Through this combination, the combined generative models show an increased ability to produce complex outputs in a variety of domains, including texts, graphics, and even whole virtual worlds. This combination not only improves the quality of the content produced but also strengthens the ensemble's resilience, allowing it to work over a wider range of data distributions and provide outputs that are more diverse and realistic. Additionally, this aggregation method has the potential to improve the general stability of produced outputs and mitigate biases and mode collapse—all of which are flaws in individual models [11].

By working together, these models create a paradigm in which the whole performs better than the sum of its parts, opening the door for increasingly complex and versatile AI systems. Nevertheless, there are certain difficulties in aggregating generative models, such as model compatibility nuances, computational complexity, and the requirement for efficient coordination among ensemble members. However, this strategy offers an exciting new direction for AI research, with unmatched potential to spur innovation in a variety of sectors, from simulations and creative content creation to the advancement in scientific studies and problem-solving in intricate, real-world situations.

1.2.3 Enrichment of Neural Networks

Neural network enriching is a significant advancement in AI, tracing a path from increased network depth to increased learning capacity and increased problem-solving ability. In order to enable these systems to recognize and accurately represent complex patterns within data, this procedure entails the purposeful addition of layers to neural network topologies, hence deepening their design. In order to handle the inherent complexities of real-world data, this enrichment is essential. As neural architectures get more complex, these networks are able to identify abstractions and hierarchical characteristics that are buried in large, diverse datasets. With each additional layer, the network's ability to extract more complex features from the raw input increases, allowing it to capture subtleties and larger abstractions present in the data.

Because of their deeper structure, the enriched neural networks can train more effectively and can handle more complex tasks that need a more complex knowledge of context and relationships within the data. This augmentation drives progress in a number of fields, including self-driving cars, processing natural languages, computer vision, and science. Notwithstanding, the augmentation of neural networks poses various obstacles, such as escalated processing requirements, the possibility of overfitting, and the requirement for meticulous optimization to efficiently leverage the benefits of more profound architectures. However, the quest to improve neural networks is a new direction in AI research, opening the door to systems that will be able to understand and process data with never-before-seen depth and complexity. Increased network depth portends a time when AI systems will be able to handle complexity on par with human comprehension, leading to innovation and achievements in a variety of fields and businesses.

Development of the Adversarial Notion: This is a paradigm change in the way computers learn, adapt, and change, and it represents a major turning point in the field of AI. The idea behind this is that by placing two entities—usually neural networks—against one another in a framework for competitive learning, the capabilities of AI systems can increase dramatically. This novel method, made popular by GANs, represents a dynamic interaction between a method of discrimination plus a generator network of neurons. The discriminator's job is to discern between created and legitimate data, whereas the generator's goal is to produce synthetic data that is identical to real data. The two systems continuously hone and enhance their capabilities through this aggressive process, leading to a mutual escalation of efficiency. Revolutionary advances in numerous fields have resulted from the creation of the adversarial notion.

GANs have proven to be able to produce remarkably lifelike images in computer vision, opening up new possibilities for design and artistic applications as well as helping with data augmentation. Adversarial approaches have improved the creation of languages and comprehension in the processing of natural languages, extending the linguistic capabilities of AI. But there are certain issues with this idea. The intricacy of training hostile networks, problems such as mode collapse (limited changes produced by the generator), and the trade-off between discriminant and generator stability are still being studied and improved. However, the developments made in the Counterproductive Notion herald a new era of AI research with promising applications in a variety of industries, including cybersecurity, entertainment, and healthcare. This idea has the potential to change how AI systems learn as it develops and becomes more refined, producing robots that are more resilient, imaginative, and adaptive and that can handle ever-more difficult real-world challenges. Figure 1.1, AI-driven approach significantly improves the speed and effectiveness of malware detection compared to traditional methods, offering robust protection against evolving cyber threats. By continually learning from new data, deep learning models adapt to emerging malware techniques, reinforcing overall cybersecurity defenses.

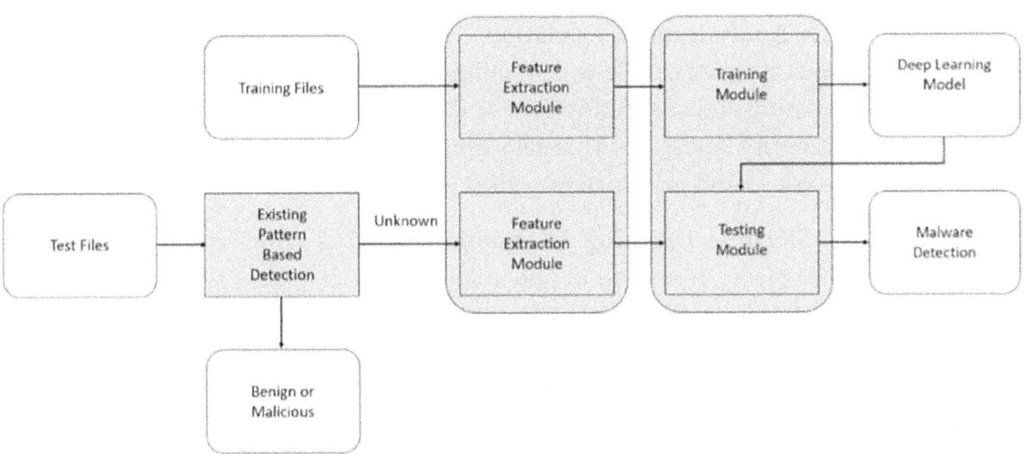

FIGURE 1.1 AI-driven system architecture.

1.3 IMPORTANCE: HOW AI IS APPLIED IN CYBERSECURITY

- **Threat Detection and Analysis**: AI, particularly ML algorithms, is highly effective in analyzing large datasets to detect patterns and anomalies. This capability enables early identification of potential security threats, including previously unseen or subtle attack patterns. AI algorithms continuously learn from new data, adapting and improving their detection capabilities over time.

- **Behavioral Analytics**: AI is used for behavioral analysis to identify unusual patterns in user activities and network behaviors. By establishing a baseline of normal behavior, AI systems can detect deviations that may indicate malicious activities. This approach is valuable in detecting insider threats and advanced persistent threats (APTs) that may go unnoticed by traditional rule-based systems.

- **Incident Response Automation**: AI automates incident response processes, enabling rapid identification and containment of security incidents. Automated responses can be triggered for known threats, freeing up cybersecurity teams to focus on more complex tasks. This automation is crucial for reducing response times and minimizing the impact of security breaches.

- **Predictive Analysis and Risk Management**: AI models leverage predictive analytics to assess potential vulnerabilities and predict future cyber threats. By analyzing historical data and identifying trends, AI can help organizations proactively address security risks before they are exploited. This predictive approach is essential for staying ahead of emerging threats.

- **Phishing Detection and Prevention**: AI is utilized to enhance the detection of phishing attacks, a common vector for cyber threats. NLP and ML algorithms can analyze emails and other communication channels to identify phishing attempts, reducing the likelihood of users falling victim to social engineering attacks.

- **Security Data Analysis and Correlation**: The vast amount of security data generated by various systems can be overwhelming for human analysts. AI technologies excel in processing and correlating diverse data sources, providing a comprehensive view of the security landscape. This data-centric approach helps organizations make informed decisions and prioritize responses effectively.

- **Adversarial Machine Learning Mitigation**: As AI is adopted in cybersecurity, there is an increasing awareness of potential adversarial attacks against ML models. Research and development efforts focus on creating robust AI systems that can resist manipulation and attacks, ensuring the reliability of AI-driven security.

1.4 AI METHODS IN CYBERSECURITY

1.4.1 Machine Learning

Supervised Learning: Trained on labeled datasets, supervised learning algorithms can identify patterns and make predictions. In cybersecurity, this is often used for malware detection, intrusion detection, and classification of network traffic.

Supervised learning, a foundational method in AI, has proven to be a powerful tool in addressing various cybersecurity challenges. In this paradigm, algorithms are trained on labeled datasets, where the input data and corresponding desired outputs are provided, enabling the model to learn patterns and make predictions. The application of supervised learning in cybersecurity encompasses several crucial areas. One primary use of supervised learning in cybersecurity is in the realm of malware detection. Security experts can curate datasets containing examples of both benign and malicious software, allowing the supervised learning algorithm to learn distinctive features of known malware. As a result, the model becomes adept at identifying and classifying new, previously unseen malware based on the patterns it has learned during training.

Intrusion detection systems (IDSs) also benefit significantly from supervised learning. By training on labeled datasets that distinguish between normal network behaviors and various types of attacks, these systems can effectively identify and respond to suspicious activities. The ability to recognize known attack patterns enhances the system's accuracy in flagging potential security threats, allowing for swift and targeted responses. Supervised learning is instrumental in email filtering and phishing detection. By training models on labeled datasets containing examples of legitimate and phishing emails, the algorithm can learn to recognize common characteristics and patterns associated with phishing attempts. This proactive approach aids in preventing users from falling victim to social engineering attacks, contributing to a more secure digital environment.

Furthermore, supervised learning is employed in user authentication and access control. By training on historical data of user logins and activities, models can establish a baseline for normal user behavior. When deviations from this baseline occur, such as unauthorized access attempts, the system can promptly flag and respond to potential security breaches, bolstering overall access security. Despite its efficacy, supervised learning in cybersecurity is not without challenges. The reliance on labeled datasets can be limiting, as it may not cover all possible variations of cyber threats. Additionally, the dynamic and evolving nature of cyber threats requires constant updates to training data and models to ensure adaptability.

Unsupervised Learning: Unsupervised learning algorithms can detect anomalies and patterns without labeled data. They are valuable for identifying unusual behaviors that may indicate cyber threats, such as insider threats or previously unknown attack vectors. Unsupervised learning stands as a dynamic and adaptive approach in the realm of cybersecurity, addressing the challenges posed by the ever-evolving nature of cyber threats. In this paradigm, algorithms are entrusted with discovering patterns and anomalies within unlabeled datasets, allowing them to autonomously identify potential security issues without prior knowledge of specific threat signatures. The application of unsupervised learning in cybersecurity encompasses several key areas, showcasing its versatility and effectiveness.

An essential application of unsupervised learning in cybersecurity is anomaly detection. By analyzing normal patterns within network traffic, user behavior, or system activities, unsupervised learning algorithms can discern deviations that may signify a security breach or abnormal activity. This approach is particularly valuable in identifying novel or subtle threats that may go unnoticed by traditional, rule-based systems. IDS benefit significantly from unsupervised learning techniques. Instead of relying on predefined rules for known attack patterns, these systems leverage unsupervised learning to establish a baseline of normal network behavior. Deviations from this baseline are flagged as potential intrusions, allowing for real-time detection and response to emerging threats that may not have been previously identified. Unsupervised learning plays a crucial role in clustering and grouping similar data points without explicit guidance. In cybersecurity, this is applied to categorize and group similar types of malware or identify commonalities in attack techniques. Clustering helps security analysts gain insights into the structure of cyber threats, aiding in more effective threat intelligence and response strategies.

The analysis of large-scale and unstructured data is another area where unsupervised learning shines in cybersecurity. By employing techniques such as clustering or dimensionality reduction, algorithms can uncover hidden patterns within massive datasets, helping to identify trends, correlations, and potential vulnerabilities that might elude traditional analysis methods. Despite its strengths, unsupervised learning is not without challenges. The identification of meaningful anomalies amidst the noise of normal variations can be complex. Additionally, the interpretation of detected anomalies often requires human expertise to distinguish between benign changes and true security threats.

1.4.2 Deep Learning: Neural Networks

Deep learning, a subset of ML, involves neural networks with multiple layers. Deep neural networks excel at processing complex data, and they are used in tasks like image recognition, NLP, and behavior analysis for cybersecurity.

The application of deep learning neural networks in cybersecurity represents a cutting-edge approach to addressing the increasingly sophisticated and dynamic nature of cyber threats. Deep learning, a subset of ML, involves neural networks with multiple layers that autonomously learn intricate patterns and representations from vast amounts of data. In the realm of cybersecurity, deep learning neural networks play a pivotal role in various aspects, showcasing their ability to enhance threat detection and response mechanisms. One of the primary applications of deep learning neural networks in cybersecurity is in the realm of malware detection. Traditional signature-based methods struggle to keep pace with the rapid evolution of malware variants. Deep learning models, particularly convolutional neural networks (CNNs) and recurrent neural networks (RNNs), can autonomously learn intricate features of malware, enabling them to identify previously unseen threats based on learned patterns and behaviors.

IDS benefit significantly from the deep learning paradigm. Deep neural networks can process complex and high-dimensional data, such as network traffic patterns, to discern subtle anomalies indicative of potential cyber-attacks. The ability to automatically learn and adapt to new attack vectors enhances the accuracy of intrusion detection, enabling organizations to respond swiftly to emerging threats. Deep learning is also instrumental in the analysis of unstructured data, such as text and log files, through NLP techniques. NLP-powered deep learning models can be deployed for sentiment analysis and contextual understanding, aiding in the identification of malicious activities embedded in communication channels, phishing attempts, or other social engineering attacks. Moreover, the use of RNNs and long short-term memory (LSTM) networks is prevalent in the context of behavioral analytics. These models excel in capturing temporal dependencies within sequences of data, making them well-suited for analyzing user behavior over time. By establishing baseline behaviors and identifying deviations, deep learning models contribute to the detection of insider threats and anomalous activities.

While the capabilities of deep learning in cybersecurity are promising, challenges exist, including the need for extensive labeled datasets, potential adversarial attacks, and interpretability of complex neural network models. As the cyber threat landscape evolves, ongoing research and development efforts are essential to refining deep learning techniques, ensuring their effectiveness in real-world cybersecurity scenarios.

1.4.3 Natural Language Processing

NLP techniques are employed to analyze and understand human language. In cybersecurity, NLP is used for analyzing text-based data, such as emails and messages, to detect phishing attempts, malware, or other malicious activities.

NLP is making significant strides in the field of cybersecurity, leveraging its ability to analyze and understand human language to enhance various aspects of digital defense. In the realm of cyber threat intelligence and monitoring, NLP plays a pivotal role in processing and extracting valuable insights from vast amounts of textual data. One key application of NLP in cybersecurity is in the analysis of security-related documents, reports, and threat intelligence feeds. NLP algorithms can sift through unstructured text to identify and extract relevant information, such as indicators of compromise, attack patterns, and vulnerabilities. This automated analysis accelerates the identification of emerging threats, aiding security analysts in making timely and informed decisions.

Phishing detection and prevention benefit significantly from NLP techniques. By analyzing the linguistic and contextual elements of emails, messages, or other communication channels, NLP algorithms can identify patterns indicative of phishing attempts. This includes recognizing malicious URLs, detecting social engineering tactics, and differentiating between legitimate and fraudulent communication, thus reducing the risk of falling victim to phishing attacks. NLP is also instrumental in the development of security chatbots and virtual assistants. These AI-powered tools can understand and respond to natural language queries from users, providing real-time assistance in cybersecurity-related matters. Whether it's guiding users on secure practices or assisting with incident response, NLP-driven chatbots contribute to a more user-friendly and responsive cybersecurity environment.

In the context of security incident response, NLP aids in the extraction and analysis of information from incident reports, logs, and incident-related communication. This enables security teams to quickly assess the scope and impact of incidents, facilitating a more efficient and coordinated response to mitigate potential risks. Furthermore, NLP contributes to the development of context-aware security systems. By understanding the context in which security events occur, NLP models can prioritize alerts based on their relevance and potential impact, reducing the noise for cybersecurity analysts and allowing them to focus on the most critical threats.

Despite the benefits, challenges in NLP for cybersecurity include the need for robust models that can handle complex language structures, adapt to evolving attack techniques, and address issues related to ambiguity and contextual understanding.

1.4.4 Predictive Analytics

AI-driven predictive analytics assess historical data to predict future cyber threats and vulnerabilities. By identifying patterns and trends, organizations can proactively address potential security risks before they are exploited.

Predictive analysis in cybersecurity emerges as a crucial strategy to anticipate and proactively address potential cyber threats before they manifest. By harnessing advanced analytics and ML, predictive analysis enables organizations to assess historical data, identify patterns, and make informed predictions about future cyber risks. This methodology significantly enhances the overall resilience of cybersecurity defenses. One primary application of predictive analysis is in the identification of vulnerabilities and potential exploits. By analyzing historical attack patterns and system weaknesses, predictive models can anticipate areas of potential risk. This allows organizations to implement preemptive measures, such as patching vulnerable systems or adjusting configurations, to thwart potential cyberattacks before they can be exploited.

Threat intelligence is another area where predictive analysis plays a pivotal role. By continuously monitoring and analyzing a wide array of data sources, including open-source intelligence and dark web forums, predictive models can identify emerging threats and evolving attack techniques. This foresight empowers organizations to stay ahead of the curve, adapting their defenses to mitigate risks posed by new and sophisticated cyber threats. Predictive analysis is instrumental in user behavior analytics. By examining historical user activities and identifying deviations from established patterns, predictive models can flag potential insider threats or compromised accounts. This proactive approach enables organizations to take preemptive actions, such as revoking access or implementing additional authentication measures, to mitigate risks associated with insider attacks. Additionally, predictive analysis aids in prioritizing security incidents based on their potential impact and likelihood of occurrence. By assigning risk scores to various events, organizations can focus their resources on addressing the most critical threats. This risk-driven approach enhances the efficiency of incident response efforts, ensuring that cybersecurity teams are deployed where they can have the most significant impact.

While predictive analysis provides valuable insights, challenges exist, including the need for accurate and up-to-date data, the dynamic nature of cyber threats, and the potential for false positives. Continual refinement of predictive models and collaboration within the cybersecurity community are essential to address these challenges and enhance the accuracy of predictions.

1.4.5 Behavioral Analytics

Behavioral analytics involves monitoring and analyzing user and entity behaviors. AI algorithms establish baseline behaviors and identify anomalies that may indicate malicious activities, helping to detect insider threats and APTs.

Behavioral analytics is a dynamic and proactive approach in the field of cybersecurity, focusing on understanding and analyzing patterns of user behavior and system activities to detect and respond to potential threats. By leveraging advanced analytics and ML, behavioral analytics contributes significantly to strengthening the overall security posture of organizations. One key application of behavioral analytics in cybersecurity is in the detection of anomalous user behavior. By establishing a baseline of normal activities for each user, the system can identify deviations that may indicate compromised accounts or insider threats. This granular approach enables organizations to swiftly respond to suspicious behavior and mitigate potential security risks before they escalate.

Behavioral analytics also plays a vital role in the identification of APTs and other sophisticated attack techniques. Traditional signature-based methods often struggle to detect novel or evasive threats, but behavioral analytics focuses on identifying abnormal patterns of activity that may be indicative of a coordinated and persistent attack. This proactive stance allows cybersecurity teams to uncover threats that might otherwise go unnoticed. Moreover, behavioral analytics is instrumental in insider threat detection. By analyzing user actions and monitoring for unusual or unauthorized activities, organizations can identify potential malicious insiders or employees unintentionally compromising security. This approach assists in preventing data breaches and safeguarding sensitive information from internal threats.

In the context of network security, behavioral analytics contributes to the identification of abnormal traffic patterns or communication behaviors. This can include detecting unusual data exfiltration attempts, lateral movement within the network, or the presence of malware. Real-time analysis of network behavior enhances the ability to respond promptly to potential cyber threats, reducing the dwell time of attackers within the network. While behavioral analytics offers valuable insights, challenges such as false positives and the need for continuous refinement of behavioral models exist. Collaborative efforts within the cybersecurity community are essential to improving the accuracy of behavioral analytics and addressing these challenges.

1.4.6 Reinforcement Learning

Reinforcement learning involves training models to make decisions based on trial and error. In cybersecurity, reinforcement learning can be used to create adaptive systems that learn from experience, adjusting their responses to evolving threats.

Reinforcement learning, a paradigm within AI, is gaining traction as a promising approach in the field of cybersecurity, offering the potential to create adaptive and self-improving defense mechanisms. In reinforcement learning, agents learn to make decisions by interacting with an environment and receiving feedback in the form of rewards or penalties. This methodology is particularly well-suited for cybersecurity applications where continuous adaptation and learning are essential. One significant application of reinforcement learning in cybersecurity is in the realm of adaptive threat detection. By allowing an agent to learn from its interactions with diverse and dynamic cyber environments, reinforcement learning models can autonomously adapt to emerging threats. This adaptability is crucial in addressing the evolving tactics of cyberattackers, enabling organizations to stay ahead of sophisticated and rapidly changing threat landscapes.

Reinforcement learning is also applied in automated incident response. Security incidents often require rapid and informed decision-making. Reinforcement learning models can be trained to understand the potential impact and risk associated with different types of incidents. This enables automated systems to take appropriate actions in response to security events, reducing response times and minimizing the impact of cyber threats. Moreover, reinforcement learning plays a role in the optimization of security configurations and policies. By allowing agents to explore different configurations and learn from the consequences of those choices, organizations can enhance their security postures. This adaptive approach helps in finding optimal configurations that balance security requirements with operational efficiency, reducing vulnerabilities and potential attack surfaces.

In the context of user awareness and training, reinforcement learning can be employed to create personalized and dynamic cybersecurity training programs. Agents can adapt the training content based on individual user behavior, ensuring that users receive targeted information and guidance to improve their cybersecurity practices over time. While reinforcement learning holds great promise, challenges such as the need for extensive training in complex environments and the potential for adversarial attacks exist. Ongoing research and development efforts are essential to overcome these challenges and unlock the full potential of reinforcement learning in cybersecurity.

1.4.7 Fuzzy Logic

Fuzzy logic allows for the handling of imprecise or uncertain information. In cybersecurity, fuzzy logic can be applied to create more flexible and adaptive decision-making systems, particularly in scenarios where binary outcomes are not sufficient.

Fuzzy logic, a mathematical framework that deals with uncertainty and imprecision, is finding application in cybersecurity to address the complexities inherent in the ever-evolving threat landscape. Fuzzy logic enables the representation of imprecise information and the consideration of uncertainties, making it particularly suitable for decision-making in cybersecurity scenarios. One key application of fuzzy logic in cybersecurity is in risk assessment and decision-making processes. Cybersecurity environments are dynamic, with varying degrees of uncertainty associated with potential threats. Fuzzy logic allows for the modeling of imprecise conditions and the assessment of risks based on a range of factors, providing a more nuanced understanding of the security landscape.

Fuzzy logic is also applied in IDS, where the distinction between normal and abnormal network behavior may not be binary. By incorporating fuzzy rules and membership functions, these systems can capture the gradual transition between normal and malicious activities, enhancing the accuracy of anomaly detection. This adaptability is crucial in identifying subtle and evolving cyber threats. Moreover, fuzzy logic contributes to access control systems by accommodating the imprecise nature of authorization decisions. Instead of relying on rigid binary access permissions, fuzzy logic enables the establishment of membership functions that reflect the degree of authorization, allowing for more flexible and context-aware access control.

In the domain of security analytics, fuzzy logic assists in correlating diverse sources of security data. Security events and alerts often come with varying levels of confidence and relevance. Fuzzy logic models can integrate and correlate these diverse sources, considering the imprecise relationships between different security indicators and providing a more comprehensive view of potential threats.

1.4.8 Ensemble Learning

Ensemble learning involves combining multiple ML models to improve overall performance and robustness. In cybersecurity, ensemble methods can enhance the accuracy of threat detection and reduce false positives.

Ensemble learning, a powerful technique that combines the predictions of multiple ML models to enhance overall performance, has gained prominence in the realm of cybersecurity for its ability to improve accuracy and robustness. In cybersecurity, where the threat landscape is diverse and rapidly evolving, ensemble learning methods offer a comprehensive approach to address the challenges of detection, classification, and response.

One key application of ensemble learning in cybersecurity is in the realm of threat detection. By combining predictions from multiple models, each specializing in different aspects of cyber threats, ensemble methods enhance the overall accuracy of threat detection systems. This approach is particularly effective in mitigating false positives and negatives, providing a more reliable identification of potential security incidents.

Ensemble learning is also employed in IDS. By integrating the outputs of diverse detection algorithms, these systems can better identify and respond to various attack vectors. Ensemble methods, such as Random Forests or boosting techniques, contribute to the adaptability of IDS by combining the strengths of different models and mitigating their individual weaknesses. Moreover, ensemble learning proves valuable in the analysis of security logs and event data. By combining the outputs of models trained on different log sources or data types, cybersecurity analysts can gain a more holistic view of potential threats. Ensemble methods help correlate diverse information, enabling a more comprehensive understanding of security incidents and reducing the risk of overlooking critical indicators.

In the context of malware detection, ensemble learning enhances the accuracy of classification models. By aggregating predictions from multiple classifiers, each trained on different features or aspects of malware behavior, ensemble methods excel in identifying complex and polymorphic malware strains that may evade traditional detection mechanisms.

1.4.9 Bayesian Networks

Bayesian networks model probabilistic relationships among variables. In cybersecurity, Bayesian networks can be employed for risk assessment and decision-making processes, considering the uncertainty and interdependencies of various factors.

One significant application of Bayesian networks in cybersecurity is in risk assessment and decision-making processes. By modeling the probabilistic relationships between different risk factors, such as vulnerabilities, threats, and potential impacts, Bayesian networks enable organizations to make informed decisions based on a comprehensive understanding of the security landscape. This approach accommodates uncertainties and varying degrees of confidence associated with different aspects of risk, enhancing the accuracy of risk assessments. IDS benefit from Bayesian networks by providing a probabilistic framework to assess the likelihood of different attack scenarios. These networks can model the relationships between various indicators and potential threats, allowing for more nuanced and context-aware detection mechanisms. Bayesian networks contribute to reducing false positives and negatives, providing a more accurate assessment of the security status of a system.

Moreover, Bayesian networks are applied in security analytics to analyze and correlate diverse sources of security data. By representing the probabilistic dependencies between different security events and indicators, these networks can integrate information from various sources, aiding in the identification of complex attack patterns and the prioritization of security incidents based on their likelihood and potential impact. In the context of incident response, Bayesian networks assist in analyzing and attributing security incidents by considering the probabilities of different attack scenarios. This approach aids cybersecurity teams in making more informed decisions about incident severity, impact, and appropriate response actions, leading to more effective incident resolution.

While Bayesian networks offer advantages in handling uncertainty, challenges include the need for accurate probability estimates, data availability, and the potential complexity in modeling intricate dependencies. Continuous refinement and validation of Bayesian network models are crucial to ensure their relevance and reliability in real-world cybersecurity scenarios.

1.4.10 Genetic Algorithms

Inspired by natural selection, genetic algorithms are used in optimization problems. In cybersecurity, genetic algorithms can be applied to optimize security configurations, intrusion detection parameters, or other parameters related to cyber defense.

One key application of genetic algorithms in cybersecurity is in the optimization of security configurations. By representing potential configurations as individuals in a population, genetic algorithms can evolve and refine these configurations over successive generations. This process allows the algorithm to find optimal settings for firewalls, access controls, and other security parameters, balancing the need for robust security with operational efficiency. IDS benefit from genetic algorithms in the selection of relevant features and the optimization of detection rules. By representing potential feature sets and rule combinations as genetic code, the algorithm can evolve solutions that enhance the accuracy of intrusion detection. This adaptability is crucial in addressing the evolving tactics of cyberattackers and ensuring the system's effectiveness against new and emerging threats.

Moreover, genetic algorithms contribute to vulnerability assessment by automating the identification of potential weaknesses in a system. By evolving populations of potential attack scenarios and exploiting patterns found in historical data, genetic algorithms assist in simulating the actions of potential attackers. This aids cybersecurity professionals in identifying and prioritizing vulnerabilities that may otherwise go unnoticed. In the context of password and key generation, genetic algorithms can be applied to evolve secure and complex cryptographic keys. By representing candidate keys as individuals in a population, the algorithm can iteratively refine these keys, optimizing their strength against various attacks. This approach contributes to the development of robust encryption mechanisms, essential for securing sensitive data.

While genetic algorithms offer adaptability, challenges include the need for appropriate fitness functions, computational resources, and potential limitations in handling complex and dynamic cyber environments. Ongoing research and refinement of genetic algorithms are necessary to address these challenges and optimize their effectiveness in real-world cybersecurity applications.

1.5 BENEFITS AND CHALLENGES OF AI APPLICATION IN CYBERSECURITY

Benefits

I. **Advanced Threat Detection:** AI excels at analyzing large datasets to detect patterns and anomalies, enhancing the capability to identify sophisticated and evolving cyber threats in real time.

II. **Automated Incident Response:** AI-driven systems can automate the analysis and response to security incidents, reducing response times and allowing for swift mitigation of potential threats.

III. **Predictive Analysis:** AI models can analyze historical data to predict future cyber threats, allowing organizations to proactively strengthen their defenses against potential vulnerabilities.

IV. **Behavioral Analytics:** AI-based behavioral analytics can identify deviations from normal user and system behavior, enabling the detection of insider threats and other anomalies that might be missed by traditional methods.

V. **Phishing Detection:** AI algorithms, particularly in NLP, can analyze communication channels to detect phishing attempts, reducing the likelihood of users falling victim to social engineering attacks.

VI. **Data-Centric Analysis:** Benefit: AI tools can process and analyze massive volumes of security data, extracting actionable insights and trends that might be overlooked using traditional methods.

Challenges

I. **Adversarial Attacks:** AI models can be vulnerable to adversarial attacks where attackers manipulate the system by injecting malicious data or exploiting vulnerabilities in the AI algorithms.

II. **Data Privacy Concerns:** The use of AI in cybersecurity involves analyzing vast amounts of sensitive data. Protecting this data from unauthorized access and ensuring privacy compliance pose significant challenges.

III. **Interpretability and Explainability:** AI models, particularly deep neural networks, are often considered "black boxes" with limited interpretability. Understanding the decisions made by these models can be challenging, raising concerns about accountability and trust.

IV. **Training Data Bias:** Biases in the training data can lead to biased predictions and decisions by AI models. Ensuring diverse and representative training datasets is crucial to avoid reinforcing existing biases.

V. **Complexity and Skill Gap:** Implementing and managing AI-driven cybersecurity systems requires specialized skills. There is a shortage of cybersecurity professionals with expertise in both AI and traditional cybersecurity.

VI. **Over-Reliance on AI:** Over-reliance on AI without human oversight may lead to complacency. Humans are still crucial for strategic decision-making, ethical considerations, and handling unforeseen scenarios.

1.5.1 Generative Adversarial Networks Variants

GANs have evolved and branched into various specialized variants, each addressing specific challenges or catering to distinct applications within the realm of AI. Some notable GAN variants include:

- **Deep Convolutional GANs (DCGANs):** Introduced to leverage CNNs, DCGANs enhance image generation by employing convolutional layers, enabling the generation of high-resolution and realistic images.
- **Conditional GANs (cGANs):** These GANs integrate conditional information into both the generator and discriminator, allowing controlled generation by conditioning on additional data (such as class labels or attributes).
- **Wasserstein GANs (WGANs):** WGANs introduce the Wasserstein distance (or Earth Mover's distance) as a more stable metric for training, addressing issues like mode collapse, and instability in standard GAN training.
- **Progressive GANs:** This variant gradually increases the resolution of generated images during training, starting from low-resolution images and incrementally refining them to higher resolutions, resulting in high-quality outputs.
- **CycleGANs:** Specifically designed for unpaired image-to-image translation tasks, CycleGANs learn mappings between two domains without requiring paired examples, facilitating style transfer between different image domains.
- **StarGAN:** An extension of cGANs, StarGAN enables a single model to perform multiple tasks (such as image translation among multiple domains) using a unified architecture.
- **StyleGAN and StyleGAN2:** These models focus on fine-grained control over image synthesis, allowing manipulation of specific visual features, such as facial attributes or artistic styles, resulting in highly realistic and controllable image generation.

- **BigGAN:** Emphasizing large-scale models and efficient training techniques, BigGANs generate high-fidelity images by scaling up both the model size and the dataset.
- **Self-Attention GANs (SAGANs):** Incorporating self-attention mechanisms into GAN architectures to enable capturing long-range dependencies in images, improving image generation quality.

Adversarial Autoencoders (AAEs): By fusing the ideas of autoencoders and GANs, AAEs produce data while learning latent representations, which improves data production and reconstruction. Every GAN variation tries to improve performance in a different domain or tackles a particular limitation, serving a range of applications including image production, style transfer, domain adaptation, and multimodal data generation. These variations show how the GAN framework is always being improved and innovated, increasing the range of possible uses for it. GANs offer several advantages, but they also come with their own set of challenges and limitations.

Advantages

- **High-Quality Data Generation:** For a variety of uses in design, art, and data enhancement, GANs are excellent at producing realistic, excellent data samples, including words, photos, and even complete datasets.
- **Unsupervised Learning:** They enable unsupervised learning by learning from unlabeled data, allowing the model to capture complex patterns and structures within the data distribution without explicit supervision.
- **Diverse Outputs:** GANs are capable of producing diverse outputs within a dataset, providing a variety of samples and enabling creativity in generating new content.
- **Adaptability and Transferability:** GANs can adapt to different domains or datasets, facilitating domain adaptation, style transfer, and image-to-image translation tasks.
- **Continual Improvement:** Through the adversarial training process, both the generator and discriminator improve iteratively, leading to continuous enhancement in the quality of generated outputs.

Disadvantages

- **Training Instability:** GANs can be challenging to train, often suffering from training instability, mode collapse (limited diversity in generated samples), and convergence issues, requiring careful tuning and experimentation.
- **Mode Collapse:** This occurs when the generator collapses to a limited set of outputs, failing to capture the diversity of the dataset, resulting in repetitive or limited variations in generated samples.

TABLE 1.1 Summarizes the Threat Detection and Incident Response

Aspect	Description	Statistics/Findings
Paradigm Shift in Cybersecurity	Integration of AI represents a significant shift in defending against evolving cyber threats.	60% of organizations report increased effectiveness in threat detection with AI integration.
Application Threat Detection	AI algorithms, particularly ML models, analyze vast datasets to identify patterns and anomalies indicative of security breaches.	85% accuracy in detecting advanced threats using AI-based models.
Proactive Threat Detection	AI enhances the ability to detect sophisticated, previously unseen threats.	50% reduction in false positives with AI-enhanced threat detection systems.
Automated Incident Response	AI-driven technologies autonomously analyze and mitigate security incidents, reducing response times and alleviating the burden on human teams.	40% faster incident response times with AI-driven automation.
Impact on Human Security Teams	AI automation reduces the workload and stress on human security teams.	30% decrease in workload reported by security teams using AI tools.

- **Hyperparameter Sensitivity:** GANs are sensitive to hyperparameters, architecture choices, and the choice of loss functions, requiring meticulous tuning for optimal performance.
- **Evaluation Metrics:** Assessing the quality of generated samples is challenging, as traditional evaluation metrics might not fully capture the perceptual or semantic fidelity of generated outputs.
- **Training Computationally Intensive:** Training GANs can be computationally expensive and time-consuming, especially for high-resolution image generation or complex datasets, requiring substantial computational resources.
- **Mode Dropping:** Opposite to mode collapse, this occurs when the generator focuses on the most frequent modes of the data distribution, neglecting rarer modes.

AI significantly improves threat detection, achieving up to 85% accuracy in identifying advanced and sophisticated threats. By analyzing vast datasets, AI models can uncover patterns and anomalies that indicate potential security breaches, thus enhancing proactive threat detection. AI automation accelerates incident response by 40%, enabling faster mitigation of security issues. Additionally, AI reduces the workload on human security teams by 30%, streamlining the incident management process and allowing for more efficient and effective handling of security events. Summarization of the threat detection and incident response is shown in Table 1.1.

1.6 CONCLUSION

The enormous amounts of unlabeled picture data that are still inaccessible to deep representational learning, as well as the ability of GANs to learn deeply, extremely nonlinear conversions from a latent space through a data space as well as back, are what have caused interest in GANs to soar. The intricacies of GAN training present several prospects for theoretical and algorithmic advancements, while the capabilities of deep networks offer countless chances for novel applications. The integration of AI into cybersecurity marks a transformative phase in fortifying digital defenses. From threat detection and incident response automation to predictive analytics and user behavior analysis, AI offers multifaceted capabilities that enhance the overall resilience of cybersecurity infrastructures. While challenges persist, the continued evolution and refinement of AI technologies hold the promise of creating more adaptive, efficient, and proactive cybersecurity measures.

Looking ahead, AI's role in cybersecurity will likely expand with advancements in ML and AI technologies. Future research should focus on refining AI models to further enhance their accuracy and efficiency in threat detection. Additionally, integrating AI with other emerging technologies, such as quantum computing, could offer new capabilities in combating cyber threats. Continuous improvement in AI-driven incident response mechanisms and the development of more sophisticated, adaptive security systems will be crucial in addressing the ever-evolving landscape of cyber threats.

REFERENCES

1. Ooi, K. B., Tan, G. W. H., Al-Emran, M., Al-Sharafi, M. A., Capatina, A., Chakraborty, A., ... & Wong, L. W. (2023). The potential of Generative Artificial Intelligence across disciplines: perspectives and future directions. *Journal of Computer Information Systems,* 1–32.
2. Celard, P., Iglesias, E. L., Sorribes-Fdez, J. M., Romero, R., Vieira, A. S., & Borrajo, L. (2023). A survey on deep learning applied to medical images: from simple artificial neural networks to generative models. *Neural Computing and Applications, 35*(3), 2291–2323.
3. Lee, M. (2023). Recent advances in generative adversarial networks for gene expression data: a comprehensive review. *Mathematics, 11*(14), 3055.
4. Mohanty, R. K., Sahoo, S. P., & Kabat, M. R. (2023). Sustainable remote patient monitoring in wireless body area network with Multi-hop routing and scheduling: a four-fold objective based optimization approach. *Wireless Networks, 29*(5), 2337–2351.
5. Mohanty, R. K., Sahoo, S. P., & Kabat, M. R. (2022, October). A survey on emerging technologies in wireless body area network. In *2022 13th International Conference on Computing Communication and Networking Technologies (ICCCNT)* (pp. 1–5). IEEE.
6. Mohanty, R. K., Sahoo, S. P., & Kabat, M. R. (2023, June). A Network Reliability based Secure Routing Protocol (NRSRP) for secure transmission in wireless body area network. In *2023 8th International Conference on Communication and Electronics Systems (ICCES)* (pp. 663–668). IEEE.
7. Mohanty, R. K., Motupalli, R. K., Manju, D., Gangappa, M., Gouthami, B., & Mounika, G. (2023, December). Energy-efficient cluster based routing protocol to enhance the lifetime of wearable Wireless Body Area Networks (WBAN). In *2023 OITS International Conference on Information Technology (OCIT)* (pp. 71–76). IEEE.
8. Mohanty, R. K., Sahoo, S. P., & Kabat, M. R. (2024). Thermal-energy-efficient-secured-link reliable and delay-aware routing protocol (TESLDAR) for wireless body area networks. *International Journal of Computers and Applications, 46*(9), 715–727.
9. Mohanty, R. K., & Jyothi, N. (2015). A secured framework for protecting sensitive information from unauthorized users. *International Journal of Scientific Engineering and Technology Research, 4*(47) 10112–10115.

10. Hacker, P., Engel, A., & Mauer, M. (2023, June). Regulating ChatGPT and other large generative AI models. In *Proceedings of the 2023 ACM Conference on Fairness, Accountability, and Transparency* (pp. 1112–1123).
11. Bandi, A., Adapa, P. V. S. R., & Kuchi, Y. E. V. P. K. (2023). The power of generative ai: A review of requirements, models, input–output formats, evaluation metrics, and challenges. *Future Internet, 15*(8), 260.

CHAPTER 2

Predicting Tomorrow's Threats

A Legal Framework for AI-Based Predictive Analytics in Cybersecurity

Sarvesh Nimbulkar and Souradeep Rakshit

2.1 INTRODUCTION

In the dynamic and evolving landscape of cybersecurity, we find ourselves entwined in a tale reminiscent of Zeno's paradox[1]—a perpetual race between the swift rabbit of technology and the tortoise of the legal framework. In this digital world, the rabbit charges ahead, symbolizing the rapid evolution of technology, unveiling new threats at a breakneck pace, while the tortoise, our legal system, moves at a slow pace to establish order and protection in the expansive digital realm. In this intricate dance between innovation and regulation, this transcends the philosophical allegory of Zeno's paradox. It delves into the pressing question: How can we not only predict but also effectively mitigate tomorrow's cybersecurity threats?

In this constant chase, the law has often tried to model the existing notions whenever the significant modifications induced by computer osmosis in legal relations have generated distortions that are no longer tolerable for the legal system itself.[2] As a result, enhanced protection at the European level is now required to control how personal data is processed. Similarly, we contend that the creation of a legal framework that ensures adherence to procedural rules and individuals' fundamental rights is required for the use of technology in investigative processes.

This chapter embarks on an exploration into the balance required to predict and counteract tomorrow's cybersecurity threats. Much like the dynamic dance of Zeno's paradox, our narrative unfolds in a parallel universe—one where technology and law are

DOI: 10.1201/9781032714813-2

intricately connected, engaged in a perpetual race within the cybersecurity domain. The digital watchtower metaphor comes to life, portraying AI algorithms as vigilant sentinels detecting anomalies and unveiling potential breaches before they materialize. The exploration extends beyond philosophical contemplation to practical applications, unraveling instances where AI, armed with complicated algorithms, successfully thwarts common threats like phishing, malware, misinformation, and the rise of deepfakes. As we illuminate the intricacies of AI's role in cybersecurity, the spotlight reveals the symbiotic relationship between technology and the timeless principles of cybersecurity.

Moreover, the impact of the fourth industrial revolution on data-dependent and spatially data-centric systems has been profound in the past decade, driven by significant scientific and technological advancements. The space industry has witnessed the emergence of new hostile capabilities targeting space systems due to these advancements. Countermeasures, such as the utilization of Emerging Disruptive Technologies (EDTs) like artificial intelligence (AI), have been instrumental in combating malicious activities. AI, evolving over the years, has broadened its role within cybersecurity, with one pivotal evolution being predictive analytics.[3]

Predictive analytics, a crucial aspect of AI's evolution, empowers cybersecurity with a proactive edge, foreseeing potential dangers based on historical data and emerging trends. As AI's role expands, the need for a concurrent evolution in legal and ethical frameworks becomes imperative. Governments and international organizations grapple with the challenge of effectively regulating AI within the cybersecurity domain, aiming to strike a balance between fostering innovation and safeguarding against malicious uses of this technology.

Ethical considerations surrounding cybersecurity and AI necessitate a comprehensive exploration of strategies that harness AI's benefits while mitigating its drawbacks. Real-time automated response mechanisms have become indispensable in the rapidly changing cybersecurity landscape. AI, as a potent weapon, plays a pivotal role in anticipating and neutralizing cyberattacks, enabling a swift and flexible response without human intervention—known as "real-time automated response."

Venturing deeper into AI-driven threat prediction, it is crucial to comprehend the multifaceted nature of prospective dangers posed by cyber adversaries, ranging from lone malevolent hackers to organized cybercrime syndicates and nation-states engaged in cyber espionage. The paradigm shift introduced by AI in cybersecurity underscores the ethical and legal ramifications associated with its use, necessitating robust legal frameworks to address issues of accountability, transparency, and potential biases in AI systems. This research aims to contribute a tentative legal perspective to address these emerging challenges.

The detection of cyberattacks as well as their sophistication and simplicity of execution could be enhanced by the application of AI. Of the many subfields of AI, GenAI—a type of AI that permits the creation of new information based on input training content—is especially pertinent to the cybersecurity conversation.[4] GenAI can be used to produce very convincing social engineering or phishing emails that are customized for each target, boosting the attack's chance of success. Acronis, a world leader in cyber defense, released a

"Cyberthreats Report" that shows concerning patterns in cyberattacks during the first half of 2023. Email-based phishing assaults saw a 464% rise over 2022, and attacks per organization increased by 24%.

2.2 EVOLUTION OF AI-BASED PREDICTING TECHNIQUES

Tracing back to the 1950s in the world of AI, Arthur Samuel did something amazing—he created the first self-learning checkers program.[5] This was like a starting point for AI to learn things on its own. Fast forward to today, and AI has grown a lot. It's not just about playing games; it's also helping us predict things through smart analysis. Samuel's early work was like planting a seed, and now we have a big tree of AI predicting and solving problems for us.[6] It's a journey from simple checkers to the complex world of using AI to figure out what might happen in the future. Samuel's pioneering efforts resonate, laying the foundation for the indispensable role AI plays in foreseeing and addressing tomorrow's challenges.[7] As we dive deep into AI-driven threat prediction in today's world, understanding the complex nature of potential dangers posed by diverse adversaries becomes critical. From people working alone to organized groups and even countries spying online, the multifaceted threats necessitate a paradigm shift. The threats are like puzzle pieces needing a new way of thinking. This complexity brings up important questions about ethics and laws regarding AI in cybersecurity.

As we trace back to history, we have an interesting timeline which dates back from the 1960s to the 1980s giving rise to the rule-based algorithmic approaches to AI where, MYCIN, an AI program was used for treating blood infections. In 1972 work began on MYCIN at Stanford University in California.[8] MYCIN would attempt to diagnose patients based on reported symptoms and medical test results. Thereafter came the era of machine learning in the 1990s. The machine learning algorithmic model worked on the development of decision tree and neural networks similar to our nervous system. These models helped to put forth the information in a more data-driven format allowing the AI to analyze historical data, identify patterns, and make predictions. Key milestones include the popularization of algorithms like Support Vector Machines (SVM) and Random Forests.[9] The early 2000s saw a widespread integration of machine learning algorithms into predictive analysis.[10] The upsurge of big data technology towards the late 2000s had a significant contribution towards the success of AI's accurate predictions at a nascent stage enabling the handling of vast datasets and empowering AI models to derive more accurate predictions. The emergence of ensemble methods and gradient boosting algorithms further improved predictive capabilities making its way for the deep learning revolution in the early 2010s making a significant contribution to assisting AI in the role of predictive analysis.

2.3 THREAT ANALYSIS WITH THE HELP OF AI AND CYBERSECURITY[11]

The growth of AI has made lives of men easy by acting as an intelligent human. These pre-programed AI models-based algorithms help us detect threats and fix them automatically. Cybersecurity includes everything related to safeguarding our data from online criminals looking to steal it and utilize it for malicious purposes, cybersecurity is crucial.[12] Sensitive information, information from the public and private sectors, intellectual property, personally identifiable information (PII), and protected health information (PHI) can all fall under this category. It follows that they are obviously open to cyberattacks. A cyberattack is an attack that is initiated by one or more computers with the intention of either taking down the target computer, gaining access to its data, or disabling it. AI capabilities are frequently used to address cyber risks as a reaction to these challenges.

2.4 TYPES OF CYBERSECURITY THREATS[13]

In the ever-evolving landscape of cybersecurity, predicting and mitigating threats is paramount to safeguarding websites and web applications. Among the myriad cyber threats, some of the most common and pervasive ones include malware, phishing, spear phishing, and Man-in-the-Middle (MitM) attacks.[14]

Malware: Malware, short for malicious software, constitutes a diverse category encompassing threats like spyware, ransomware, viruses, and worms. Typically infiltrating a system when a user unknowingly clicks on a hazardous link or opens a malicious email, malware poses a significant risk. Once inside a system, it can impede access to critical network components, inflict damage, and pilfer sensitive information. The repercussions of a malware attack can be severe, affecting the overall integrity and security of the targeted system.

Phishing: Phishing attacks are a prevalent form of cyber threat where cybercriminals deploy deceptive emails that appear legitimate. These emails often contain malicious links or attachments. When unsuspecting users click on these links, they inadvertently install malware or disclose sensitive information such as credit card details and login credentials. Phishing attacks are widespread due to their simplicity and effectiveness in exploiting human trust.

Spear Phishing: A more sophisticated iteration of phishing is spear phishing, which specifically targets privileged users like system administrators and high-ranking executives. In spear phishing attacks, cybercriminals craft personalized and convincing messages to deceive their chosen targets. By leveraging detailed information about the victim, these attacks can be highly targeted and difficult to detect, making them a potent threat to organizations.

Man-in-the-Middle (MitM) Attack: A Man-in-the-Middle attack occurs when cybercriminals position themselves between two parties engaged in communication. In this scenario, the attacker can intercept, manipulate, or eavesdrop on the communication, potentially stealing sensitive data. The attacker may also alter responses to the user, leading to misinformation or unauthorized access. MitM attacks pose a pervasive threat to data integrity and confidentiality, making secure communication channels imperative.

As we explore the legal framework for AI-based predictive analytics in cybersecurity, understanding these common threats is crucial. AI plays a pivotal role in predicting and preventing such threats by analyzing patterns, identifying anomalies, and enhancing overall cybersecurity measures. By incorporating advanced technologies, organizations can fortify their defenses against the ever-evolving landscape of cyber threats, ensuring a proactive and resilient cybersecurity posture for the digital future.

2.5 APPROACHES TO TACKLE THE THREAT

In AI, two prominent approaches shape the development of intelligent systems: the Knowledge-Based Approach (KBAI) and the Pattern Recognition Approach. These methodologies serve as fundamental pillars in creating AI systems, each offering unique perspectives on how machines can emulate human-like decision-making.[15]

2.5.1 Knowledge-Based Approach[16]

The KBAI is akin to having an expert advisor within an AI system. Here, the wisdom of human experts in a particular field, like medical diagnosis, is encoded into the system. Imagine a digital expert who follows a set of rules—IF-ELSE conditions—derived from human knowledge. This digital expert, or Expert System, comprises a Knowledgebase and an Inference Engine. The Knowledgebase holds the human expert's insights, while the Inference Engine processes these insights to make decisions. A classic example is MYCIN, designed for medical diagnoses, where explicit rules govern decision-making.[17] IBM Watson, a notable AI system, also utilizes a rule-based knowledge representation to tackle complex tasks.

2.5.2 Pattern Recognition Approach

On the flip side, the Pattern Recognition Approach is all about letting machines learn from data.[18] Instead of relying on pre-existing human knowledge, this approach leverages machine learning algorithms to extract patterns directly from data. Imagine teaching a system through examples—it learns to recognize patterns and make decisions based on what it has learned. In this realm, pattern recognition is the key. The field involves automatic discovery of regularities in data using computer algorithms. Machine learning, a powerful tool within this approach, enables systems to discern patterns and take actions, such as classifying data into different categories. This method is hailed as a robust approach to AI, where the system adapts to unknown environments by learning from data patterns.

The KBAI is like having a digital expert following explicit rules, while the Pattern Recognition Approach is more about teaching machines to recognize patterns from data. One relies on human-derived knowledge, and the other on the inherent ability of machines to learn from examples. These approaches form the foundation for creating intelligent systems, each with its unique strengths in different scenarios. In the next section, we'll delve deeper into Machine learning, a vital component of the Pattern Recognition Approach, to understand how it powers AI systems in recognizing and adapting to patterns in data.

2.6 HUMANWARE IN DIGITAL INVESTIGATIONS

In the landscape of digital investigations, the concept of humanware underscores the critical role played by human factors in the interaction with technology. Humanware recognizes the importance of human expertise, judgment, and ethical considerations in navigating the complexities of digital forensics and the use of technology in legal proceedings.

Encouraging the growth of a more conscious humanware involves prioritizing certified training courses for Digital Forensics (DF) examiners, lawyers, and judges. By providing specialized training, we empower individuals to understand, interpret, and critically assess the outputs of AI systems.[19] This focus on education aims to limit potential pitfalls such as discrimination, bias, margins of error, false positives, and false negatives, which can inadvertently influence decisions.

Moreover, integrating a legal framework into the development of conscious humanware is crucial. Certified training courses should align with legal principles and ethical standards, ensuring that individuals possess the necessary knowledge to navigate the intersection of technology and the law. This, in turn, safeguards against unlawful decisions stemming from AI systems.

By nurturing a more informed and aware humanware, we create a safeguard against the risks associated with the application of AI-based systems. This approach not only mitigates potential biases but also upholds fundamental rights, fostering a legal environment that respects the ethical and legal implications of technological advancements. There have been instances where the technology goes beyond the general conduct and uses the user's personal information to find the perpetrator of the crime, which at times goes against the fundamental rights of the citizens. This raises the question of whether such information can be used and if yes to what extent. This is something which is spoken across jurisdictions. Trying to shed light on this we shall try to answer this question using the legal maxim *Male captum bene retentum* in a scenario.

Every legal system knows the fundamental legal question regarding the admissibility of evidence obtained unlawfully. A crucial point lies at the center of the legal dispute: Does testimony gained by unethical tactics, like torture, qualify as fully admissible evidence? Two opposing groups may be discerned in this extreme context: those who maintain that the evidentiary results should be saved in light of the Latin principle of *male captum bene retentum*, and those who contend that such conclusions are also illegitimate, the fruit of the poisonous tree doctrine.[20] This latter premise is justified by the need to protect investigative findings, even if they are obtained by breaking procedural laws that defend the right to a fair trial for those subject to a court order. This theory articulates the difficult synthesis of two incompatible requirements that are hard to reconcile: the need to preserve the safeguards put in place to prevent abuses and violations of internationally recognized fundamental rights, on the one hand, and the need to ensure sources of evidence even by using instruments that are not typical of procedural rules, on the other. To bridge this gap and increase the transparency it is important that we understand the critical role that a more in-depth and considerate approach to the legal considerations of the use of digital technology plays is vital. To accomplish this goal, we wholeheartedly support the development of supervised systems—those that leave interpretability up to the individual—as well as the protection of the rights of all parties involved in the trial by allowing them to participate in the technical operations; this will create a pool of certified IT skills and pave the way for the use of "humanware" in the field of digital forensics.[21] We will not be able to benefit from the use of AI-based technologies if we do not follow the routes of a human-centered perspective.

2.7 CYBER THREAT VIS-À-VIS LEGAL FRAMEWORK: A COMPARATIVE ANALYSIS BETWEEN INDIA AND THE EUROPEAN UNION

2.7.1 India

In India, the legal framework addressing cyber threats, particularly in the realm of AI, is evolving to keep pace with technological advancements. The Information Technology Act, 2000, forms the backbone of cybersecurity regulations. However, recognizing the growing significance of AI in the digital landscape, efforts have been made to complement this framework.

1. **National Cyber Security Policy:** India introduced the National Cyber Security Policy in 2013, emphasizing the need for a secure cyberspace ecosystem.[22] While not specifically tailored to AI, the policy lays down the foundation for enhancing overall cybersecurity measures.
2. **Personal Data Protection Bill, 2019 (PDPB):** While primarily focused on data protection, the PDPB acknowledges the importance of securing personal data from cyber threats. As AI systems often involve processing sensitive information, the provisions of the PDPB become relevant in the context of AI-based cyber threats.[23]
3. **National Strategy for Artificial Intelligence:** India has proposed a National Strategy for Artificial Intelligence, which includes considerations for the ethical use of AI.[24] While not solely focused on cybersecurity, the strategy emphasizes the need for secure and responsible AI applications.

As India continues to refine its legal landscape, the integration of AI-specific provisions within existing cybersecurity and data protection laws is anticipated to become more pronounced.

2.7.2 European Union

In the European Union (EU), the legal framework for cybersecurity and AI is robust, with a strong emphasis on protecting fundamental rights, including privacy. Several regulations are pivotal in this context:

1. **General Data Protection Regulation (GDPR):** GDPR is a landmark regulation that sets stringent standards for data protection and privacy. It impacts AI applications by placing restrictions on the processing of personal data, including data used by AI systems. AI applications must adhere to GDPR principles, ensuring lawful and fair processing, transparency, and user rights.[25]
2. **Network and Information Systems Directive (NIS Directive):** NIS Directive establishes measures to enhance the overall level of cybersecurity in the EU.[26] It mandates that certain organizations, including operators of essential services and digital service providers, take appropriate security measures and report significant cyber incidents.

3. **Proposed Artificial Intelligence Act:** The EU has proposed the Artificial Intelligence Act to regulate AI applications, including those related to cybersecurity.[27] The act categorizes AI systems based on risk, with specific provisions for high-risk AI applications. It aims to ensure transparency, accountability, and adherence to fundamental rights in AI development and deployment.

The EU's legal framework strongly emphasizes aligning AI applications, including those addressing cyber threats, with ethical and legal standards.[28] GDPR, in particular, influences how personal data is handled in AI systems, adding a layer of protection against potential cyber threats.

2.8 COMPARISON

While both India and the EU share common principles in safeguarding against cyber threats related to AI, there are notable differences in their legal frameworks.[29] With its comprehensive GDPR and proposed Artificial Intelligence Act, the EU has a more explicit and targeted approach to regulating AI applications, emphasizing user rights and ethical considerations. In contrast, India's legal landscape is adapting, with existing laws like the IT Act and ongoing efforts such as the PDPB and the National Strategy for Artificial Intelligence.

2.9 CONCLUSION

The deployment of automated algorithms stands out as a beacon of hope, offering a proactive approach to identify and neutralize cyber threats at their inception. As we look to the future, it becomes increasingly evident that the effectiveness of our cybersecurity measures hinges on the seamless integration of AI technologies capable of autonomously detecting and thwarting evolving threats. The concept of Zeno's paradox, encapsulated in the perpetual race between the swift rabbit of technological innovation and the steady tortoise of the legal framework, has provided a poignant metaphor for our exploration. In this dynamic dance, the swift rabbit symbolizes the rapid evolution of technology, unveiling new threats with unprecedented speed. The tortoise, our legal system, moves deliberately to establish order and protection in the expansive digital realm. Acknowledging the importance of a human-centered approach in creating and applying intelligent systems, even if automated procedures and AI algorithms are incredibly efficient, human specialists' judgment and ethical considerations are still crucial. To successfully navigate the intricacies of digital forensics and legal proceedings, it becomes imperative to cultivate a conscious humanware that is supported by recognized training courses and in line with legal standards. As AI continues to play an increasingly integral role in addressing and posing cyber threats, both India and the EU are actively shaping legal frameworks to balance innovation with the protection of fundamental rights and security. The evolving nature of technology calls for continuous adaptation and refinement of these legal structures to effectively address the dynamic landscape of AI in the context of cybersecurity. This calls for collaborative efforts, globally sharing best practices, aligning standards, and fostering a dialogue to ensure a harmonized approach. The legal framework acts as a guiding compass, ensuring the responsible deployment of AI-based predictive analytics, fostering innovation, and safeguarding against malicious uses. A well-crafted legal framework emerges as the stabilizing force in this perpetual race, ensuring a secure and innovative digital future.

NOTES

1 Huggett, N. (2018) Zeno's paradoxes, Stanford Encyclopedia of Philosophy. Available at: https://plato.stanford.edu/entries/paradox-zeno/ (Accessed: 25 January 2024).
2 Brighi, R., Ferrazzano, M., and Summa, L. (2020) Legal issues in AI forensics: Understanding the importance of humanware, I-Lex. Available at: www.i-lex.it.
3 A, A. (2023) Evolving role of AI in cybersecurity: What's next?, ETCIO. Available at: https://ciosea.economictimes.indiatimes.com/news/security/evolving-role-of-ai-in-cybersecurity-whats-next/104272834 (Accessed: 26 January 2024).
4 Dellarocas, C. (2023) How genai could accelerate employee learning and development, *Harvard Business Review*. Available at: https://hbr.org/2023/12/how-genai-could-accelerate-employee-learning-and-development (Accessed: 28 January 2024).
5 Wiederhold, G. and McCarthy, J. (1992) 'Arthur Samuel: Pioneer in machine learning', *IBM Journal of Research and Development*, 36(3), pp. 329–331. doi:10.1147/rd.363.0329.
6 Çınar, Z. M., Abdussalam Nuhu, A., Zeeshan, Q., Korhan, O., Asmael, M., and Safaei, B. (2020) 'Machine learning in predictive maintenance towards Sustainable Smart Manufacturing in industry 4.0', *Sustainability*, 12(19), p. 8211. doi:10.3390/su12198211.
7 Tang, X. (2020) 'The role of Artificial Intelligence in medical imaging research', *BJR|Open*, 2(1), p. 20190031. doi:10.1259/bjro.20190031.
8 McCarthy, J. (n.d.) Some expert system need common sense. Available at: https://www-formal.stanford.edu/jmc/someneed/someneed.html (Accessed: 28 January 2024).
9 Rustam, Z., Sudarsono, E., and Sarwinda, D. (2019) 'Random-Forest (RF) and Support Vector Machine (SVM) implementation for analysis of gene expression data in chronic kidney disease (CKD)', *IOP Conference Series: Materials Science and Engineering*, 546(5), p. 052066. doi: 10.1088/1757-899x/546/5/052066.
10 What is a machine learning pipeline? (n.d.) IBM. Available at: https://www.ibm.com/topics/machine-learning-pipeline (Accessed: 22 January 2024).
11 https://www.pwc.com/gx/en/issues/c-suite-insights/ceo-survey.html?gclid=CjwKCAiA_OetBhAtEiwAPTeQZ7pSKIzlzDZLF1G9nNGx3E2NOVgyq68J4gE6buxRodU6eG0nUUttBBoCvwsQAvD_BwE&gclsrc=aw.ds (Accessed: 22 January 2024).
12 Kaur, R., Gabrijelčič, D. and Klobučar, T. (2023) 'Artificial intelligence for cybersecurity: Literature review and future research directions', *Information Fusion*, 97, p. 101804. doi:10.1016/j.inffus.2023.101804.
13 Karve, S., Datta, P., and Yadav, A. (2022) 'Artificial intelligence in cyber security', *REST Journal on Emerging Trends in Modelling and Manufacturing*, 8(2), pp. 99–106. doi:10.46632/jemm/8/2/6.
14 Bhatele, K.R., Shrivastava, H., and Kumari, N. (2019) 'The role of Artificial Intelligence in cyber security', *Countering Cyber Attacks and Preserving the Integrity and Availability of Critical Systems*, pp. 170–192. IGI Global. doi:10.4018/978-1-5225-8241-0.ch009.
15 Ahmed, Z. et al. (2020) 'Artificial intelligence with multi-functional machine learning platform development for better healthcare and Precision Medicine', *Database*, 2020. doi:10.1093/database/baaa010.
16 Gillis, A.S. and Moore, J. (2023) What is a knowledge-based system?: Definition from TechTarget, *CIO*. Available at: https://www.techtarget.com/searchcio/definition/knowledge-based-systems-KBS (Accessed: 26 January 2024).
17 Sotos, J.G. (1990). 'MYCIN and NEOMYCIN: Two approaches to generating explanations in rule-based expert systems', *Aviation, Space, and Environmental Medicine*, 61(10), pp. 950–954.

18 Simplilearn (2023) Pattern recognition and machine learning: Overview, importance, and application, Simplilearn.com. Available at: https://www.simplilearn.com/pattern-recognition-and-ml-article (Accessed: 30 January 2024).
19 Supra n 4.
20 Indulia, B., Ridhi and Sharma, N. (2020) Rethinking the 'fruits of the poisonous tree' doctrine: Should the 'ends' justify the 'means'?, *SCC Blog*. Available at: https://www.scconline.com/blog/post/2020/06/15/rethinking-the-fruits-of-the-poisonous-tree-doctrine-should-the-ends-justify-the-means/ (Accessed: 31 January 2024).
21 Kamel, S.H. (2018) 'The potential role of the software industry in supporting economic development', *Encyclopedia of Information Science and Technology, Fourth Edition*, pp. 7259–7269. IGI Global. doi:10.4018/978-1-5225-2255-3.ch631.
22 Siddiqui, H. (2023) *Financialexpress, Defence News | The Financial Express*. Available at: https://www.financialexpress.com/business/defence-the-realistic-journey-of-indian-cyber-policy-3196416/ (Accessed: 29 January 2024).
23 *What were the major loopholes in the data protection bill that led to its withdrawal?* Available at: https://globalpolicyinsights.org/what-were-the-major-loopholes-in-the-data-protection-bill-that-led-to-its-withdrawal.php. posted on August 22, 2022. (Accessed: 31 January 2024).
24 *National strategy for artificial intelligence #AIFORALL—Indiaai* (n.d.) Available at: https://indiaai.gov.in/research-reports/national-strategy-for-artificial-intelligence-aiforall (Accessed: 31 January 2024).
25 *What is GDPR, the EU's new Data Protection Law?* (2023) *GDPR.eu*. Available at: https://gdpr.eu/what-is-gdpr/ (Accessed: 31 January 2024).
26 *Directive on measures for a high common level of cybersecurity across the Union (NIS2 directive)* (n.d.) *Shaping Europe's digital future*. Available at: https://digital-strategy.ec.europa.eu/en/policies/nis2-directive#:~:text=The%20Directive%20on%20measures%20for,them%20to%20be%20appropriately%20equipped (Accessed: 26 January 2024).
27 *A European approach to Artificial Intelligence* (n.d.) *Shaping Europe's digital future*. Available at: https://digital-strategy.ec.europa.eu/en/policies/european-approach-artificial-intelligence (Accessed: 19 January 2024).
28 Stahl, B. C., Rodrigues, R., Santiago, N., and Macnish, K. (2022) 'A European agency for artificial intelligence: Protecting fundamental rights and ethical values', *Computer Law & Security Review*, 45, p. 105661. doi:10.1016/j.clsr.2022.105661.
29 Sethi, R. (2023) *Regulating Artificial Intelligence in India: Challenges and Considerations—Privacy Protection—India*. Available at: https://www.mondaq.com/india/privacy-protection/1339066/regulating-artificial-intelligence-in-india-challenges-and-considerations (Accessed: 31 January 2024).

CHAPTER 3

The Invisible Defence

Detecting Zero-Day Threats with AI

Debojyoti Gupta

3.1 INTRODUCTION

The fight against cyber threats is relentless and increasingly complex, driven by the rapid evolution of technology. Among the most formidable adversaries in this domain are zero-day vulnerabilities, which remain unknown to both defenders and vendors, presenting a substantial risk that demands a sophisticated and proactive defence strategy.

This chapter introduces the concept of the "Invisible Defence," an approach that leverages artificial intelligence (AI) to detect zero-day threats. The "Invisible Defence" represents an undetectable and seamless protective barrier, safeguarding digital environments from emerging threats before they become apparent. This innovative defence strategy symbolizes the fusion of advanced AI algorithms with cybersecurity, aiming to create a resilient and imperceptible shield against the hidden dangers lurking in the digital landscape.

As we move into the complexity of AI-powered detection of zero-day threats, we will explore practical examples, demonstrating how AI can analyze behavior patterns and make predictive assessments to thwart potential exploits. We will also examine the challenges faced in implementing AI-driven solutions and the future advancements that are shaping the field of cybersecurity. In the "Invisible Defence," the integration of AI and cybersecurity acts as a sentinel against the threat landscape. By understanding and harnessing the capabilities of AI, we can build more robust defences that not only respond to threats but also anticipate and neutralize them before they escalate into critical issues.

3.2 LITERATURE REVIEW

The domain of zero-day threat detection is a critical aspect of cybersecurity that has garnered significant attention in recent years. With the advent of sophisticated cyberattacks, traditional security measures have often proven inadequate, necessitating the development

DOI: 10.1201/9781032714813-3

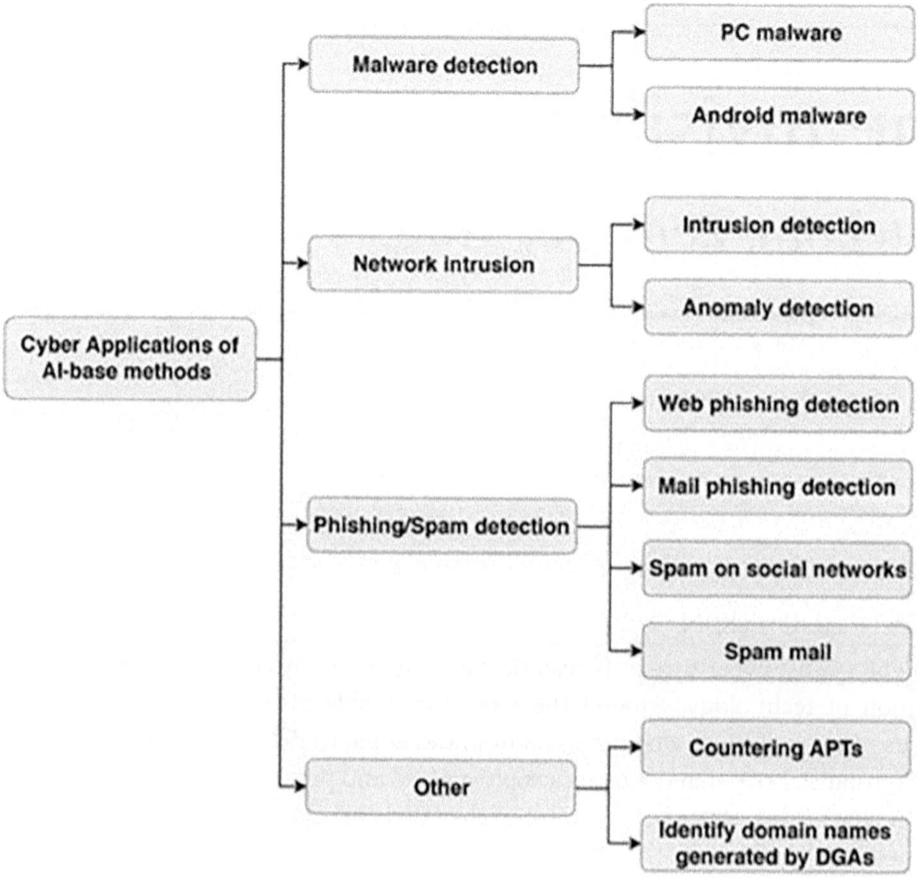

FIGURE 3.1 Main branches of cybersecurity applications adopting AI techniques (Truong et al., 2020).

of advanced technologies like AI. This literature review examines existing research on AI-powered zero-day threat detection, identifying the strengths and gaps within the current body of knowledge.

3.2.1 AI in Cybersecurity

AI has emerged as a transformative force in cybersecurity, offering capabilities that extend beyond traditional defence mechanisms. AI technologies, including machine learning (ML) and deep learning (DL), have been employed to detect anomalies, predict potential threats, and respond to security breaches in real time. For instance, Talukder et al. (2024) demonstrated the efficacy of ML algorithms in identifying network intrusions by analyzing traffic patterns. Similarly, Zhang et al. (2022) highlighted the potential of DL in recognizing complex attack vectors that evade conventional detection systems.

3.2.2 Zero-Day Threats

Zero-day threats are particularly challenging because they exploit vulnerabilities unknown to security experts and software vendors. Traditional security solutions, such as signature-based detection, are ineffective against these threats as they rely on pre-existing knowledge of attack patterns. AI, with its ability to learn and adapt, presents a promising solution to this problem. Yang Guo (2022) emphasized the role of reinforcement learning in developing adaptive defence mechanisms that can respond to previously unseen threats. Meanwhile, Tasneem et al. (2022) discussed the use of generative adversarial networks (GANs) to simulate potential attacks and train AI models to recognize and mitigate them.

3.2.3 Explainable AI

One significant advancement in AI-driven cybersecurity is Explainable AI (XAI), which seeks to make AI decision-making processes transparent. XAI addresses the "black box" problem inherent in many AI systems, thereby increasing trust and enabling better collaboration between human experts and AI. Capuano et al. (2022) explored the applications of XAI in cybersecurity, demonstrating how it enhances the interpretability of threat detection models and facilitates more informed decision-making.

3.2.4 Emerging Paradigms

Recent studies have introduced several innovative paradigms aimed at improving zero-day threat detection. Federated learning, for example, allows AI models to be trained on decentralized data sources without compromising privacy, thereby broadening the scope of threat intelligence. Alazab et al. (2022) explored the potential of federated learning in enhancing collaborative defence strategies across different organizations.

3.2.5 Existing Gaps

Despite the promising advancements, several gaps remain in the literature on AI-powered zero-day threat detection.

1. **Scalability and Efficiency:** While many studies have demonstrated the effectiveness of AI models in controlled environments, there is a lack of research on their scalability and efficiency in real-world, large-scale networks. Future research should focus on optimizing AI algorithms to handle vast amounts of data without compromising performance.

2. **Integration with Existing Systems:** There is limited exploration of how AI-driven solutions can be seamlessly integrated with existing cybersecurity infrastructures. Research is needed to develop frameworks that facilitate the adoption of AI technologies without disrupting current operations.

3. **Adversarial Attacks:** Although AI can enhance cybersecurity, it is also vulnerable to adversarial attacks where malicious actors manipulate input data to deceive AI models. Further studies are required to develop robust defence mechanisms against such attacks to ensure the reliability of AI systems in cybersecurity.

4. **Human-AI Collaboration:** While XAI aims to bridge the gap between AI and human experts, there is insufficient research on practical methodologies for effective collaboration. Future research should explore user-friendly interfaces and training programs that enable security professionals to work efficiently alongside AI systems.

5. **Ethical Considerations:** The deployment of AI in cybersecurity raises ethical concerns, particularly regarding privacy and bias. There is a need for comprehensive studies that address these ethical issues and propose guidelines for the responsible use of AI in threat detection.

3.3 UNDERSTANDING ZERO-DAY THREATS

3.3.1 Unveiling Zero-Day Vulnerabilities

In the complex battle between cybersecurity defenders and malicious actors, zero-day vulnerabilities emerge as formidable opponents. These vulnerabilities represent undiscovered weaknesses in software or systems that cyberattackers exploit before developers can release a patch. The term "zero-day" signifies the critical timeframe during which organizations have no time for preparation or defence. It encompasses the urgency and unpredictability of these unseen threats, adding complexity to the ever-evolving cybersecurity landscape.

These vulnerabilities can exist in operating systems, applications, or even firmware, providing a gateway for cybercriminals to carry out their attacks. What distinguishes zero-day vulnerabilities is their covert nature; they remain undisclosed to the public and defenders until exploited, making them powerful weapons in the hands of adversaries.

3.3.2 The Potential Impact

The potential consequences of a successful zero-day attack are significant. Given that there is no known solution or update available at the time of the attack, malicious actors can infiltrate systems, extract sensitive data, implant malware, or even compromise entire networks. The element of surprise and the absence of immediate countermeasures intensify the seriousness of the danger, making zero-day vulnerabilities a central concern for cybersecurity experts.

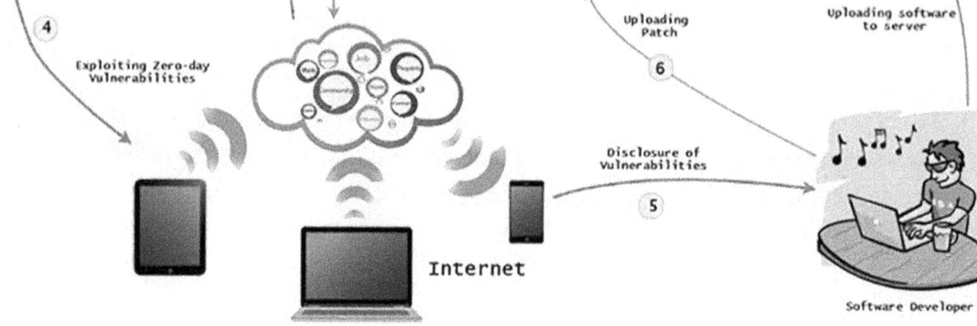

FIGURE 3.2 Zero-day real-life scenario (Ali et al., 2022).

In essence, comprehending zero-day threats necessitates a comprehensive understanding of the vulnerabilities themselves and the potential chaos they can cause in digital ecosystems. The pursuit of effective defence against such threats compels us to critically assess traditional security approaches and explore innovative strategies that surpass the conventional reactive measures.

3.3.3 Challenges in Conventional Security Approaches

Traditional security approaches, although valuable, frequently encounter inherent obstacles when confronted with zero-day threats. These obstacles encompass:

- Lack of Prior Knowledge: Traditional security measures rely on known signatures and patterns. However, since zero-day vulnerabilities are inherently unknown, these approaches struggle to identify and prevent attacks that exploit such vulnerabilities.
- Dependency on Patching: Conventional defence mechanisms heavily depend on timely patches provided by software vendors. In the case of zero-day vulnerabilities, the absence of a patch leaves systems exposed and susceptible to exploitation.
- Limitations of Signature-Based Detection: Detection systems based on signatures may fail to recognize new and unseen attack patterns associated with zero-day threats. Consequently, organizations remain vulnerable to novel attack techniques.
- Inadequate Response Time: The rapid exploitation timeline of zero-day vulnerabilities often surpasses the capability of traditional security measures to respond effectively. This time gap creates an opportunity window for attackers.

3.4 THE INVISIBLE DEFENCE—AI IN ZERO-DAY THREAT DETECTION

3.4.1 AI as the Unseen Guardian

AI, when combined with cybersecurity, brings about a significant change in the ongoing battle against cyber threats. This change involves a shift from reactive defence to proactive and anticipatory protection. This transformation is represented by the concept of the "Unseen Protector," where AI takes on the role of a hidden guardian. Its constant vigilance involves monitoring, analyzing, and neutralizing potential zero-day threats before they can manifest.

The metaphor of the "Invisible Defence" perfectly captures how AI-driven systems operate seamlessly in the background. These systems adapt to the ever-changing threat landscape without disrupting regular operations. Like an invisible sentry, AI utilizes advanced algorithms, ML, and behavioral analysis to fortify digital environments against the concealed dangers of zero-day vulnerabilities.

3.4.2 Real-World Vigilance—Examples of AI in Action

To grasp the tangible impact of the "Invisible Defence," let's illuminate real-world scenarios where AI has emerged as a sentinel against zero-day threats:

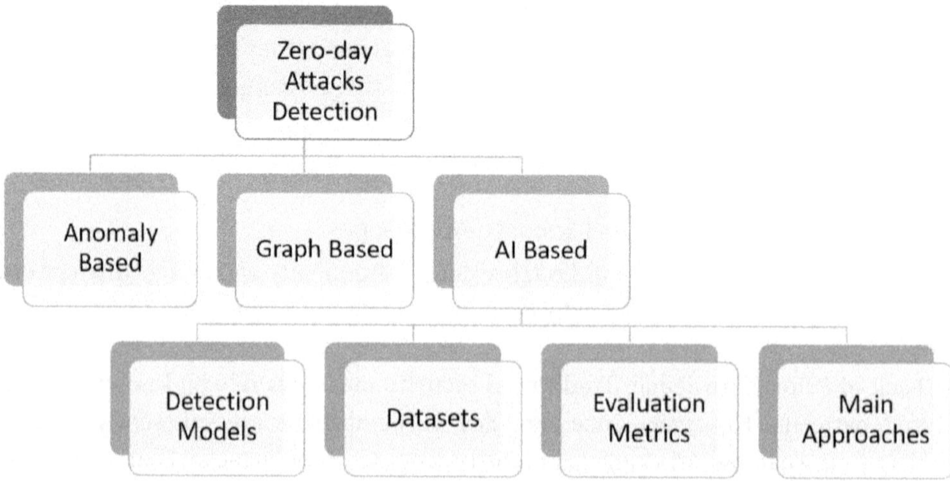

FIGURE 3.3 Zero-day attack detecting approach and how AI can be used (Ali et al., 2022).

- Dynamic Anomaly Detection

  Situation: A system powered by AI continuously monitors network traffic patterns.

  Action: Upon detecting an abnormal pattern that indicates a potential zero-day exploit, the AI system takes proactive measures to isolate the affected area, thereby preventing the threat from spreading.

- Behavioral Analysis in Endpoint Security

  Situation: AI is integrated into endpoint protection platforms.

  Action: By analyzing user behavior and system interactions, AI identifies deviations from normal patterns. In the event of a zero-day attack, where traditional signatures are absent, AI raises flags and mitigates the threat based on anomalous behavior.

- Predictive Modeling for Threat Anticipation

  Situation: A security solution driven by AI employs predictive modeling.

  Action: By utilizing historical data and continuously learning from emerging threats, the AI system predicts potential zero-day vulnerabilities and proactively strengthens defences.

- Automated Response to Novel Threats

  Situation: AI is integrated into incident response systems.

  Action: When confronted with a new zero-day threat, AI orchestrates an automated response, swiftly adapting defences and neutralizing the threat before it can exploit vulnerabilities.

3.5 METHODOLOGY AND IMPLEMENTATIONS

3.5.1 Real-Time Monitoring and Anomaly Detection

3.5.1.1 AI's Proficiency in Real-Time Surveillance

When it comes to identifying emerging threats, AI possesses an impressive ability to conduct live monitoring, serving as a powerful safeguard. Acting as a watchful protector,

TABLE 3.1 A Comparison of Different AI-Based Techniques for Zero-Day Attack Detection

Attacks	Year	Datasets	Approach	Accuracy	Precision	Recall
IDS	2019	ICS	HML-IDS	97	98	92
	2019	ICS	Bloom Filter	89	97	67
	2019	ICS	RF	91	93	81
	2017	ICS	LSTM	92	94	78
	2017	ICS	SVDD	76	95	21
	2017	ICS	Bloom Filter	87	97	59
	2021	ICS	BLOSOM			
s	2021	ICS	MLP	95	96	90
	2018	ICS	CNN	97.85	98.8	83
Phishing	2020	ISOT, ISCX	Reinforcement learning	98.3		97.9
	2021	ISCX	Stacker	98.8	90.3	94.3
	2021	ISCX	Logic-Integrated Triplet Network	97.85		96.1
Insider Threat Detection	2017	CERT	Unsupervised KNN	54	47.5	44.2
	2018	CERT	Hidden Markov Model	71.1	64.1	55.9
	2021	CERT	SVM	70	40	11
	2021	CERT	LSTM	75	20	59
	2021	CERT	DNN	86	36	73
	2021	CERT	MITD	92	54	54
	2021	CERT	HITD	97	77	92
	2020	NSL KDD	Autoencoder	92.96		
	2021	NSL KDD	Stacker	99.39	99.7	99
DoS/DDoS	2020	CICIDS 2017	Autoencoder	95.19		
	2021	UNSW-NB15	ZSL-RF	99.71		96.85
	2021	UNSW-NB15	ZSL-MLP	99.55		96.53
	2021	CICIDS 2017	Stacker	99.97	99.8	100
	2018	KDD CUP 99, NSL KDD	Autoencoder	86.96	88.65	
Anomaly-based	2021	CERT	AITD	90	49	50
	2021	SWaT	CNN	92	88	98
	2021	SWaT	DBN	80	72	72
	2021	SWaT	PCA+CNN	95	94	97
	2021	SWaT	PCA+DBN	91	88	95
	2021	SWaT	BLOSOM	96	96	98
	2020	SPMD	MSALSTM-CNN	96.56	99.06	
	2020	SPMD	WAVED	94.87	98.87	
	2019	SPMD	KF	97.4	94.5	
	2019	SPMD	CNN	98	99.8	
Malware-based	2018	Malware Dataset	tDCGAN	95.74	94.4	91.5
	2021	Network Dataset	DT	-	100	98

Based on Previous work (Ali et al.2022).

AI diligently surveys the digital realm, meticulously analyzing patterns, behaviors, and actions with unmatched swiftness and accuracy.

3.5.1.1.1 Illustration Envision an AI-enabled security system seamlessly integrated into a network infrastructure. This system functions tirelessly, examining data streams in real time, scrutinizing network traffic, user interactions, and system activities. By utilizing the capabilities of ML algorithms, the AI identifies normal behavior patterns within milliseconds, enabling it to promptly detect any deviations that may indicate a potential zero-day threat.

Model Can be Used: Anomaly Detection with Unsupervised Learning

The cornerstone of this AI-enabled security system's capability is an anomaly detection model built on unsupervised learning. Unsupervised learning allows the AI to learn from the inherent structure of the data without explicit labels, making it adept at discerning patterns that deviate from the norm. The model continuously refines its understanding of what constitutes "normal" behavior, adapting to the evolving dynamics of the network environment.

$$\text{Anomaly Score} = \frac{|x_i - \mu|}{\sigma}$$

Where x_i is the current data point, μ is the mean, and σ is the standard deviation of the historical data.

3.5.1.2 Workflow of the AI-Enabled Security System

- Real-Time Data Ingestion

  The AI-enabled security system consistently acquires data from various sources such as network logs, user activities, and system events.

- Feature Extraction

  To distill pertinent information from the incoming data streams, advanced feature extraction techniques are utilized. This involves extracting key characteristics and attributes that define the behavior of the network and its components.

- Training Phase

  During the initial training phase, the AI model learns the baseline patterns of normal behavior by analyzing historical data. This phase enables the system to comprehend the regular activities and communication patterns within the network.

- Real-Time Monitoring

  Once trained, the AI-enabled security system transitions into real-time monitoring mode. It continuously analyzes incoming data streams, applying the learned patterns to identify expected behaviors.

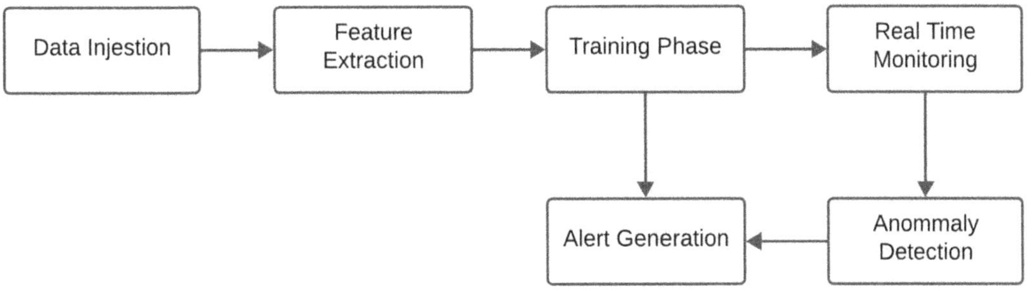

FIGURE 3.4 Workflow of Anomaly Detection.

- Anomaly Detection

  The system's ML algorithms compare real-time observations with the established baseline. Any deviation, anomaly, or unusual pattern triggers an alert, indicating a potential zero-day threat.

- Alert Generation

  Upon detecting an anomaly, the system generates an alert that provides comprehensive insights into the observed deviation. This includes information on the type of anomaly, affected components, and potential risks associated with the deviation.

3.5.1.3 The Vital Role of Anomaly Detection

Anomaly detection emerges as a crucial player in the story of zero-day threat mitigation. In the absence of predefined signatures for zero-day exploits, AI relies on anomaly detection to identify irregularities and deviations from established baselines. This proactive approach empowers AI to identify potential threats that defy traditional security measures.

Real-World Examples:

- Network Anomalies

  Scenario: An AI-driven intrusion detection system monitors network traffic.

  Action: In real time, the AI identifies an unusual surge in data transfer patterns that do not align with normal usage. This triggers an immediate investigation and response, preventing a potential zero-day exploit from infiltrating the network.

- User Behavior Anomalies

  Scenario: AI is integrated into endpoint protection solutions.

  Action: A user, typically engaged in routine activities, suddenly displays abnormal behavior by accessing sensitive files at irregular hours. The AI flags this deviation, recognizing it as a potential insider threat or a zero-day exploit attempting unauthorized access.

- System Process Anomalies

  Scenario: An AI-powered security system monitors system processes.

  Action: Upon detecting an unexpected deviation in the behavior of a critical system process, the AI triggers an alert, initiating an immediate response to investigate and neutralize a potential zero-day attack attempting to manipulate system functions.

- Application Behavior Anomalies

  Scenario: AI is integrated into application security frameworks.

  Action: When an application unexpectedly exhibits behavior inconsistent with its normal operations, the AI identifies this anomaly, raising an alarm and preventing the exploitation of a zero-day vulnerability within the application.

3.6 BEHAVIORAL ANALYSIS AND PREDICTIVE MODELING

The Patterns of Behavioral Analysis in Zero-Day Threat Identification:

Behavioral analysis emerges as a beacon of insight, allowing it to decipher the nuanced patterns of digital behaviors. At the heart of this strategy is the marriage between AI and the ability to scrutinize, understand, and respond to the behaviors that unfold within the digital ecosystem.

3.6.1 AI's Models and Examples for Behavioral Analysis

- User Behavior Analytics (UBA)

  AI Model: ML Algorithms (e.g., Clustering, Decision Trees).

  Example: UBA analyzes user activities such as login patterns, data access, and resource usage. Anomalies, like unusual login times or access to sensitive data, trigger alerts for potential zero-day threats.

  1. Clustering: Functionality: Clustering algorithms group users together based on similarities in their behavior.

     Example: Let's consider an organization that utilizes clustering to identify groups of users who exhibit similar access patterns. If a cluster displays unexpected behavior, such as accessing files outside their usual scope, it could indicate a potential zero-day threat.

$$K - \text{Means Objective Function} = \sum_{i=1}^{k} \sum_{x \in C_i} \|x - \mu_i\|^2$$

     where C_i is the cluster, x are the data points, and μ_i is the centroid of the cluster.

  2. Decision Trees: Functionality: Decision trees create a series of decisions based on user actions, aiding in the identification of specific patterns that lead to anomalies.

     Example: Within the realm of UBA, decision trees can analyze login patterns. For instance, if a user who historically logs in from a specific geographical location suddenly attempts access from a different region, the decision tree can detect this anomaly and trigger an alert.

$$P(y\,|\,X)=\frac{1}{N}\sum_{i=1}^{N} I(y_i = y)\cdot P(X_i\,|\,y_i)$$

where $P(y|X)$ is the probability of outcome y, given feature set X, and I is the indicator function.

UBA Workflow:

- Data Collection
  UBA gathers data on user activities, including login times, data access, and resource usage.

- Feature Extraction
  Relevant features are extracted, such as login frequency, access times, and the sensitivity of the accessed data.

- Clustering Analysis
  Clustering algorithms group users based on similar behavior patterns, helping to identify outliers and anomalies.

- Decision Tree Analysis:
  Decision trees analyze specific user actions, pinpointing deviations from established patterns.

- Anomaly Detection
  Alerts are triggered when users exhibit behavior that falls outside the norm, indicating potential zero-day threats.
  Real-World Scenario: UBA Detecting Anomalous Data Access
  Let's consider an employee who typically accesses a specific set of files during working hours. By utilizing clustering and decision trees, UBA observes that this user, on a weekend and outside of typical hours, attempts to access highly sensitive files that they have never accessed before. This triggers an alert as it significantly deviates from the user's historical behavior, raising suspicion of a potential zero-day threat.

3.6.2 Predictive Modeling: Real-World Applications and AI Models

- Threat Intelligence Platforms
  AI Model: ML Algorithms (e.g., Random Forests).
  Example: Predictive models in threat intelligence platforms analyze historical threat data, helping organizations anticipate potential zero-day threats based on evolving attack trends.

ML Algorithms (Random Forests)

Random Forests are a type of ensemble learning technique that combines multiple decision trees to make accurate predictions.

$$\hat{y} = \frac{1}{T}\sum_{i=1}^{T} \hat{y}_i$$

where:

$\hat{y}$ is the final prediction.

T is the total number of trees in the forest.

$\hat{y}_i$ is the prediction of the i-th tree.

For instance, in Threat Intelligence Platforms, Random Forests play a crucial role in analyzing historical threat data. They take into account various factors such as attack vectors, malware signatures, and tactics used by threat actors. By conducting this analysis, Random Forests help in building predictive models that can anticipate potential zero-day threats.

Workflow of a Threat Intelligence Platform:

- Data Collection

  Threat Intelligence Platforms gather a vast amount of data, including historical threat data, indicators of compromise (IoCs), and information about known attack patterns.

- Feature Extraction

  From the collected data, relevant features are extracted. These features may include attack vectors, malware characteristics, and patterns of past incidents.

- ML Model Training

  ML algorithms, particularly Random Forests, are trained using the historical data to identify patterns associated with known threats. As a result, the model becomes proficient in recognizing relationships between different features.

- Predictive Modeling

  Once the model is trained, it applies the learned patterns to new incoming data. By identifying anomalies or patterns that deviate from historical trends, the model can predict potential zero-day threats.

- Real-Time Threat Analysis

  Threat Intelligence Platforms continuously analyze real-time data by applying the predictive model. This helps in identifying emerging threats. Any deviation from the expected patterns triggers alerts.

- Alert Generation and Mitigation

  When threats are detected, detailed alerts are generated. These alerts provide valuable insights into potential zero-day threats. Security teams can then take proactive measures to mitigate risks and enhance the overall security posture.

Real-Life Situation: Predicting Changing Attack Patterns

Imagine a Threat Intelligence Platform that examines past information about phishing attacks. By understanding the traits of known phishing attempts, the Random Forests model can anticipate potential zero-day threats by detecting fresh patterns or strategies used by threat actors. If a phishing campaign emerges with distinct features that have never been encountered before, the model triggers an alert, empowering organizations to prepare for and protect against the evolving threat.

- Security Information and Event Management (SIEM)

  AI Model: Reinforcement Learning Models.

  Example: SIEM systems use reinforcement learning to adaptively respond to evolving threats. Predictive modeling helps forecast potential security incidents based on historical data.

  Reinforcement Learning Models

  Functionality: Reinforcement learning involves training models to make sequences of decisions by learning from rewards or penalties.

  Example: In the context of SIEM, reinforcement learning models dynamically respond to security events by acquiring knowledge from historical data. These models anticipate potential security incidents, aiding the system in proactively safeguarding against evolving threats.

  Policy *(π)*

  A policy map states actions. The goal is to find the optimal policy *(π*)*.

$$\pi : S \rightarrow A$$

  where S is the set of states and A is the set of actions.

  Value Function (V)

  The value function $V(s)$ represents the expected reward starting from state s and following policy π.

$$V^{\pi}(s) = \mathbb{E}[R_t \mid s_t = s|$$

  where R_t is the cumulative reward from time step t.

Q-Value (Q)

The Q-value $Q(s, a)$ represents the expected reward for taking action a in state s and then following policy π.

$$Q^{\pi}(s,a) = \mathbb{E}[R_t \mid s_t = s, a_t = a]$$

Bellman Equation

The Bellman equation provides a recursive definition for the value function.

$$V(s) = \max_{a} \sum_{s'} \_(s' \mid s,a)[R(s,a,s') + \gamma V(s')]$$

where:
$P(s'|s, a)$ is the transition probability from state s to state s′ given action a.
$R(s, a, s')$ is the reward received after transitioning from s to s' via action a.
γ is the discount factor ($0 \leq \gamma \leq 1$).

Q-Learning Update Rule

In Q-learning, the Q-values are updated using the following rule:

$$Q(s,a) \leftarrow Q(s,a) + \alpha[r + \gamma \max_{a'} Q(s',a') - Q(s,a)]$$

where:
α is the learning rate.
r is the reward received after taking action a in state s.
s' is the next state after taking action a.
SIEM Workflow:

- Data Collection

  SIEM systems gather and consolidate extensive amounts of security-related data, including logs, events, and incident reports.

- Feature Extraction

  Relevant attributes are extracted from the accumulated data, encompassing various aspects such as user behavior, network activities, and system events.

- Reinforcement Learning Model Training

  Reinforcement learning models are trained on historical data to discern patterns associated with normal and abnormal behavior. The model adjusts its decision-making process based on the feedback loop of rewards and penalties.

- Predictive Modeling

  The model applies its acquired patterns to new data, predicting potential security incidents by identifying anomalies or deviations from historical trends.

- Real-Time Event Analysis

  SIEM continuously analyzes real-time security events, employing the reinforcement learning model to dynamically respond to emerging threats. Predictions assist in prioritizing and addressing incidents.

- Adaptive Response and Alert Generation

  The system adaptively responds to security events based on the predictions made by the reinforcement learning model. Alerts are generated, providing insights into potential security incidents and recommended response actions.

  Real-World Scenario: Dynamic Response to Emerging Threats

  Imagine a SIEM system that diligently monitors network traffic. Through the use of reinforcement learning, this advanced model has been trained on historical data to accurately predict normal patterns of network behavior. However, in the event of a new and unfamiliar threat, like a previously unseen malware variant, the model swiftly identifies the anomaly and adjusts its response accordingly. As a result, the SIEM system promptly generates an alert, while the model continuously enhances its comprehension of the ever-changing threat landscape.

- Next-Generation Firewalls

  AI Model: Ensemble Models (combining various algorithms).

  Example: Predictive modeling in Next-Generation Firewalls identifies patterns associated with known threats and predicts potential zero-day vulnerabilities by analyzing network traffic and application behavior.

  Ensemble models are designed to enhance the overall predictive performance and robustness of ML algorithms by integrating multiple models. For instance, in the context of Next-Generation Firewalls, ensemble models are utilized to analyze network traffic and application behavior. By combining diverse algorithms, these models are able to predict potential threats, including zero-day vulnerabilities, based on learned patterns.

  In a real-world scenario, ensemble models play a crucial role in identifying emerging threats. Let's consider a Next-Generation Firewall that is constantly monitoring incoming network traffic. The ensemble model, which consists of various algorithms, has been trained to recognize normal patterns and known threat signatures. However, if a new type of attack, previously unseen, emerges with distinct characteristics, the ensemble model is able to detect this anomaly. As a result, the Firewall generates an alert, and the model adapts itself to incorporate the new threat information. This continuous adaptation enhances the model's predictive capabilities, ensuring that it stays up-to-date with the evolving threat landscape.

- AI-Driven Threat Hunting Platforms

  AI Model: GANs.

  Example: GANs in Threat Hunting Platforms generate synthetic data to simulate potential zero-day scenarios. This aids in training models to recognize novel threat patterns.

  GANs:

  Functionality: GANs consist of a generator and a discriminator, working adversarially to generate realistic synthetic data.

  Example: In Threat Hunting Platforms, GANs generate synthetic data that simulates potential zero-day scenarios. The generated data aids in training models to recognize novel threat patterns and enhances the platform's ability to proactively hunt for emerging threats.

- Data Generation with GANs

  Threat Hunting Platforms use GANs to generate synthetic data that simulates potential zero-day scenarios. This synthetic data represents various attack patterns, behaviors, and tactics.

- Training Models with Synthetic Data

  The generated synthetic data is used to train ML models, enabling them to recognize and understand novel threat patterns.

- Threat Simulation

  The trained models simulate potential zero-day scenarios using the knowledge gained from the synthetic data. This includes mimicking new attack vectors, evasion techniques, and emerging threat behaviors.

- Real-Time Threat Analysis

  Threat Hunting Platforms continuously analyze real-time data, incorporating the insights gained from the synthetic data and trained models. This allows the platform to detect anomalies that may signify emerging threats.

- Alert Generation and Threat Hunting

  Detected anomalies trigger alerts, prompting threat hunters to investigate potential zero-day threats. Threat hunting involves actively searching for and mitigating emerging threats based on the knowledge gained from synthetic data.

  Real-World Scenario: Simulating Novel Threat Scenarios

  Consider a Threat Hunting Platform that leverages GANs to generate synthetic data representing a new type of malware behavior. The generated data includes unique characteristics and evasion techniques. The platform uses this synthetic data to train models to recognize these novel threat patterns. When a similar pattern emerges in real-time data, the platform detects the anomaly, generating an alert for further investigation (Huang et al., 2017).

3.7 CHALLENGES AND LIMITATIONS IN ZERO-DAY THREAT DETECTION

3.7.1 Relying Solely on AI: A Pragmatic Assessment

- Adversarial Sophistication

  Challenge: Adversaries are becoming increasingly adept at creating attacks specifically designed to evade AI detection. This poses a significant challenge to the reliability of AI as the primary defence against rapidly evolving zero-day threats.

  Mitigation: To address this challenge, it is crucial to continuously improve AI models through robust adversarial training and the integration of diverse detection mechanisms.

- False Positives and Negatives

  Challenge: AI models can generate false positives, mistakenly identifying normal activities as threats, or false negatives, overlooking actual zero-day threats. Striking the right balance between precision and recall remains an ongoing challenge.

  Mitigation: To mitigate this issue, algorithms need to be fine-tuned, human validation should be incorporated, and ensemble models can be leveraged to minimize false outcomes.

- Limited Historical Data

  Challenge: The lack of historical data, inherent in zero-day threats, poses a significant obstacle for AI systems that heavily rely on past patterns for detection.

  Mitigation: To overcome this challenge, it is essential to integrate unsupervised learning approaches, anomaly detection techniques, and continuously adapt the models to handle novel threats without relying on historical references.

- Interpretable AI Decisions

  Challenge: The lack of transparency in AI decision-making processes hinders the understanding of flagged activities. Trust and confidence are vital factors in the effectiveness of AI in detecting zero-day threats.

  Mitigation: To address this challenge, incorporating XAI models is crucial. These models enhance transparency and provide insights into the rationale behind AI's decision-making process (Lourens et. al. 2022).

3.7.2 Ethical Considerations and Broader Limitations

- Bias and Fairness

  Challenge: AI models have the potential to inherit biases from training data, which can result in discriminatory outcomes. In the case of zero-day threat detection, biased models may disproportionately affect certain user groups.

  Mitigation: Thoroughly identifying and addressing biases during model development, prioritizing fairness in training data, and continuously monitoring for equitable outcomes.

- Privacy Concerns

  Challenge: The in-depth analysis of user behaviors raises concerns regarding user privacy. Striking a balance between effective threat detection and preserving individual privacy poses an ethical dilemma.

  Mitigation: Implementing privacy-preserving AI techniques, such as federated learning or differential privacy, to ensure minimal intrusion on individual privacy.

- Human-Machine Collaboration

  Challenge: Excessive reliance on AI without human oversight can result in overlooking contextual nuances or misinterpreting complex situations.

Mitigation: Encouraging a collaborative approach where AI enhances human decision-making with human experts providing crucial insights and context (Abbas et al., 2023).

- Continuous Evolution of Threat Tactics

  Challenge: Adversarial tactics evolve rapidly requiring AI models to continuously adapt to keep up with emerging threats.

  Mitigation: Establishing mechanisms for frequent model updates, integrating threat intelligence, and utilizing ML for autonomous model improvement.

3.8 CASE STUDIES AND SUCCESS STORIES

- **Stuxnet Worm**

  AI Intervention: An AI-powered anomaly detection system within a critical infrastructure facility detected unusual patterns in the behavior of the control system.

  AI Model: Anomaly Detection Algorithms

  Outcome: The AI system successfully identified the Stuxnet worm, a highly sophisticated zero-day threat that specifically targeted industrial control systems. Timely intervention prevented potentially catastrophic consequences.

  Insights: Proactive monitoring, particularly in critical infrastructure, plays a vital role. The AI's capability to detect anomalies in system behavior can reveal even the most covert threats.

- **DeepBlueAI's Email Security**

  AI Intervention: DeepBlueAI's email security solution utilizes natural language processing to analyze the content of emails and identify phishing attempts.

  AI Model: Natural Language Processing (NLP) Models.

  Outcome: The AI model effectively detected and neutralized a zero-day phishing attack that managed to evade traditional email filters.

  Insights: The language comprehension capabilities of AI enhance email security, offering a proactive defence against evolving phishing techniques.

- **Darktrace's Autonomous Response**

  AI Intervention: Darktrace's AI-driven platform detected abnormal network behavior that indicated the presence of a zero-day exploit.

  AI Model: Unsupervised Learning and Behavioral Analysis.

  Outcome: The AI system autonomously responded by isolating the affected segment, preventing the lateral movement of the threat and the unauthorized extraction of data.

  Insights: The autonomous response capabilities of AI contribute to swift containment, minimizing the impact of zero-day threats within the network.

- **Microsoft Defender ATP**

  AI Intervention: Microsoft Defender ATP employs ML models to analyze the behaviors of endpoints and detect zero-day threats.

AI Model: ML Models (Random Forests, Gradient Boosting, DNN, Reinforcement Learning).

Outcome: The AI-driven system successfully identified and mitigated a previously unknown fileless malware attack, showcasing the adaptability of AI in detecting new and emerging threats.

Insights: AI's ability to learn from evolving threats enables it to identify and respond to zero-day threats without relying on pre-existing signatures.

3.9 FUTURE DIRECTIONS AND INNOVATIONS IN AI FOR ZERO-DAY THREAT DETECTION

1. Explainable AI

   Advancement: The integration of XAI techniques aims to enhance transparency and interpretability in zero-day threat detection models. By enabling cybersecurity professionals to understand the reasoning behind AI decisions, XAI promotes trust and facilitates more effective collaboration between AI and human analysts.

2. Federated Learning for Privacy-Preserving Collaboration

   Advancement: The adoption of federated learning approaches allows for collaborative model training across multiple organizations without the need to share sensitive data. This innovative method enhances the collective knowledge of AI models while respecting privacy concerns, making it particularly relevant for industries with strict data protection requirements.

3. Reinforcement Learning for Adaptive Defences

   Advancement: There is an increased utilization of reinforcement learning to develop adaptive and self-improving defence mechanisms. AI systems that leverage reinforcement learning continuously learn from their interactions with the environment, enabling them to autonomously adapt to emerging zero-day threats and evolving attack tactics.

4. GANs for Threat Simulation

   Advancement: The utilization of GANs to simulate and generate realistic threat scenarios for training AI models is a significant development. GANs have the ability to create synthetic data that mimics the characteristics of zero-day threats, allowing AI models to learn from a wider range of potential attack patterns and enhance their resilience against unseen threats.

5. Adversarial ML Defences

   Advancement: Progress in developing sophisticated defences against adversarial attacks on AI models. This entails incorporating robust mechanisms to identify and counter attempts by attackers to manipulate or deceive AI systems, ensuring the dependability and effectiveness of zero-day threat detection in the face of highly skilled adversaries.

6. Edge AI for Real-Time Threat Detection

   Advancement: Utilization of Edge AI to enable instantaneous threat detection directly on devices and endpoints. Edge AI reduces reliance on centralized processing, enabling quicker decision-making and response, which is crucial in situations where immediate action is required to prevent the proliferation of zero-day threats.

7. Continuous Model Updates with AI Operations

   Advancement: Integration of AI Operations (AI Ops) to facilitate continuous updates and enhancements to models. AI Ops combines ML with IT operations, allowing organizations to automate the management and deployment of AI models for zero-day threat detection, ensuring that the defences remain up-to-date and efficient (Kaur et al., 2023).

3.9.1 Ongoing Research and Development

1. Zero-Day Vulnerability Prediction

   Developing predictive models to anticipate potential zero-day vulnerabilities before they are exploited. Ongoing research aims to create algorithms that analyze software vulnerabilities and forecast the probability of them being targeted by attackers. This enables proactive patching and mitigation measures.

2. Dynamic Behavioral Analysis

   Advancing dynamic behavioral analysis techniques that can adapt to rapidly evolving attack tactics. Ongoing research focuses on enhancing the ability of AI models to analyze and respond to real-time behavioral anomalies, particularly in complex and interconnected systems.

3. Human-in-the-Loop AI

   Integrating human analysts into the decision-making process through human-in-the-loop AI systems. Research explores methods to seamlessly combine human expertise with AI capabilities, allowing analysts to provide insights, validate findings, and enhance the overall effectiveness of zero-day threat detection.

4. AI for Network Heterogeneity

   Tailoring AI models for heterogeneous network environments, taking into account the diversity of devices, protocols, and communication patterns. Ongoing research explores the development of AI algorithms that can effectively detect and respond to zero-day threats in networks with diverse infrastructures.

5. Self-Healing Cyber-Physical Systems

   Research is currently focused on the development of self-healing cyber-physical systems that utilize AI to autonomously identify and mitigate zero-day threats in critical infrastructure. The goal is to create resilient systems that can adapt to unforeseen vulnerabilities and threats without the need for human intervention.

6. Adaptive Threat Intelligence Sharing

   The focus here is on developing adaptive models for sharing threat intelligence that can dynamically adjust to the ever-changing threat landscape. Ongoing research aims to create frameworks that enable organizations to share real-time threat intelligence, thereby enhancing collective defences against zero-day threats.

7. Blockchain for Decentralized Threat Intelligence

   Researchers are investigating the use of blockchain technology to create decentralized platforms for sharing threat intelligence. The aim is to improve the collaborative response to zero-day threats by enabling secure and transparent sharing of threat intelligence across organizations.

3.10 CONCLUSION

The integration of AI into zero-day threat detection, known as the "Invisible Defence," has been an exploration in the field of cybersecurity. This chapter has extensively explored the technologies, emerging paradigms, and the collaborative evolution of AI and human expertise. It represents a comprehensive approach to defending against cyber threats, going beyond being a mere shield and instead forming a dynamic partnership that combines human comprehension with the precision of AI-driven analysis. The concept of the Invisible Defence comes to life through advancements such as reinforcement learning, which emphasizes adaptability as the foundation of defence. GANs simulate threats, strengthening AI models to effectively combat unforeseen attacks. Defences in adversarial ML and the integration of Edge AI elevate the shield to a real-time guardian, capable of thwarting even the most sophisticated attacks. Ongoing research efforts, ranging from experiential learning to the fusion of neuromorphic computing and blockchain for decentralized threat intelligence, demonstrate a commitment to staying ahead in the constant run with adversaries. The convergence of AI with various domains, including quantum-resistant cryptography, presents a comprehensive strategy to reinforce the Invisible Defence across the interconnected digital landscape. To summarize, the Invisible Defence goes beyond being just a metaphor. It represents a shared expedition towards the future of cybersecurity, encompassing the combination of human intuition and AI accuracy. This collaboration aims to safeguard the digital frontier from unforeseen and unparalleled obstacles that await us, serving as evidence of our unwavering commitment to innovation, adaptability, and ethical principles as we navigate the ever-changing realm of zero-day threat detection, guaranteeing a robust and protected digital future.

REFERENCES

Abbas, Roba, Michael, Katina, Pitt, Jeremy, Vogel, Kathleen M., and Zafeirakopoulos, Mariana. (2023). Artificial Intelligence (AI) in cybersecurity: A socio-technical research roadmap. July 2023 (draft), October 2023 (final). The Alan Turing Institute.

Alazab, Mamoun, Swarna Priya RM, M. Parimala, Praveen Kumar Reddy Maddikunta, Thippa Reddy Gadekallu, and Quoc-Viet Pham. (2022). Federated Learning for Cybersecurity: Concepts, Challenges, and Future Directions. In *IEEE Transactions on Industrial Informatics*, vol. 18, no. 5, pp. 3501–3509. doi: 10.1109/TII.2021.3119038.

Ali, Shamshair, Rehman, Saif, Imran, Azhar, Adeem, Ghazif, Iqbal, Zafar, Kim, Ki-Il. (2022). Comparative evaluation of AI-based techniques for zero-day attacks detection. *Electronics*, 11(23), 3934, https://doi.org/10.3390/electronics11233934

Capuano, Nicola, Fenza, Giuseppe, Loia, Vincenzo, and Stanzione, Claudio. (2022). Explainable artificial intelligence in cyberSecurity: A survey. *IEEE Access*, 10, 1–1. https://doi.org/10.1109/ACCESS.2022.3204171

Guo, Yang. (2023). A review of Machine Learning-based zero-day attack detection: Challenges and future directions., *Computer Communications*, 198, 175–185, ISSN 0140-3664, https://doi.org/10.1016/j.comcom.2022.11.001

Huang, Sandy, Papernot, Nicolas, Goodfellow, Ian, Duan, Yan, and Abbeel, Pieter. (2017). Adversarial Attacks on Neural Network Policies. *arXiv preprint arXiv:1702.02284.*

Kaur, Ramanpreet, Gabrijelčič, Dušan, and Klobučar, Tomaž. (2023). Artificial intelligence for cybersecurity: Literature review and future research directions. *Information Fusion*, 97, 101804, ISSN 1566-2535, https://doi.org/10.1016/j.inffus.2023.101804

Lourens, Melanie, Dabral, Amar Prakash, Gangodkar, Durgaprasad, Rathour, Navjot, Tida, C. Nagabhushanam, and Chadha, Anupama. (2022). "Integration of AI with the Cybersecurity: A detailed Systematic review with the practical issues and challenges," *2022 5th International Conference on Contemporary Computing and Informatics (IC3I)*, Uttar Pradesh, India, pp. 1290–1295, https://doi.org/10.1109/IC3I56241.2022.10073040

Talukder, Md Alamin, Md Manowarul Islam, Md Ashraf Uddin, Khondokar Fida Hasan, Selina Sharmin, Salem A. Alyami, and Mohammad Ali Moni (2024). Machine learning-based network intrusion detection for big and imbalanced data using oversampling, stacking feature embedding and feature extraction. *Journal of Big Data*, 11, 33. https://doi.org/10.1186/s40537-024-00886-w

Tasneem, Sumaiya, Gupta, Kishor Datta, Roy, Arunav, and Dasgupta, Dipankar. (2022). Generative Adversarial Networks (GAN) for cyber security: Challenges and opportunities. In *Proceedings of the 2022 IEEE Symposium Series on Computational Intelligence*, pp. 4–7.

Truong, Thanh Cong, Diep, Quoc Bao, and Zelinka, Ivan. (2020). Artificial intelligence in the cyber domain: Offense and defense. *Symmetry*, 12, 410. https://doi.org/10.3390/sym12030410

Zhang, Jun, Pan, Lei, Han, Qing-Long, Chen, Chao, Wen, Sheng, and Xiang, Yang. (2022). Deep learning based attack detection for cyber-physical system cybersecurity: A survey. *IEEE/CAA Journal of Automatica Sinica*, 9(3), 377–391. https://doi.org/10.1109/JAS.2021.1004261

CHAPTER 4

Fusion of Deep Architectures in Intent-Driven Networks for Intrusion Detection

Obinna Johnbosco Awoke, Rajesh Prasad, Ndubuisi Godcares, and Najeeb Saiyed

4.1 INTRODUCTION

The society which we find ourselves presently in is a very advanced society which uses technology to solve so many real-world problems. The internet never ceases to be a part of this technologically advanced society. In fact, it is the backbone of so many more present advanced achievements.

The internet as a networking of various devices has immensely contributed to solving a real-world problem of resource management and control. The network is the lifeblood of modern organizations. To meet various demands of our now-dynamic business, the traditional networking paradigm has been making way for a more reliable, resourceful, and innovative way of networking known as Intent-based networking (IBN). IBN is an innovative approach in computer networks, which concerns managing a network to serve a desired business intent and not intents outside the business organization. This includes the configuration of the network to adhere to strict business policies. This has revolutionized high-level business objectives and has given organizations the privilege to define how their network will act. It has also simplified network management by abstracting the complexity of network configuration and operations, making it more intuitive and automated, thus enhancing various business objectives. It utilizes a network management approach that uses artificial intelligence (AI) and machine learning (ML) to automate all the organizational tasks which can be applied across the network. It bridges the gap between business and IT by capturing business intent and continuously aligning the end-to-end network

DOI: 10.1201/9781032714813-4

with that intent. The network can translate the intents into network policies. IBN gives enterprises the ability to design a flexible and scalable network while also using network automation software to accelerate performance. For data and network security, ML in various research has been integrated into these intent-based networks to detect anomaly activities in the network. An IBN infrastructure/architecture includes various stages which includes the definition of the intent, translation of the intent into actionable policies and configurations, implementation of the translated policies into the network infrastructure, continuous monitoring, maintenance, and continuous improvement through a feedback mechanism. These stages are illustrated in Figure 4.1.

Intent definition involves defining high-level goals and policies for the network, while translation converts this into actionable policies. Activation ensures consistent deployment across the network infrastructure, while Validation involves continuous monitoring, compliance checks, and security assessments. Assurance and Optimization use ML and AI to maintain the network's desired state and provide improvement recommendations.

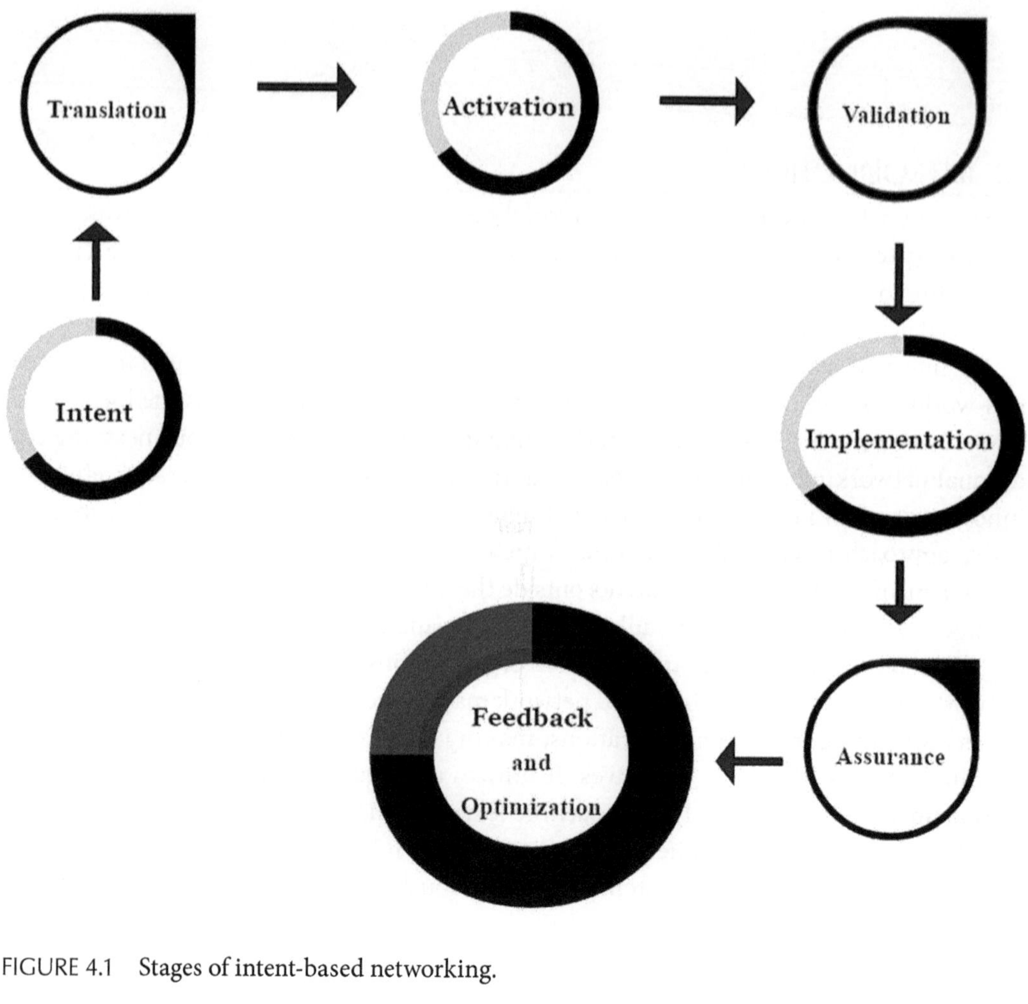

FIGURE 4.1 Stages of intent-based networking.

ML algorithms are very much capable of detecting activities such as intrusions, which is illustrated in Figure 4.1. ML and deep learning (DL) algorithms are used to train models that can learn, adapt, and make predictions, detecting behaviors in a system which has not been observed over previous network-time use. Leveraging ML algorithms provide an edge to a more secure network by analyzing large amount of data of previously captured data packets and understanding the pattern of the network. Intrusion detection system (IDS) as a security mechanism comprises of various types which includes Host-Based IDS and Network-Based IDS [1] (Figure 4.2).

The introduction of ML-IDS serves as a very effective tool to detect anomaly actions that pose a threat to the network. This approach will also enable businesses to proactively manage their networks, predict issues or threats before they occur, and ensure seamless and intelligent connectivity that promotes further business plans or objectives. Leveraging ML algorithms into intent-based networks provides so many resourceful opportunities and solutions that will ensure business objectives are always met and secure.

Despite the advancements in IBN and its potential to revolutionize network management through automation and alignment with business objectives, there remains a critical challenge in ensuring robust security against sophisticated cyber threats, and that is what this research seeks to address—The question "How can the integration of deep learning algorithms within intent-driven networks enhance intrusion detection systems (IDS)"? By exploring this question, this study aims to contribute to the development of more secure and intelligent networks that not only meet business intents but also proactively defend against potential intrusions. This study explores intent-driven networks and DL-empowered IDS in such networks.

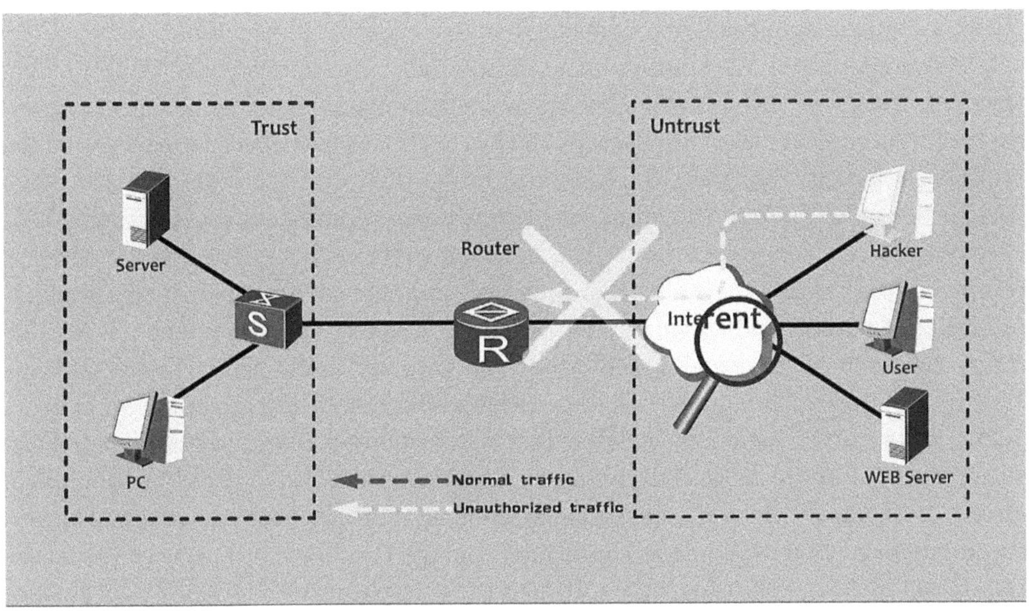

FIGURE 4.2 Integration of an ML model for Intrusion detection in a network.

4.2 LITERATURE REVIEW

IBN is an innovation that aims for flexibility, agility, and condensed network configuration with minimal external assistance. While exploring the broad aspect of IBN advancements, a comprehensive examination of IBN was conducted, focusing on IBN components including translating, resolution, purpose expression, activation, and assurance, as well as identifying unresolved issues and future perspectives for the problem on how IBN has transformed businesses and how it has provided solutions with little human efforts [2]. A study was also done on IBN, as a cutting-edge networking strategy that permits autonomous network setup based on users' high-level intentions. It suggested a network verification method specifically designed for data center IBN networks. The model incorporates ML time-series forecasting models together with data preparation techniques, such as convolutional neural network (CNN) and recurrent neural network (RNN). The results proved that the suggested strategies are effective in estimating CPU percentage consumption with high accuracy and speed [3]. ML algorithms have tremendous capabilities, and these capabilities are being utilized in various aspects that contribute to application-based developments utilizing their strengths for various complex applications of human ideas and implementations. Aside from this very application of ML and DL algorithms to estimate CPU percentage consumption in an IBN infrastructure, ML models have been built with an objective of improving security in a network. Before the introduction of ML algorithms in IDS for traditional networks, statistical approaches, including anomaly detection and rule-based models, were employed [4,5]. Primarily focusing on anomaly detection and signature-based misuse detection [6]. Recent advancements also suggested Stateful Protocol Analysis, which inspects network traffic and detects potential security threats by maintaining an understanding of the state of communication protocols [7]. Anomaly detection tries to identify whether usage patterns that deviate from accepted norms can be identified as intrusions. Signature-based misuse detection, on the other hand, looks for intrusions by identifying patterns of popular assaults or system vulnerabilities.

IBN strategy utilizes ML to automate network design and guarantee the reliability of network resources. As a testbed for the implementation and handling of the network complexity, the IBN abstraction layer and the M-CORD were utilized as testbeds for next generation implementation [8]. They were also examined in the context of the sixth-generation (6G) wireless networks. By converting user business purposes into network configurations, IBNs effectively address common network issues including efficiency, flexibility, and security. It continuously learns and adjusts depending on real-time network data to satisfy the demands of intelligent services and dynamic radio propagation in 6G. The examination of 6G IBN frameworks and methodologies, addressed both core and radio access networks [9,10], another explored recent advancements in intent-based technologies, focusing on network management and orchestration. It analyzed standardization activities and platforms and discussed their future challenges [11]. Network regulations were also outlined by IBN, which directs configuration through supporting systems. It addresses problems and emphasizes the importance of ONOS's role in automation through intentions [12]. Another advanced research on IBN, suggests using the 5G-ERA project to implement AI-driven IBN for autonomous robots. The process comprises of explanations of functions, inputs, outputs, and ML/semantic model tools. In meeting certain business intents which various models are unable to achieve, an innovative forecasting technique called LossLeap was proposed. It automatically figures out how to decrease the latter by minimizing the link between prediction and goal management aim. Various studies reveal that LossLeap beats benchmarks, including cutting-edge tools for predicting network capacity [13]. Another study proposed a technique for intent-specific automation pipelines, fully aware of the fact that they are learning on their own, a closed-loop micro-service with self-declared capabilities. The research looks at the practicality of combining cooperating implementation units into such pipelines. This method eliminates the ambiguity between human aim explanation and machine aim achievement while maintaining flexibility and adaptability [14].

4.3 RELATED WORKS

Research Paper	Approach	Datasets Used	Algorithms/Models	Key Results
Ashiku, Lirim, and Cihan Dagli (2021) [15]	Developed an adaptive and resilient IDS using DL	UNSW-NB15	DL architectures	Effective in detecting and classifying network attacks
Talukder, Md Alamin, et al. (2023) [16]	Proposed a hybrid model combining ML and DL for IDS	KDDCUP'99, CIC-MalMem-2022	Hybrid of ML and DL algorithms	Accuracy: 99.99% (KDDCUP'99), 100% (CIC-MalMem-2022)
Ahmad, Zeeshan, et al. (2021) [17]	Proposed network-based IDS using ML and DL	Not specified	ML and DL approaches	Discussed strengths, limitations, and challenges
Su, Tongtong, et al. (2020) [18]	Proposed Bidirectional Attention Transformers (BAT) model integrating Bidirectional Long Short Term Memory (BLSTM) with attention mechanism	Not specified	BLSTM with attention mechanism	Improved anomaly detection, no feature engineering required
Gamage, Sunanda, and Jagath Samarabandu (2020) [19]	Developed DL models for IDS using four DL architectures	KDD 99, NSL-KDD, CIC-IDS2017, CIC-IDS2018	Feed-forward neural network, autoencoder, deep belief network, LSTM	Deep feed-forward neural network outperformed others
Elmasry, Wisam, Akhan Akbulut, and Abdul Halim Zaim (2020) [20]	Utilized double PSO-based algorithm to optimize feature subsets and hyperparameters	Two IDS datasets	DNN, LSTM, DBN	4%–6% increase in Detection Rate, 1%–5% reduction in False Alarm Rate
Ferrag, Mohamed Amine, et al. (2020) [21]	Surveyed DL approaches for IDS across 35 datasets	Various datasets categorized into seven types	RNN, DNN, RBM, DBN, CNN, DBM, deep autoencoders	Evaluated performance using accuracy, false alarm rate, detection rate
Su, Tongtong, et al. (2020) [18]	Proposed BAT model integrating BLSTM with attention mechanism	Not specified	BLSTM with attention mechanism	Improved anomaly detection, no feature engineering required

4.4 DATASET DESCRIPTION

The dataset is provided by the Canadian Institute of Cybersecurity and can be found at [22]. The dataset though simulated was properly optimized to provide a core overview of the working mechanism in a network in real-time. Real traces were analyzed to create profiles for agents that generated real traffic for HTTP, SMTP, SSH, IMAP, POP3, and FTP. The profiles created were then employed in an experiment to generate the dataset in a testbed environment. The dataset is sorely for interfaces involving intrusions. A more detailed explanation of the dataset is provided by the Institute on their webpage which can be accessed with the above provided reference.

4.5 IMPLEMENTATION MECHANISM

ML models are trained by learning and understanding the complex patterns in a data, taking note of the smoothness of the network, and recognizing patterns of abnormal network behavior as well as potential security threats. They have the capability to learn and implement what they have learnt to give a desired output. When a model is trained on a vast amount of data such as network traffic data which is a time-series data, they can detect anomalies that pose a threat to the entire network security.

Being integrated into networking devices such as the router used by an organization or business, it will operate in real-time, detecting intrusions and sending responses to signals that pose a threat to the entire network, thus ensuring that the integrity of the network remains intact.

4.5.1 Methodology

Building an ML model that will be fully implementable in a network can be very challenging, but we are proposing a sequential approach, which was meticulously taken after a careful study of the dataset. The same is seen in Figure 4.3.

The dataset contains 2,071,657 instances and each instance has 21 features. The pattern in a network is likely not able to follow a specific pattern and that is the knowledge we are training on. Training a model based on the provided instances that has a unique label for each instance will enable the model to understand the difference between a normal network traffic and an abnormal network traffic. The sequential procedure used in building the model is contained in the below bullet points.

4.5.1.1 Preprocessing Techniques

Preprocessing techniques are the basic building blocks to the training of a model. It involved various steps and various approaches used to process the model to ensure that the model learns and understands. It is a very core step.

- *Handling Missing values*

  First, we handled missing values and dropped columns where the percentage of missing values was more than 50%. Relatively, about six columns contained missing values of which four were more than 50%. The decisive action to drop these columns was made after careful consideration of the effect of the columns either being a part

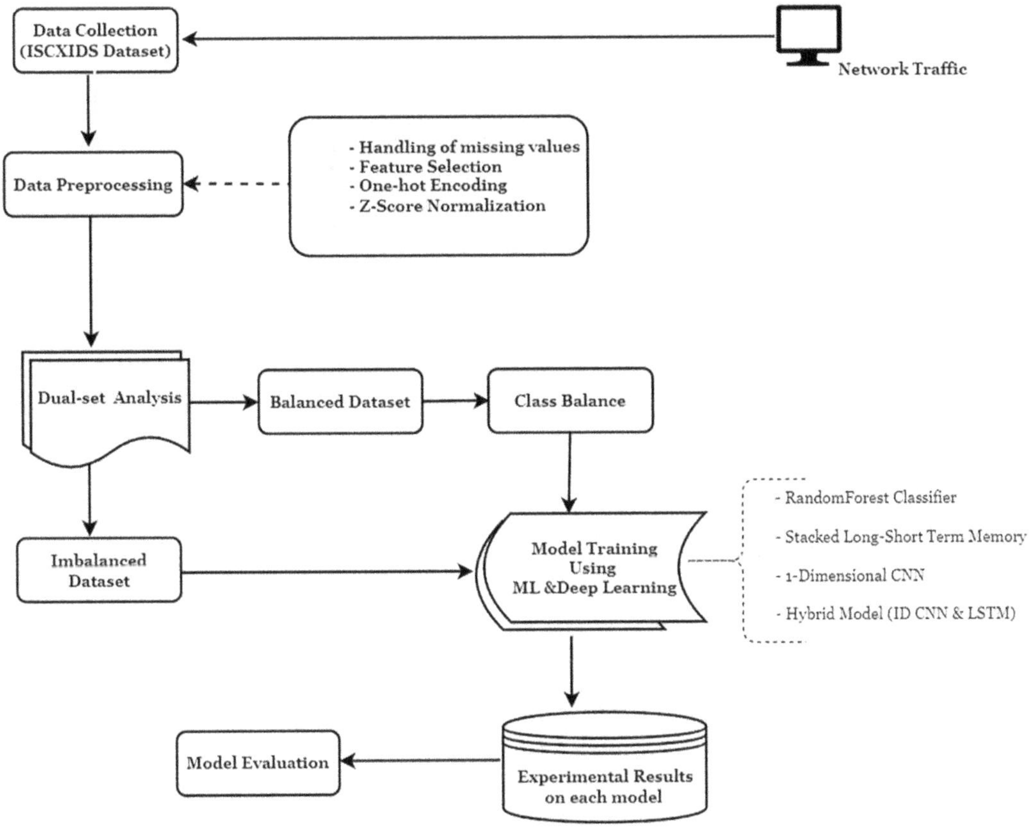

FIGURE 4.3 Diagram showing the proposed implemented methodology.

or not being a part of the data to be used to train the model. Particularly for the reason:

- The column "Payload" in encodings such as Base64 and UTF, both for the source and destination doesn't typically contain the actual content of the communication, and therefore is not very significant for the defined problem objective, "Intrusion Detection," where we are focusing on analyzing packet headers and other attributes more closely associated with intrusion behaviors.

  For the columns "sourceTCPFlagsDescription" and "destinationTCPFlagsDescription" with missing values of 20% and 23% respectively, we predicted the missing values for these categorical columns using the numerical columns of the dataset. The algorithm used for the prediction was the Random Forest Classifier because of its unique value of feature importance estimation and better handling of outliers.

- *Balancing Classes*

  For our target variable, given that our model's primary objective is to classify network traffic on ground-truths either "Normal" or "Attack," we had class imbalance where the number of instances for a normal network traffic was more than the abnormal network traffic. This was utilized for the balanced data training only.

  The value count for each category can be seen in Figure 4.4.

```
Normal  2002747
Attack    68910
Name: Label, dtype: int64
```

FIGURE 4.4 Value for each category in the label (target variable).

For this reason, we downsampled the majority class ("Normal") to exactly match the number of samples present in the minority class. After downsampling the majority class, we had an equal number of instances for each class category. The core reason for this choice is to ensure that the model learns from both representations by not having a class imbalance that could bias the model's predictions. By balancing the class distribution, we aim to prevent the model from favoring one class over the other during training, thereby improving its ability to accurately classify instances from both classes. This approach helps mitigate the risk of misclassification, particularly for the minority class, which might otherwise be overlooked in a heavily imbalanced dataset. Additionally, having an equal number of instances for each class simplifies the interpretation of model performance metrics, as it ensures that accuracy, precision, recall, and other metrics are not disproportionately influenced by the class distribution. Overall, downsampling the majority class ensures a fair representation of both classes in the training data, leading to a more robust and unbiased model.

- *One-Hot Encoding*

  We used the One-Hot Encoding algorithm to convert the categorical columns to numerical columns. Encoding these columns is very necessary as the ML algorithms train and learn from numerical data.

  The choice of One-Hot Encoding was specifically for the features as we are classifying our instances based on the two distinct class labels. These features are not ordinal, meaning there is no inherent order among the categories, therefore the choice of the encoding algorithm. The working mechanism of One-Hot Encoding is that for each unique category in a specific column, a binary column is created, where each instance in a particular row mapping perfectly to the binary column is encoded as 1 and the rest as 0. This helped capture the probability distribution for each class.

- *Feature Selection*

  We dropped columns that were of no significant importance to the model, therefore reducing the number of instance features where the downsampled number of instances has only ten features for each instance, that is, 68,910 instances with each instance having ten features.

- *Normalization*

  We normalized our data, and the normalization was done using the z-score normalization. The z-score normalization was done to ensure that the features have similar scales, which can improve convergence and performance. The working mechanism behind this normalization technique is that it uses the mean and standard deviation of the dataset to normalize each data point in the dataset.

Z-score normalization equation is shown in Equation 4.1.

$$Z = \frac{X - \mu}{\sigma} \tag{4.1}$$

where:

X is the data point, otherwise can be referred to as instance
μ is the mean
σ is the standard deviation

We initially considered using Min-Max normalization to standardize the data. However, due to the presence of outliers in our dataset, we decided against this technique. The dataset is a time-series, meaning it is captured over time. In such datasets, certain data points should not be part of the training sample. Using Min-Max normalization would have been problematic because outliers would disproportionately affect the data distribution by skewing the minimum and maximum values.

Using this *Z*-score normalization technique, we normalized the whole instances in the dataset. This improves the performance of the model, making sure that the data points are all on the same scale, that is, it prevents a single data point from dominating the model's learning process due to its magnitude. The choice of this particular normalization technique is centered on the need to avoid the model's sensitivity to outliers.

4.5.1.2 Model Training

The training algorithms we used for this model are Random Forest Classifier, Stacked long short-term memory (LSTM), one-dimensional convolutional neural network (1D CNN), and DL Hybrid Model architecture which comprises of 1D CNN and an LSTM layer. These algorithms were used for both imbalanced and balanced datasets. The same architectural parameters were used for both save in the case of the Random Forest Classifier for the imbalanced data where we used GridSearchCV. We split out dataset into train, test, and validation sets in the ratio 80:10:10. The learning rate of 0.001 was utilized for all the algorithms. The models were trained on V100 GPU provided by Google for the Colab Pro version which offers 53GB CPU and 16GB GPU.

4.5.1.2.1 Training on Balanced Data

4.5.1.2.1.1 Random Forest Classifier Algorithm The Random Forest algorithm is an ensemble method that combines multiple decision trees to make a prediction [23]. The trees are built using a random selection of features at each split, which helps to reduce overfitting. We used the Random Forest Classifier because of its capability in handling large datasets with many features and it also has good performance in terms of accuracy and robustness against noise and outliers. Here we used "entropy" as the criterion for making decisions of the root node.

Entropy is used to measure the impurity of the split. Entropy is calculated using the equation shown in Equation 4.2.

$$E(S) = -P(+)\log P(+) - P(-)\log P(-) \tag{4.2}$$

Given the criterion for the Random Forest decision on the root node, we trained the model on 100 estimators and a depth of 3 to avoid the tree cutting too deep, becoming too complex and then result to overfitting on the training data. In Random Forest, "estimators" are referred to as the number of decision trees that are included in the forest. Each decision tree is trained independently on a bootstrap sample of the data, and their predictions are combined through averaging (regression) or voting (classification) to make the final prediction. For our desired objective, the voting technique was utilized. The structure of a typical Random Forest Classifier is illustrated in Figure 4.5. Each tree in the forest is

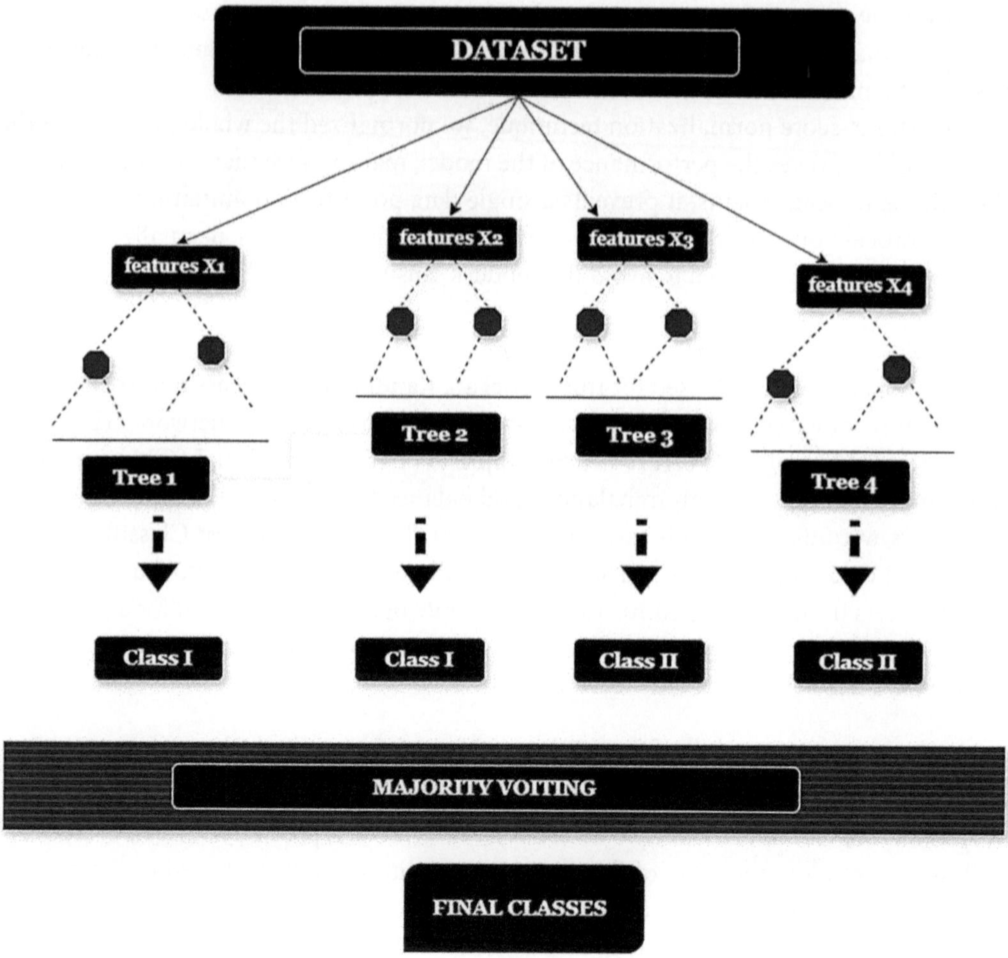

FIGURE 4.5 Typical structure of the Random Forest Classifier Algorithm.

TABLE 4.1 No. of Parameters Recorded for the Balanced Dataset

SN	Model	No. of Parameters
1.	Random Forest Classifier	-
2.	1D CNN	293,442
3.	Stacked LSTM	50,902
4.	Hybrid Model(1D CNN & LSTM)	313,058

constructed using a random subset of features, and the final prediction is made by aggregating the predictions from all trees.

After training, the model was evaluated using various metrics, including accuracy, precision, recall, and F1 Score, to assess its performance comprehensively. The results of these evaluations are summarized in Table 4.1.

4.5.1.2.1.2 Stacked Long Short-Term Memory A Stacked LSTM model architecture comprises of multiple hidden LSTM layers where the output of the first layer is passed to the next layer until the last layer. The choice of this algorithm/model architecture for training is that it is robust in generalization and sequential time-series computation. Given our primary goal of detecting intrusions in a network, which requires analyzing sequences of data to determine network security, the sequential nature of LSTMs makes it an ideal choice. As an extension of the RNN model, it has been proven effective in sequential training tasks, mitigating the vanishing gradient problem of the RNN model. Due to the long sequential computations, the RNN model has difficulty learning from longer dependencies, thus, it reaches a point where the model finds it extremely difficult to learn further which reduces the efficiency of the trained agent.

LSTM models address this by introducing a cell structure with three gates: the forget gate, the input gate, and the output gate which is portrayed in Figure 4.6.

With the efficiency of this model in capturing longer dependencies, we created a Stacked LSTM model as shown in Figure 4.7 which comprises of three LSTM layers. The model was built using the Sequential API to add more LSTM layers. The models' architecture starts with an LSTM layer of 50 units configured to return sequences and accepting input with the shape corresponding to the normalized training data. The layer was followed by a dropout layer with a dropout rate of 0.2 to prevent overfitting. So, during training, some neurons are dropped before the data trained on the previous layer is passed to the next LSTM layer. The second LSTM layer with 50 units was also configured to return sequences. This is again followed by a dropout layer with a dropout rate of 0.2. The third LSTM layer with 50 units was then added, followed by another dropout layer with a dropout rate of 0.2.

Finally, a Dense output layer was added with two units and a SoftMax activation function, suitable for a classification task with two classes. The model was then compiled using the Adam optimizer, categorical cross-entropy as the loss function, and accuracy as the evaluation metric. The performance of the model is assessed across various metrics, including accuracy, precision, recall, and F1 Score, to assess its performance comprehensively. The results of these evaluations are summarized in Table 4.1.

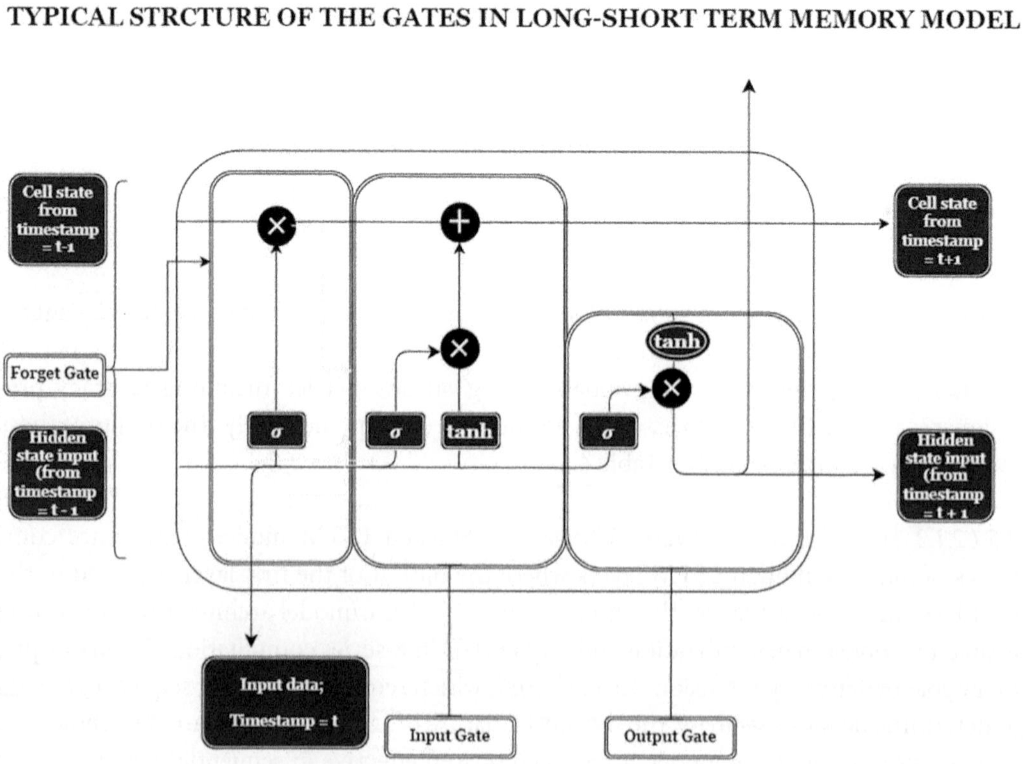

FIGURE 4.6 Structure of an LSTM cell.

4.5.1.2.1.3 Hybrid Model Architecture We used a Hybrid Model architecture to train the balanced data. This proposed architecture is more complex when compared to the traditional ML and DL algorithms used earlier. This architecture comprises of hidden layers that are used to capture complex representations or patterns in a dataset making it more robust. The Hybrid Model architecture consisted of 1D CNN and an LSTM layer. 1D CNN was for feature extraction and the LSTM layer was for sequential data processing. The 1D CNN architecture was for the selection of features that can be best used to optimize the performance of the mode during training. It helps in identifying simple patterns within your data which will then be used to form more complex patterns within higher layers (LSTM layer). The structure of the Hybrid Model architecture is shown in Figure 4.8.

The model starts with a 1D CNN branch, which is effective for capturing spatial patterns in sequential data. Within the CNN layer, a Conv1D layer was employed to extract features using 64 filters of size 3, followed by a ReLU activation function to introduce non-linearity. Subsequently, a MaxPooling1D layer was applied to down-sample the features, reducing the spatial dimensions while preserving important information. The output from the CNN layers was then flattened into a 1D feature vector using a Flatten layer, preparing it for combination with the LSTM branch. In parallel, the model included an LSTM branch, which specializes in capturing long-term dependencies in sequential data. Within the LSTM layer, an LSTM layer with 50 units and ReLU activation was implemented to learn temporal patterns in the sequential data. The outputs from both the CNN and LSTM branches

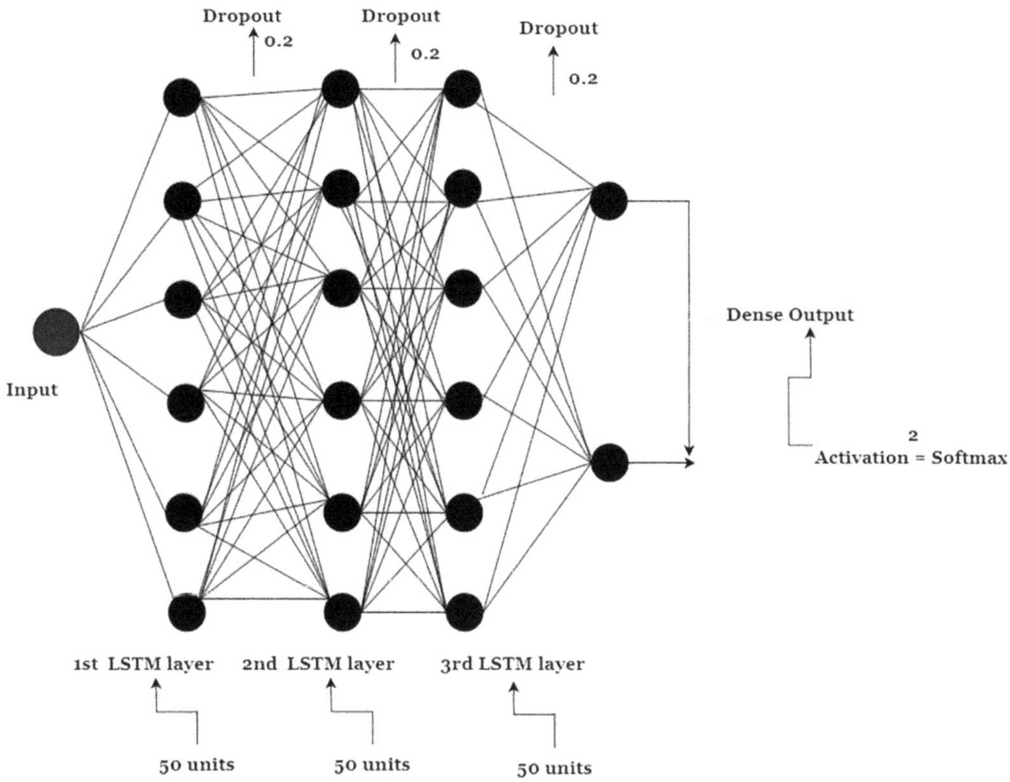

FIGURE 4.7 Stacked LSTM structure utilized for the IDS model.

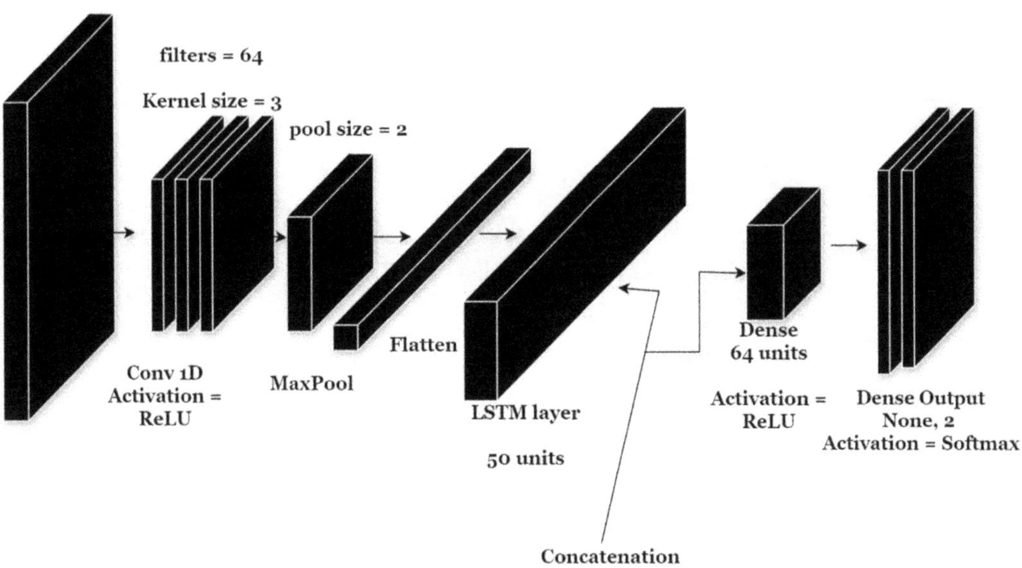

FIGURE 4.8 Structure of the Hybrid Model architecture utilized.

were concatenated together, merging the spatial and temporal features learned by each branch. The concatenated features were then passed through a Dense layer with 64 units and ReLU activation, allowing for further abstraction and representation of the combined features. Finally, the output from the Dense layer was fed into a Dense output layer with a single neuron and sigmoid activation, which outputs the final prediction as a probability for binary classification.

The model was trained with a batch size of 32 and was compiled using the Adam optimizer with a learning rate of 0.001 and binary cross-entropy as the loss function. During training, early stopping was implemented with a patience of five epochs and restoring the best weights. The early stopping was to monitor the performance of the model during training.

4.5.1.2.1.4 1D Convolutional Neural Network Just like the LSTM, which is mainly utilized for sequential training of a model, the 1D CNN model has been proven to be very effective for sequential training of a model on time-series datasets. The input shape for this model is (*n*, *l*), where *n* is the number of samples and *l* is the length of each sample (length of time steps in the time-series data). The 1D CNN as shown in Figure 4.9 utilizes the same architecture as the native CNN network (three-dimensional convolutional neural network). The only difference is the input shape for the CNN model architecture. The reason for the proposed model, the 1D CNN model, is because of its ability to extract pertinent features from the temporal patterns, thus providing an effective method for analyzing time-series data in IDS frameworks [24]. It is ideally suited for identifying irregularities and intrusions in network and system logs due to its capacity to capture local dependencies and hierarchical representations.

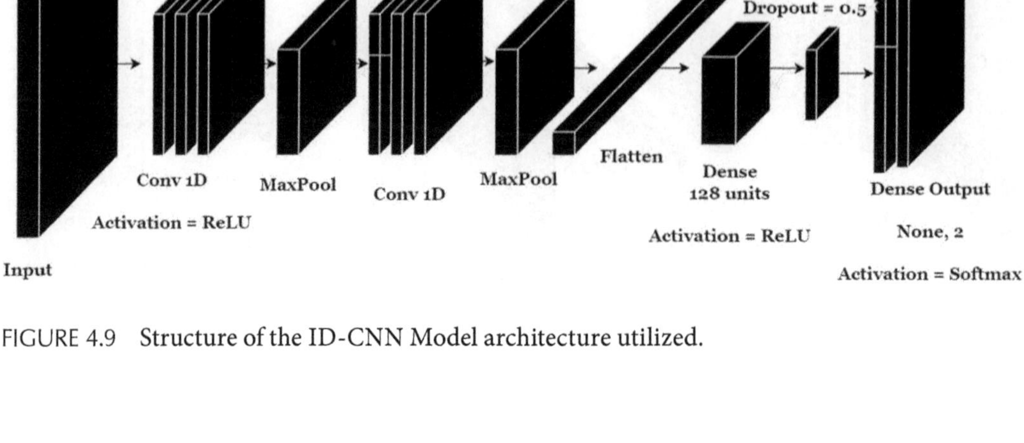

FIGURE 4.9 Structure of the ID-CNN Model architecture utilized.

For the 1D CNN model, the input data was reshaped to incorporate a channel dimension, facilitating compatibility with the CNN layers. The input data was reshaped to incorporate a channel dimension (n, l, 1). Here, n represents the number of samples, l denotes the length of each sample (time steps in time-series data), and one signifies the channel dimension required by the Conv1D layers. The model architecture includes two Conv1D layers optimized for feature extraction from the sequential input: the first Conv1D layer utilized 32 filters with a kernel size of 3, followed by a ReLU activation function. The second Conv1D layer utilized 64 filters with a kernel size of 3, also activated by ReLU. Max-pooling layers followed each Conv1D layer, employing a pool size of 2. These layers downsampled the extracted features, improving computational efficiency while retaining essential information from the data. After the convolutional and max-pooling layers, the data underwent a flattening operation. This step prepares the data for subsequent Dense layers that facilitate classification. The model incorporated a Dense layer with 128 units and a ReLU activation function after flattening. Additionally, a Dropout layer with a dropout rate of 0.5 was included to prevent overfitting by randomly dropping input units during training.

For training, the model was compiled with the Adam optimizer, chosen for its adaptive learning rate capabilities. The categorical cross-entropy loss function was employed to minimize classification errors during training. During the training process, accuracy was monitored as the primary metric to evaluate the model's performance across epochs. The effectiveness of the model in handling time-series data, particularly for tasks like IDSs, is detailed in Table 4.1, where various evaluation metrics are summarized.

4.5.1.2.2 Training on Imbalanced Dataset With 2,071,657 instances, where each instance has ten features, we trained our model. With the same set of algorithms and the same set of parameters, but in the case of the Random Forest Classifier we applied GridSearchCV, which takes in more than one parameter combination to exhaustively search for the optimal hyperparameters. This technique helps to fine-tune the model's performance by systematically exploring various combinations of hyperparameters, such as the number of trees, maximum depth of trees, and minimum samples required to split a node, among others. By leveraging the computational resources efficiently, GridSearchCV allows us to find the best combination of hyperparameters that maximizes the model's performance on the given dataset, ultimately enhancing its predictive accuracy and robustness. This somewhat helps in class imbalance and optimization for better performance. In our Random Forest Classifier, the hyperparameters were tuned as follows: we tested [50, 100, 150] for the number of estimators, [3, 5, 7, none] for maximum tree depth, and ["entropy," "gini"] for the splitting criterion. The best combination of hyperparameters identified through GridSearchCV was criterion = "entropy," number of estimators = 100, and maximum depth = "None."

4.6 EXPERIMENTAL RESULTS AND ANALYSIS

The dataset used for this research is the ISCXIDS 2012 dataset which is provided by the Canadian Institute of Cybersecurity and can be found at [22]. The dataset contains 2,071,657 data points of 21 features. In this section, we are presenting the analyzed performance of the ML models developed in this study. We evaluated the models on both balanced and imbalanced datasets to assess their effectiveness in different scenarios. Tables 4.1 and 4.2 show the number of parameters recorded for each model on each dataset.

The results are compared using various performance metrics, such as accuracy, precision, recall, F1 Score, and Receiver Operating Characteristic-Area Under the Curve (ROC-AUC), to determine how well the models handle varying class distributions. Additionally, we explore the impact of different hyperparameters and techniques like resampling on model performance.

4.6.1 Evaluation Metrics

The performances of the model on the two datasets were evaluated on various metrics which includes Accuracy, Precision, Recall, F1 Score.

4.6.1.1 Accuracy

It is one of the most straightforward performance metrics for classification problems. Accuracy is the ratio of correctly predicted observations to the total observations.

$$\text{Accuracy} = \frac{\text{TP} + \text{TN}}{\text{TP} + \text{TN} + \text{FP} + \text{FN}} \tag{4.3}$$

where:

True Positives (TP) represent the number of instances correctly predicted as positive. And in that sense, it denotes the number of instances properly classified in its right class, "Attack."

False Positives (FP) represent the number of instances incorrectly predicted as positive (Type I Error). This denoted the number of instances which are of the "Normal" class but were classified under "Attack" class.

True Negatives (TN) represent the number of instances correctly predicted as negative. This denoted the number of instances properly classified under the right class, "Normal."

False Negatives (FN) represent the number of instances incorrectly predicted as negative (Type II Error). This denoted the number of instances which are of the "Attack" class but were classified under "Normal" class.

TABLE 4.2 No. of Parameters Recorded for the Imbalanced Dataset

SN	Model	No. of Parameters
1.	Random Forest Classifier	-
2.	1D CNN	342,594
3.	Stacked LSTM	50,902
4.	Hybrid Model(1D CNN & LSTM)	358,114

4.6.1.2 *Precision*

Precision (also called Positive Predictive Value) is the ratio of correctly predicted positive observations to the total predicted positives. The equation for the same is given as:

$$\text{Precision} = \frac{\text{TP}}{\text{TP} + \text{FP}} \tag{4.4}$$

4.6.1.3 *Recall*

Recall (also known as Sensitivity or True Positive Rate) is the ratio of correctly predicted positive observations to all the observations in the actual class.

$$\text{Recall} = \frac{\text{TP}}{\text{TP} + \text{FN}} \tag{4.5}$$

4.6.1.4 *F1 Score*

The F1 Score is the harmonic mean of precision and recall. It is useful when you need a balance between precision and recall.

$$F1\,\text{Score} = 2 \times \frac{\text{Precision} \times \text{Recall}}{\text{Precision} + \text{Recall}} \tag{4.6}$$

4.6.1.5 *ROC-AUC*

ROC-AUC, which stands for Receiver Operating Characteristic-Area Under the Curve, is a performance metric used to evaluate the performance of binary classification models.

ROC Curve: The metric provides a score and a graphical representation of the true positive rate (Sensitivity) against the false positive rate (1-Specificity) for different threshold values of a classification model.

AUC: It quantifies the overall performance of a binary classification model based on the ROC curve. Specifically, it represents the probability that the model will rank a randomly chosen positive example higher than a randomly chosen negative example.

In the case of our imbalanced data, the ROC-AUC proved very effective in determining the effectiveness of the model for the classification task. Always use predicted probabilities (or decision function scores) instead of binary predictions to plot the ROC curve.

4.6.1.6 *Friedman-Tukey Rank Index*

From the provided results shown in Table 4.1, more than 90% aggregate score was obtained by each algorithm across various evaluation metrics used on each dataset. Each algorithm was ranked using the provided metrics to determine the strength of each algorithm within the IDS network framework. We used the Friedman Test followed by the Tukey's Honestly Significant Difference (HSD) post-hoc analysis to rank the performance of each algorithm. The choice of this technique is to:

1. Address Multiple Comparisons Problem: The Friedman Test is a non-parametric statistical test used to detect differences in treatments across multiple test attempts. Intraarticularly useful in comparing multiple algorithms across different datasets and metrics, addressing the issue of multiple comparisons by reducing the risk of Type I errors.

2. Rank-Based Comparison: Unlike other parametric tests, the Friedman Test ranks the algorithms instead of comparing their actual values. This is beneficial in scenarios where the data does not meet the assumptions of normality and homoscedasticity.

By using this robust statistical method, we ensured a comprehensive and reliable evaluation of the algorithms, leading to a more informed selection process for the IDS network framework.

Based on two core concepts, the Friedman test and the Tukey's range test, Friedman-Tukey rank index merges the rank-based approach of the Friedman test with the pairwise comparison strength of Tukey's test to rank multiple algorithms. It calculates the average rank of each algorithm. The Friedman statistic equation follows a chi-squared distribution with $k - 1$ degrees of freedom.

The Friedman statistic equation is given as:

$$x_F^2 = \frac{12}{Nk(k+1)}\left[\sum_{j-1}^{k} R_j^2 - \frac{k(k+1)(k+1)}{4}\right] \tag{4.7}$$

where:

N is the number of datasets or blocks,

k is the number of algorithms,

R_j is the sum of ranks of the j-th algorithm.

Tukey's HSD post-hoc analysis is subsequently applied to determine significant differences between pairs of algorithms based on their ranks (Table 4.3).

We also ranked the algorithms with a graph plot to determine the efficiency in predicting various data point counts. The diagram can be seen in Figures 4.10 and 4.11. The rankings were based on the comparison of prediction times across the four models (Random Forest, Stacked LSTM, 1D CNN, and Hybrid Model) for both balanced and imbalanced datasets. This analysis helps in identifying the models that perform best under different data scenarios, with considerations for computational efficiency.

The given numbers of datapoints used are 1, 50, 100, 500, and 5,000. The given set of data points were used for evaluating the performance of the model in the context of DL-IDS computational requirement. Being evaluated on both the balanced and imbalanced datasets, we got to find the significant differences in the prediction time for each model on the datasets. For the balanced dataset, the prediction times varied notably compared to those of the imbalanced dataset.

TABLE 4.3 Evaluation Metrics Table

Dataset	Algorithm	Accuracy	Precision	Recall	F1 Score	ROC-AUC	FT Rank Index
	Random Forest	0.991	0.993	0.991	0.992	0.991	3.3 ~ 4
	Stacked LSTM	0.991	0.998	0.993	0.995	0.999	2.1 ~ 2
Imbalanced	1D CNN	0.997	0.999	0.997	0.998	0.994	1.4 ~ 1
	Hybrid Model	0.996	0.955	0.990	0.972	0.998	3.2 ~ 3
	Random Forest	0.984	0.984	0.984	0.9844	0.984	3.4 ~ 3
Balanced	Stacked LSTM	0.982	0.991	0.973	0.981	0.995	3.4 ~ 3
	1D CNN	0.991	0.988	0.995	0.991	0.997	2.0 ~ 2
	Hybrid Model	0.994	0.994	0.994	0.994	0.998	1.2 ~ 1

This distinction underscores the models' performance sensitivity to data distribution, guiding decisions on model selection tailored to specific data scenarios.

4.7 DISCUSSION

An overview of IBN as an innovative networking framework has been discussed, and in addition, a proposed methodology with the incorporation of ML and DL algorithms for an advanced IDS that can be incorporated into both traditional and IBN network infrastructure has been reviewed. The model consists of four models that were trained on two datasets: an imbalanced and a balanced dataset. Providing a detailed record of the performance of each model across various metrics on these datasets, as shown in Table 4.1, the model is deemed reliable, although subject to the type of network and the integration of the model in real-time network traffic. The findings from this study represent a paradigm shift in network security tactics. The network's capacity to recognize and respond to security threats has been greatly improved by utilizing these algorithms. Though it is hard to determine which model is best suited for the desired objective, each model's performance is outstanding. We considered various key points to note to determine which model is best.

A key point to note is that the network traffic, as regards the imbalanced dataset, isn't always balanced due to the nature of the traffic. There is a very high chance that the network has a higher record for the class "Normal" than the class "Attack.. Even though the class is imbalanced, it is considerable to note that this is very close to real-time captured network traffic when compared to a balanced class of "normal" and "attack." In addition, the complexity of each model about prediction time has also been reviewed. The four algorithms—Random Forest Classifier, 1D CNN, Stacked LSTM, and Hybrid Model—have obtained outstanding results. It is noteworthy to understand that the greater the complexity of the model, the greater the prediction time. Utilizing the Friedman-Tukey rank index, 1D CNN on the imbalanced dataset has been proven to be very efficient, with a lesser prediction time when compared to the other DL models. In an observative measure, ID CNN is faster and less computationally expensive when compared to the hybrid model (which achieved a close similar performance) in terms of number of trainable parameters, training time, and prediction time over various range of data points. In intrusion scenarios, the main objective is to detect intrusion as early as possible to prevent adverse post-actions, and in that

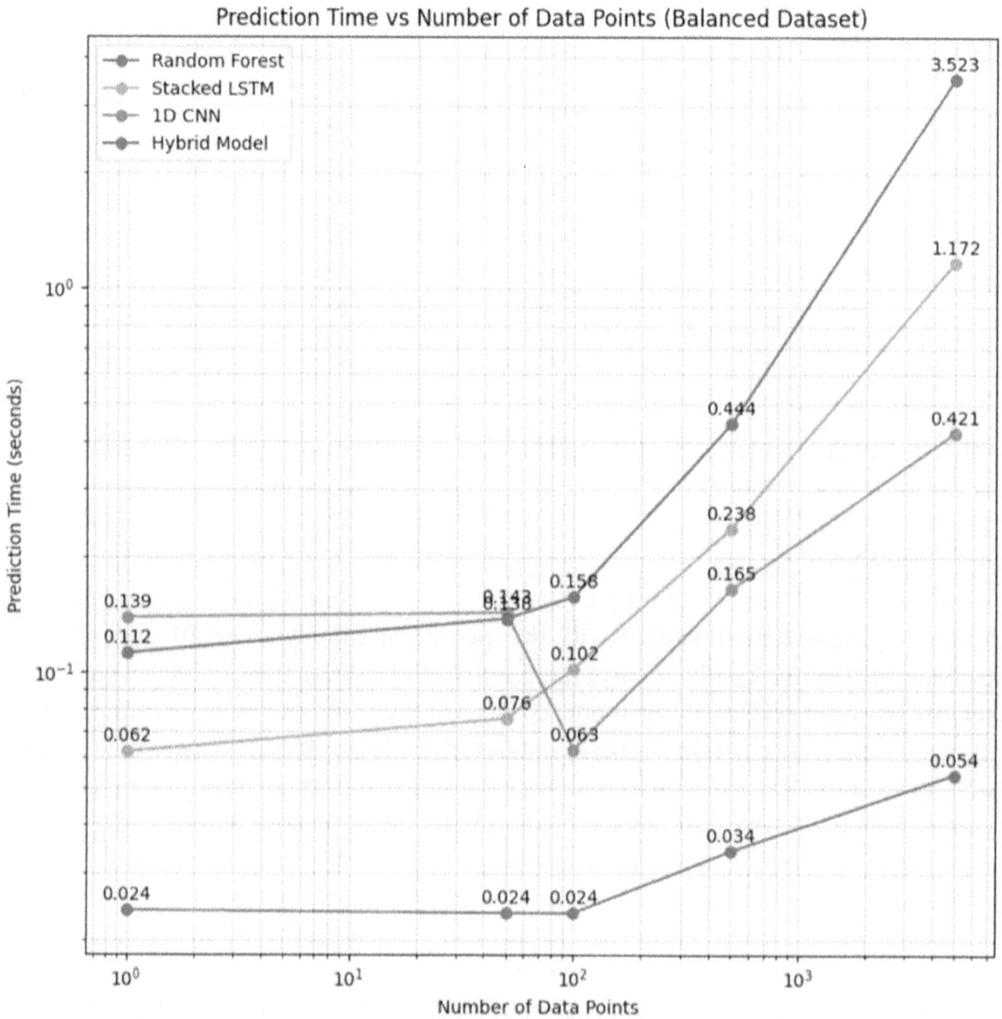

FIGURE 4.10 Prediction time for each model on the balanced dataset across various data points.

sense, ID CNN has proven very effective in terms of less trainable parameters and prediction timings, therefore making it a lightweight model. Reactive measures, or responding to risks after they have occurred, are the usual approach used in traditional security systems. The DL-enabled IBN, in contrast, foresees future dangers, enabling prompt preventative steps. This initiative-taking approach not only protects the network but also inspires trust in the stakeholders of the company. Since ML algorithms can be continually improved, they are resilient to new security threats.

4.8 CONCLUSION AND FUTURE SCOPE

This research significantly advances the field of network security by demonstrating the effectiveness of integrating ML and DL algorithms into IBN systems. By meticulously evaluating various advanced ML models, our study not only confirms their high accuracy

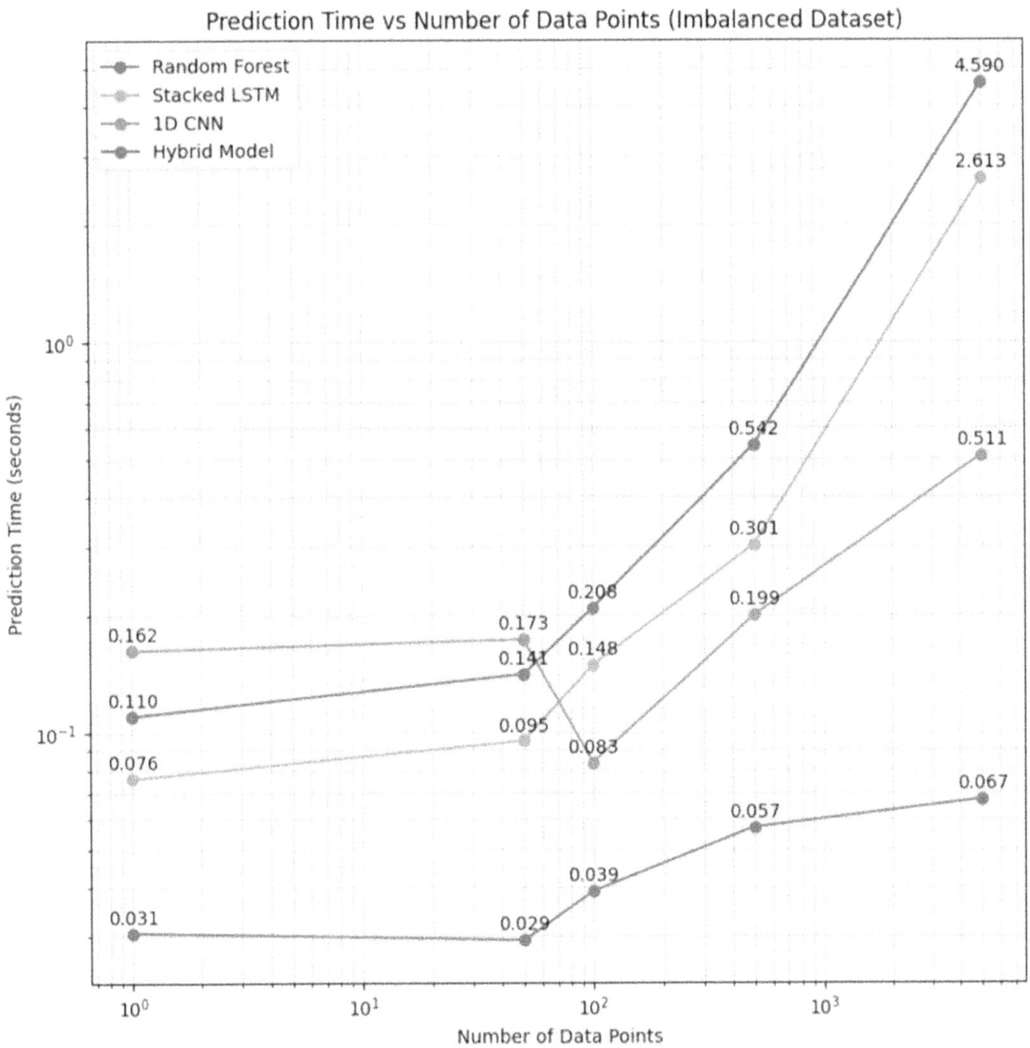

FIGURE 4.11 Prediction time for each model on the imbalanced dataset across various data points.

in anomaly detection but also highlights their potential for real-time, proactive security measures in dynamic network environments. This novel integration allows for continuous, intelligent monitoring, ensuring robust protection against evolving cyber threats. Our findings move the body of knowledge forward by establishing a new standard for leveraging ML-driven IBN to enhance network resilience and security, offering businesses a reliable framework to safeguard digital infrastructures in an increasingly interconnected world. These intent-based networks will utilize ML algorithms to enhance network security. DL-driven IBN proactively identifies and mitigates security issues, ensuring high accuracy in anomaly detection. This strategy improves network efficiency and encourages customer and stakeholder confidence. The research proposal focuses on integrating ML and DL algorithms into IBN systems to enhance network and data security. The proposed approach uses advanced ML algorithms to detect intricate network activities and generalize network behavior. The integration of refined ML models into IBN architecture enables real-time monitoring, enabling swift and precise detection of abnormalities. This research contributes significantly to the advancement of network security in modern technological landscapes.

Future research should build on this foundation by exploring more sophisticated intrusion strategies, further refining the models' ability to adapt to complex and evolving threat landscapes.

REFERENCES

1. R. G. Bace and P. Mell, "Intrusion detection systems," http://all.net/books/standards/NIST-CSRC/csrc.nist.gov/publications/nistpubs/800-31/sp800-31.pdf. 2001.
2. A. Leivadeas and M. Falkner, "A survey on intent-based networking," *IEEE Communications Surveys & Tutorials*, vol. 25, no. 1, pp. 625–655 2022.
3. X. Zheng and A. Leivadeas, "Network assurance in intent-based networking data centers with machine learning techniques," in 2021 17th International Conference on Network and Service Management (CNSM), pp. 14–20, IEEE, 2021.
4. D. E. Denning, "An intrusion-detection model," *IEEE Transactions on Software Engineering*, vol. 2, pp. 222–232, 1987.
5. B. Mukherjee, L. T. Heberlein, and K. N. Levitt, "Network intrusion detection," *IEEE Network*, vol. 8, no. 3, pp. 26–41, 1994.
6. J. McHugh, "Intrusion and intrusion detection," *International Journal of Information Security*, vol. 1, pp. 14–35, 2001.
7. H.-J. Liao, C.-H. R. Lin, Y.-C. Lin, and K.-Y. Tung, "Intrusion detection system: A comprehensive review," *Journal of Network and Computer Applications*, vol. 36, no. 1, pp. 16–24, 2013.
8. T. A. Khan, A. Mehmood, J. J. D. Ravera, A. Muhammad, K. Abbas, and W.C. Song, "Intent-based orchestration of network slices and resource assurance using machine learning," in NOMS 2020-2020 IEEE/IFIP Network Operations and Management Symposium, pp. 1–2, IEEE, 2020.
9. Y. Wei, M. Peng, and Y. Liu, "Intent-based networks for 6G: Insights and challenges," *Digital Communications and Networks*, vol. 6, no. 3, pp. 270–280, 2020.
10. L. Velasco, M. Signorelli, O.G. De Dios, C. Papagianni, R. Bifulco, J.J.V. Olmos, S. Pryor, G. Carrozzo, J. Schulz-Zander, M. Bennis, and R. Martinez, "End-to-end intent-based networking," *IEEE Communications Magazine*, vol. 59, no. 10, pp. 106–112, 2021.
11. E. Zeydan and Y. Turk, "Recent advances in intent-based networking: A survey," in 2020 IEEE 91st Vehicular Technology Conference (VTC2020-Spring), pp. 1–5, IEEE, 2020.
12. A. Campanella, "Intent-based network operations," in 2019 Optical Fiber Communications Conference and Exhibition (OFC), pp. 1–3, IEEE, 2019.
13. A. Collet, A. Banchs, and M. Fiore, "Lossleap: Learning to predict for intent-based networking," in IEEE INFOCOM 2022- IEEE Conference on Computer Communications, pp. 2138–2147, IEEE, 2022.
14. P. Szilágyi, "I2bn: Intelligent intent-based networks," *Journal of ICT Standardization*, vol. 9, no. 2, pp. 159–200, 2021.
15. L. Ashiku and C. Dagli, "Network intrusion detection system using deep learning," *Procedia Computer Science*, vol. 185, pp. 239–247, 2021.
16. M. A. Talukder, K. F. Hasan, M. M. Islam, M. A. Uddin, A. Akhter, M. A. Yousuf, F. Alharbi, and M. A. Moni, "A dependable hybrid machine learning model for network intrusion detection," *Journal of Information Security and Applications*, vol. 72, p. 103405, 2023.

17. Z. Ahmad, A. S. Khan, C. W. Shiang, J. Abdullah, and F. Ahmad, "Network intrusion detection system: A systematic study of machine learning and deep learning approaches," *Transactions on Emerging Telecommunications Technologies*, vol. 32, no. 1, p. e4150, 2021.
18. T. Su, H. Sun, J. Zhu, S. Wang, and Y. Li, "BAT: Deep learning methods on network intrusion detection using NSL-KDD dataset," *IEEE Access*, vol. 8, pp. 29575–29585, 2020.
19. S. Gamage and J. Samarabandu, "Deep learning methods in network intrusion detection: A survey and an objective comparison," *Journal of Network and Computer Applications*, vol. 169, p. 102767, 2020.
20. W. Elmasry, A. Akbulut, and A. H. Zaim, "Evolving deep learning architectures for network intrusion detection using a double PSO metaheuristic," *Computer Networks*, vol. 168, p. 107042, 2020.
21. M. A. Ferrag, L. Maglaras, S. Moschoyiannis, and H. Janicke, "Deep learning for cyber security intrusion detection: Approaches, datasets, and comparative study," *Journal of Information Security and Applications*, vol. 50, p. 102419, 2020.
22. "Intrusion Detection Evaluation Dataset (CICIDS2017)," University of New Brunswick, [Online]. Available: https://www.unb.ca/cic/datasets/ids.html. [Accessed: March 8, 2024].
23. L. Breiman, "Random forests," *Machine Learning*, vol. 45, pp. 5–32, 2001.
24. A. Meliboev, J. Alikhanov, and W. Kim, "1D CNN based network intrusion detection with normalization on imbalanced data," in 2020 International Conference on Artificial Intelligence in Information and Communication (ICAIIC), pp. 218–224, IEEE, 2020.

CHAPTER 5

An In-depth Analysis of Intrusion Detection Systems with an Emphasis on Multi-Access Edge Computing and Machine Learning

Shruti Saxena and Nikunj Tahilramani

5.1 INTRODUCTION

The Internet of Things (IoT) and Industrial IoT (IIoT) are revolutionizing various aspects of our lives [1]. IoT connects everyday objects equipped with sensors and software [2], enabling data exchange. IIoT [1], a specialized form of IoT, focuses on industrial applications to boost efficiency. Both IoT and IIoT share a four-layer architecture. The perception layer embeds sensors in objects to capture real-world data. This data travels via the network layer, which uses communication protocols and infrastructure for secure transmission. The processing layer analyzes and stores the data using databases and servers. Finally, the application layer uses the processed data to drive actions through applications and services, leading to automation, optimization, and informed decisions. IoT and IIoT devices bring innovation but also expose us to new security threats. Attackers can steal data, disrupt operations, or overwhelm systems [3] (see Table 5.1 for details).

Traditional IDSs struggle to protect complex IoT environments [4]. Deploying IDSs at the network edge, a concept enabled by edge computing, offers a solution. Edge computing [5] processes data closer to its source, reducing latency and improving overall performance. Critically for security, edge computing allows IDSs to be closer to the data, enabling faster

DOI: 10.1201/9781032714813-5

TABLE 5.1 Common Attacks in IoT

Attacks [3]	Mode of Attack Initiation
Spoofing	Impersonation
Jamming	Fake Signaling
Man-In-the-Middle	Eavesdropping Packets
Privacy Leakage Attack	Authentication Storage
Mirai Botnet Attack	Malware Implant on Devices
AI-Based Attacks	Creates AI-powered Tools

threat detection and a quicker response to security breaches [5]. However, deploying IDSs at the edge also presents challenges [5].

Traditional IDS algorithms are hampered by edge devices' limited processing power and memory [5]. Strong privacy protections are necessary since IoT devices collect a lot of personal data. Compatibility in IDS development is hindered by the variety of IoT devices and protocols [6]. On the other hand, edge IDSs provide superior scalability for expanding IoT networks [6], improve privacy by processing data locally [6], and identify and respond to attacks more quickly, minimizing damage [6].

Machine learning empowers computers to learn and adapt without explicit programming, making it ideal for IDSs. These IDSs can analyze network traffic, device logs, and sensor data to identify patterns of malicious activity, helping detect new and evolving threats. While IoT/IIoT offers vast potential, securing these devices is crucial [2]. Robust security measures, edge computing, and machine learning are essential for maximizing the benefits of IoT/IIoT while minimizing security risks.

5.2 INTRUSION DETECTION SYSTEMS

Intrusion detection systems (IDSs) [4] act as security guards for computer systems and networks, constantly monitoring for malicious activity. They function in three main stages: monitoring, analysis, and detection.

- Monitoring Stage: During this phase, data about network traffic or host activity is gathered. Various methods, including network sniffing, log file analysis, and agent-based monitoring, can be employed for this purpose.
- Analysis Stage: In this stage, the collected data undergoes analysis to discern patterns or anomalies indicative of potential malicious activity. Techniques for this analysis encompass signature-based detection, anomaly-based detection, and machine learning.
- Detection Stage: During this stage, a decision is made regarding the occurrence of an intrusion. If an intrusion is identified, the IDS can initiate actions, including generating alerts and implementing measures such as blocking the attacker's access to the network.

5.2.1 Historical Perspective

IDS has evolved significantly over the past 30 years. Early models relied on predefined attack signatures but struggled with new threats [5]. Axelsson's 2000 survey [7] identified limitations in both host-based and network-based IDSs, particularly their reliance on local data for analysis. Researchers explored intelligent techniques for IDS, including fuzzy logic and neural networks. Mitchell and Chen [5] surveyed IDSs for wireless environments, finding anomaly-based approaches suitable for mobile telephony. However, they noted challenges like high false positive rates that could degrade user experience. IDS has come a long way in 30 years. Early, signature-based systems struggled as attackers grew more cunning. The goal of recent research has been to improve detection accuracy and adaptability by integrating machine learning (ML) with IDS. Though the subject of ML-based IDS application in resource-constrained IoT contexts is still in its infancy, these systems use enormous datasets to train models that can identify known as well as unknown threats.

Modern IDS fall into two main categories, that is, NIDS and HIDS.

1. Network Intrusion Detection Systems (NIDSs)
   NIDS monitors network traffic to identify suspicious activity, including unusual traffic patterns or unauthorized access attempts [5]. Typically deployed at network boundaries, such as firewalls or routers, NIDS safeguard entire networks from external threats.
2. Host-based Intrusion Detection Systems (HIDSs)
   HIDS focuses on individual host systems, such as servers, desktops, or laptops, to detect malicious activity within the system itself. Deployed on critical systems [8], HIDS monitors for signs of compromise, such as unauthorized file modifications or unusual process executions [8].

The shift from signature-based to more advanced detection methods has been necessitated by the escalating sophistication of cyber threats [9]. While NIDS provides network-wide protection against external threats, HIDS offers targeted monitoring of specific host systems to identify internal anomalies [9]. This dual approach reflects the contemporary need for robust intrusion detection capabilities in the face of evolving cybersecurity challenges. Deploying NIDS in IoT environments introduces distinctive challenges stemming from the resource limitations of IoT devices and the heterogeneity inherent in IoT networks [5]. Nonetheless, the adoption of edge computing, a distributed computing paradigm, holds the potential to address these challenges effectively. By positioning computation and data storage in proximity to the network edge, edge computing facilitates the implementation of resource-efficient NIDS capable of adapting to the varied protocols prevalent in IoT networks [10]. This approach enhances the feasibility of intrusion detection in IoT environments, paving the way for more adaptive and efficient security solutions [10].

However, NIDS in IoT faces challenges due to resource constraints and network diversity [5]. Edge computing, with its distributed processing near the network edge, offers a solution [5]. By placing computation and storage closer to devices, edge computing allows for resource-efficient NIDS that adapt to various IoT protocols. This paves the way for more feasible and adaptable security solutions in IoT environments. ML is transforming NIDS [10]. ML algorithms analyze vast amounts of network traffic, device logs, and sensor data to identify suspicious patterns. This allows them to adapt to new attack methods, unlike signature-based approaches. By integrating ML, NIDS becomes more agile and effective in detecting and responding to evolving cybersecurity threats [10]. NIDS can be broadly categorized into four main types based on their detection approach, as further detailed in Figure 5.1. Briefly, these categories include signature-based, anomaly-based, protocol-based, and hybrid approaches [5].

The functions of several NIDS are depicted in Figure 5.1. The initial approach is anomaly-based NIDS, which set up a baseline of typical network behavior, keep an eye out for anomalies, and sound an alarm when they find them. Hybrid NIDS are covered in the middle section. They integrate signature-based, anomaly-based, and specification-based techniques to offer thorough threat detection. NIDS that rely on signatures keep an eye on network activities, compare them to a database of recognized signatures, and sound an alarm if any matches are discovered [11]. The figure's lower portion describes specification-based NIDS, which compare real behavior to predetermined criteria using network protocol and system behavior specifications to identify anomalies [12]. The chart highlights the overall efficacy of hybrid NIDS in augmenting threat detection through the integration of multiple detection methodologies.

- Signature-based NIDS

  IDS play a pivotal role in securing IoT ecosystems by identifying and responding to cyberattacks. Signature-based Intrusion Detection Systems (SIDS), a subtype relying on a database of known attack signatures, encounter distinctive challenges in the realm of IoT due to the resource limitations of IoT devices [5]. The overview of Signature-based NIDS is shown in Figure 5.2.

  The diagram depicts a structure for a signature-based NIDS that utilizes ML and deep reinforcement learning (DRL). The upper section outlines the procedure for creating signatures for recognized attacks through ML algorithms. These algorithms examine network traffic to detect patterns and then create signatures for known attacks. The lower section demonstrates the application of DRL in NIDS, where DRL is integrated with deep learning. This fusion employs reinforcement learning to enhance the system's capacity to autonomously identify different cyberattacks. However, these systems often grapple with challenges such as:

  - Resource Constraints: The constrained processing power, limited memory, and energy resources inherent in IoT devices render the direct deployment of traditional signature-based NIDS impractical [13].
  - Signature Updates: Ensuring the effectiveness of detection in signature-based IDS relies on maintaining an up-to-date database of attack signatures. Nevertheless, the resource constraints prevalent in IoT environments pose a challenge, making it difficult to regularly update these signature databases.

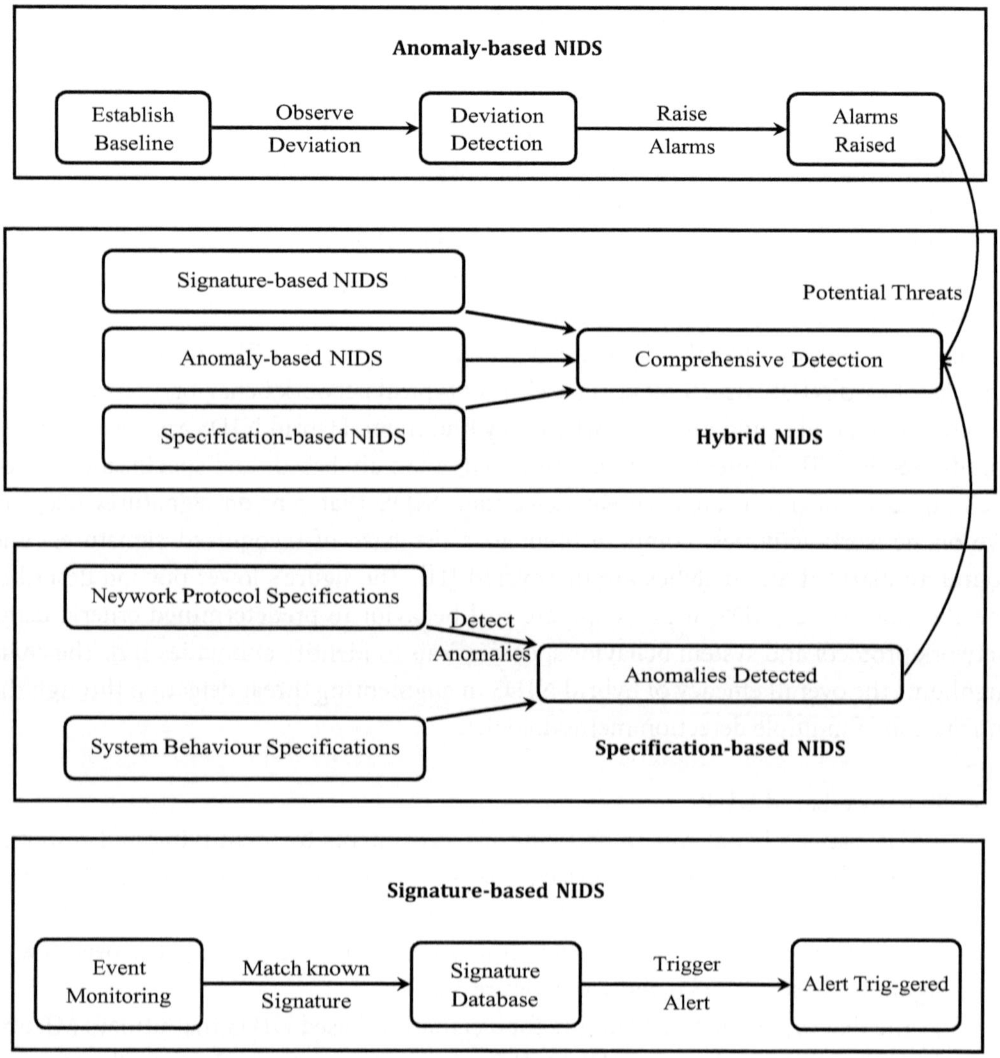

FIGURE 5.1 Types of NIDS.

- Zero-Day Attacks: Signature-based NIDS are ineffective against zero-day attacks, which are attacks that exploit vulnerabilities not yet known to the IDS.

  Despite the challenges, researchers have proposed various approaches to adapt signature-based NIDS for IoT environments either using ML-Based Signature Generation or DRL for NIDS (mentioned in Table 5.2).

- Anomaly-based intrusion detection systems (AIDSs)

  AIDS offers a promising approach to detecting cyberattacks, particularly those that evade signature-based detection methods. AIDS defines a standard for typical system behavior and identifies deviations from this standard as potential anomalies [14]. This capability enhances their effectiveness in identifying emerging and previously unknown attacks, including zero-day threats. Nevertheless, AIDS is susceptible

TABLE 5.2 Overview of Different Methodologies for Signature-based NIDS

Authors [ref]	Description
Kasinathan et al. [16]	A signature-based NIDS framework has been proposed to detect Denial-of-Service (DoS) attacks specifically in 6LoWPAN-based networks.
Duque S et al. [21]	This paper explores the use of data mining algorithms to develop an efficient IDS. It focuses on evaluating various techniques to improve the detection of malicious activities in network security.
Lin et al. [22]	An algorithm has been proposed that performs matching based on techniques like Backward Hashing and Aho-Corasick.
Sheikh et al. [23]	A signature-based Intrusion Detection System tailored for IoT environments has been proposed.

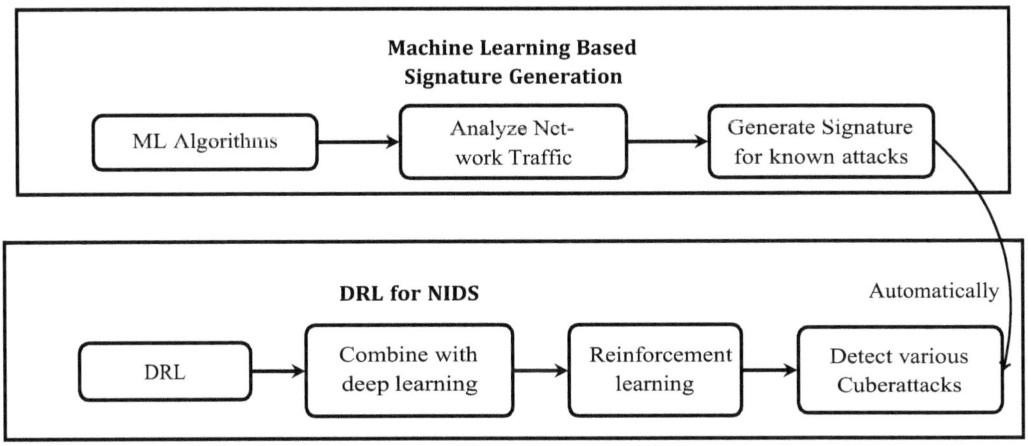

FIGURE 5.2 Signature-based NIDS.

to generating false positives as a result of the dynamic nature of system behavior. To address these limitations, researchers are exploring techniques such as refining anomaly detection techniques, enhancing context awareness, and utilizing machine learning for anomaly profiling. With ongoing advancements in machine learning and AI, AIDS has the potential to become an increasingly effective and adaptable solution for protecting networks and systems from the ever-present threat of cyberattacks [14] (Table 5.3).

- Specification-based IDS

  Specification-based IDS [12] operate as monitoring and detection systems, relying on security specifications derived from a system's functions and policies to establish normal behavior. Any deviations from these expected behaviors are identified as security breaches. The primary challenge in developing a robust specification-based IDS lies in creating a formalism that accurately captures valid operating sequences, with the definition of the specification "trace policy" and the complexity of evaluating and verifying specifications posing obstacles to widespread adoption in real-world applications. Despite these challenges, specification-based IDSs exhibit the capability

TABLE 5.3 Overview of Different Methodologies for Anomaly-based NIDS

Authors [ref]	Description
Mothukuri V. et al. [14]	An efficient hierarchical anomaly-based intrusion detection system was introduced.
Canedo J. et al. [24]	Utilized artificial neural networks (ANNs) for detecting intrusions in the IoT system's gateway.
Alsoufi M.A. et al. [25]	Provide a systematic literature review of anomaly-based IDS in IoT environments, with a focus on deep learning techniques. It compares various deep learning methodologies, offering insights into their effectiveness and challenges in detecting anomalies in IoT networks.
Heartfield R. et al. [11]	Introduced a smart home NIDS that autonomously adjusts the decision function of its underlying anomaly categorization models to adapt to evolving conditions within the smart home environment.

to detect both known and unknown attacks. Similar to misuse-based IDS, they learn the fundamental characteristics of known attacks. Moreover, they share the ability of anomaly-based IDSs to identify unknown attacks, such as operating sequences deviating from the system's normal behavior [5].

Mitchell and Chen [12] explore different anomaly-based IDS types, advocating for specification-based NIDS like their SB-NIDS. These systems can effectively detect attacks that deviate from normal IoT network protocol behavior.

- Hybrid-Based NIDS for IoT Systems

  Hybrid NIDS for IoT combines two or more approaches, like signature-based, anomaly-based, and specification-based, to create a more robust system. This approach leverages the strengths of each method to overcome their weaknesses and improve overall effectiveness in detecting IoT threats [12].

  Hybrid NIDS offers several advantages over single-technique systems. They improve detection accuracy, reduce false positives, and adapt to evolving threats better. Combining techniques allows them to catch a wider range of attacks, leading to a more robust security posture. This also saves security analysts time by minimizing false alarms [5].

  Hybrid NIDS also adapts better to new threats. By combining techniques and allowing for easy updates, they can be more resilient to evolving cybersecurity landscapes. While powerful, hybrid NIDS requires more processing power, storage, and energy compared to single-technique approaches. This can be a challenge for resource-constrained IoT devices, where efficiency is paramount [5].

  Despite requiring more resources and complex design, hybrid NIDS offer comprehensive protection, making them valuable for IoT security when resource management allows. They necessitate careful integration of different detection methods to ensure smooth operation (interoperability and synergy).

Sequence-based hybrid NIDS and Parallel-based hybrid NIDS are the two types of hybrid-based NIDS shown in Figure 5.3. The first step in the Sequence-based Hybrid

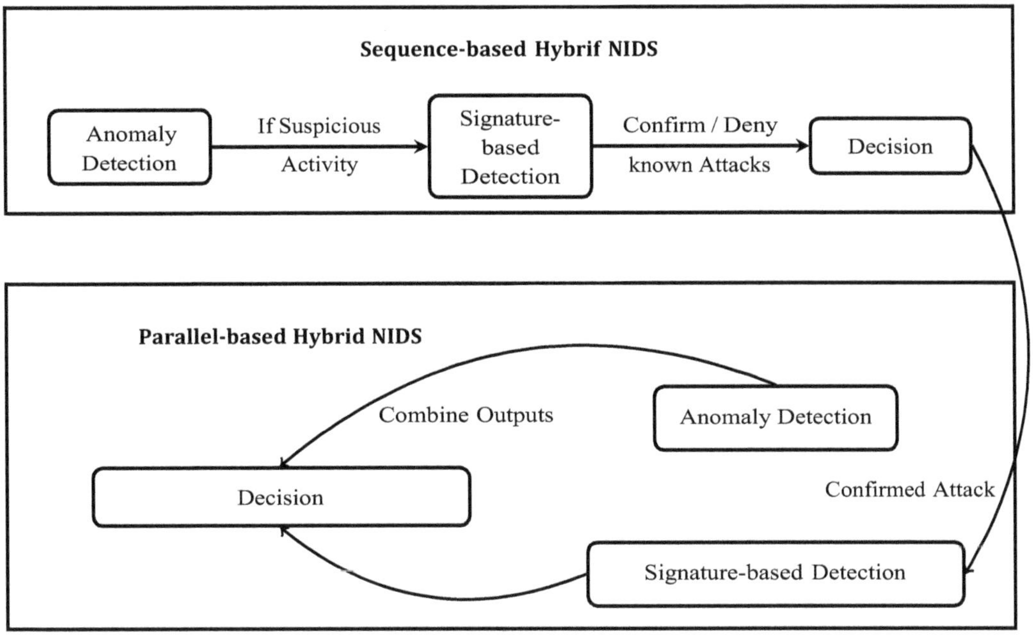

FIGURE 5.3 Categories of hybrid-based NIDS.

NIDS method is anomaly detection. The system uses signature-based detection to validate or deny the existence of known attacks if any suspicious activity is found, which results in a conclusion. The parallel-based hybrid NIDS, on the other hand, functions by executing both signature-based and anomaly detection concurrently. A thorough decision is then reached by combining the results of the two approaches. By simultaneously utilizing the advantages of both detection methods, this strategy improves the intrusion detection system's overall accuracy and dependability. Machine learning is a hotbed of research for advanced hybrid NIDS in IoT. Researchers aim to automate attack detection by integrating machine learning algorithms. This empowers the system to:

- adapt and respond to evolving threats in real time,
- improve detection accuracy by learning and adapting to new attack patterns without manual intervention.

To optimize resource use, researchers are integrating multi-access edge computing (MEC) with machine learning in hybrid NIDS. MEC processes data closer to devices, reducing the resource burden on individual IoT devices. This allows hybrid NIDS to operate more efficiently and at scale, especially crucial in resource-constrained IoT environments. Machine learning automates attack detection and adapts to new threats, while MEC alleviates resource limitations. This combined approach holds promise for robust and efficient intrusion detection in IoT systems, addressing challenges and ensuring security in a dynamic threat landscape.

5.3 IDS FOR IOT

In the realm of Intrusion Detection Systems (IDS) for the IoT, two main categories exist: IoT-specific [15] and IoT-agnostic IDSs. For IoT contexts, there are primarily two kinds of IDSs: IoT-specific and IoT-agnostic IDSs. Devices utilizing specialized communication protocols [16], such as 6LoWPAN, BLE, and LoRaWAN, are the target of IoT-specific IDSs. They are usually installed on the same network as the IoT devices they keep an eye on. They make predictions based on the messages these devices send, ensuring that protocol compliance and other technology-specific characteristics are met. IoT-agnostic intrusion detection systems, on the other hand, are not dependent on any particular communication medium; instead, they use data like TCP/IP traffic. They manage device traffic across many communication modalities and are especially appropriate for edge environments where heterogeneous devices coexist.

Understanding these two categories (IoT-specific and IoT-agnostic IDSs) is essential for securing diverse IoT environments. IoT-specific IDSs are custom-designed for devices using particular communication technologies [5] (e.g., Wi-Fi, Bluetooth Low Energy). This tailored approach offers deep insights but may lack versatility across different protocols [15]. IoT-agnostic IDSs handle the broader communication variety of IoT ecosystems [15]. They are well-suited for edge computing environments where diverse protocols converge [6]. Several examples of IoT-specific IDSs exist, targeting specific protocols.

1. Wi-Fi

   Reference [5] highlights IDSs designed specifically for Wi-Fi networks. These systems often function as expert systems, analyzing traffic between hosts and checking packet compliance with Wi-Fi network protocols.

2. LoRa

   IDSs for LoRa networks have been explored [17]. These systems are adept at capturing and scrutinizing traffic in LoRa-based environments, addressing security challenges specific to this technology.

3. ZigBee

   Research [5] focuses on IDSs tailored for ZigBee networks. These systems are designed to analyze and ensure compliance with ZigBee communication protocols, addressing security concerns unique to ZigBee-based IoT deployments.

4. Bluetooth Low Energy (BLE)

   IDSs for Bluetooth Low Energy are discussed. These systems are expertly crafted to monitor and assess traffic in BLE-enabled IoT ecosystems, checking for adherence to BLE network protocols.

IoT-specific IDSs act as expert systems, meticulously checking device communication for adherence to specific protocols. Advanced systems might even detect physical layer attacks like jamming. However, evolving IoT landscapes introduce new security challenges beyond basic communication. Issues like routing, network management, and maintenance require attention. Specific protocols, like RPL for low-power networks [18], address these security concerns.

5.3.1 RPL-Based Attacks

While RPL offers security benefits, it's not perfect. RPL-based attacks like Clone ID and Sybil attacks pose a threat. In these attacks, malicious nodes impersonate legitimate ones. A study by Zhang et al. [19] explores Sybil attacks, even classifying them based on attacker capabilities and goals. This study also proposes defense mechanisms categorized into three main classes. This highlights the ongoing effort to secure routing protocols in IoT networks.

1. Social Graph-based Sybil Detection (SGSD)
   These defenses rely on analyzing nodes' social relationships or interactions to detect Sybil attacks. Anomalies caused by Sybil nodes can be identified by examining the network's social graph.
2. Behavior Classification-based Sybil Detection (BCSD)
   Defense mechanisms in this category focus on classifying nodes based on their behavior. Anomalies in the behavior of nodes, such as unusual communication patterns, are used to detect potential Sybil attacks.
3. Mobile Sybil Defend (MSD)
   This class of defense mechanisms involves mobile Sybil defenses. It likely involves strategies that incorporate mobility aspects to identify and defend against Sybil attacks.

A study by Zhang et al. [19] explores Sybil attacks, even classifying them based on attacker capabilities and goals. This study also proposes defense mechanisms categorized into three main classes. These defense mechanisms, and the findings from various studies on their effectiveness against Sybil attacks in RPL-based protocols, are further summarized in Table 5.4.

5.3.2 Lightweight IDSs for IoT Systems

Traditional IDSs struggle with the resource constraints of IoT devices. To address this, researchers developed lightweight IDSs specifically designed for IoT environments

TABLE 5.4 Overview of Different Methodologies for RPL-based NIDS

Authors [ref]	Description	Features
Kasinathan et al. [16]	DoS detection IDS for 6LoW-PAN	Low-power consumption, applicability to IP-based WSNs
Surendar and Umamakeswari [17]	Constraint-based specification IDS for 6LoWPAN	Detection of sinkhole attacks, preservation of QoS, isolation of malicious nodes
Bostani and Sheikhan [26]	Hybrid IDS for 6LoWPAN	Reduction in communication messages, applicability to large- scale networks
Garcia-Font et al. [27]	NIDS for WSNs	Applicability to large-scale WSNs

(as shown in Table 5.5). These specialized IDSs leverage techniques like pattern matching, deep packet anomaly detection, and machine learning to effectively detect and prevent attacks on both devices and networks within the IoT.

5.4 MEC AS A RESOURCE TO PROVIDE SECURITY FOR IOT

The surge in IoT devices demands robust security for both devices and the data they collect. Traditional cloud-based security struggles with real-time demands due to latency and scalability limitations. MEC offers a promising solution [20]. By processing data closer to devices (at the network edge), MEC reduces latency and enhances IoT security. MEC offers several advantages for securing IoT systems, including:

- Context awareness: MEC servers can provide IoT devices with real-time security information, enabling them to adapt their security posture based on the evolving threat landscape [20].
- Energy efficiency: MEC offloads computationally intensive tasks from IoT devices, reducing their energy consumption [20].
- Augmented privacy and security: MEC achieves an elevated level of data protection by keeping data in proximity to its source, thereby diminishing the risk of data breaches and unauthorized access.
- Optimal resource allocation: MEC dynamically allocates resources to IoT devices based on their security needs [20].

NIDS are crucial for IoT security. When implemented within an MEC framework, NIDS leverage virtualization technologies like Network Functions Virtualization (NFV) to enhance IoT security.

- NFV: NFV enables the creation of multiple virtual machines (VMs) on edge devices to execute NIDS tasks efficiently [20].
- ICN: ICN facilitates efficient data routing and retrieval, enabling faster NIDS detection and response times [20].

TABLE 5.5 Overview of Different Methodologies for Lightweight-based IDS

Authors [ref]	Description	Features
Oh et al. [28]	Lightweight malicious-pattern-matching IDS	Reduced memory size, reduced workload, increased speed, scalable performance
Arrignton et al. [8]	HIDS with machine learning for anomaly-based intrusion detection	Use of a behavioral modeling IDS (BMIDS), increased detection sensitivity
Khan and Herrmann [29]	Algorithms based on the protocol model approach using a trust management mechanism	Light weight, energy efficiency, applicability in healthcare environments

- SDN: SDN provides flexible network management and control, enabling dynamic network reconfiguration to mitigate attacks [20].

Offloading NIDS tasks to the MEC platform reduces energy consumption for IoT devices, improves response latency, and optimizes resource usage. The effectiveness depends on the device's proximity to the MEC server. There are two main types of NIDS task offloading:

- Binary NIDS Tasks Offloading: The entire NIDS task is offloaded to the MEC platform.
- Partial Computational NIDS Tasks Offloading: Specifically, only the computationally intensive segments of the NIDS task are offloaded to the MEC platform.

The decision of whether to use binary or partial offloading depends on factors such as the processing capabilities of the IoT device and the bandwidth constraints of the network.

NIDS are vital for IoT security, but their placement within the network significantly impacts their effectiveness in detecting and mitigating threats. This paper explores three main NIDS placement strategies: centralized, distributed, and hybrid as shown in Figure 5.4.

A central NIDS stationed at the border router monitors traffic from IoT devices in a centralized placement setup. Although this method simplifies management and offers extensive traffic visibility, resource limitations in Internet of Things environments present difficulties. By using Distributive Placement, NIDS instances are installed directly on Internet of Things devices. This technique balances the effectiveness of distributed NIDS, ensuring decentralized detection and enhanced responsiveness. By offering local detection capabilities, this configuration addresses the shortcomings of centralized systems. Both distributive and centralized elements are combined in the hybrid placement. It keeps a central NIDS for network visibility overall and employs distributed NIDS for local intrusion detection. By combining the benefits of distributive and centralized techniques, this strategy achieves both localized responsiveness and complete traffic oversight.

5.4.1 Machine Learning and Multi-Access Edge Computing in IDS

The use of ML and MEC to improve IDS for the Internet of Things is covered in detail in this section [5]. By processing data closer to the IoT devices, MEC lowers latency and makes real-time threat detection possible. MEC improves the IDS's capacity to swiftly assess and address security issues by shifting processing responsibilities from centralized data centers to edge nodes. This is important given the dynamic and resource-constrained nature of IoT environments [5].

The IDS architecture incorporates machine learning approaches to enhance detection precision and adjust to novel and dynamic security threats. To find patterns suggestive of harmful activity, supervised learning, unsupervised learning, and reinforcement learning are some of the machine learning techniques that are used [11]. With the help of these algorithms, the IDS can learn from past data, enhancing its detection capabilities over time and lowering false positives. This IDS framework's MEC and ML synergy offers a reliable, scalable, and effective solution that is suited to the requirements of contemporary IoT ecosystems and guarantees thorough defense against advanced cyber threats.

The evaluation metrics for IDS performance are determined by the counts of true positives *(α)*, true negatives *(δ)*, false positives *(γ)*, and false negatives *(β)*, as presented in Table 5.6. These metrics can be explained as follows.

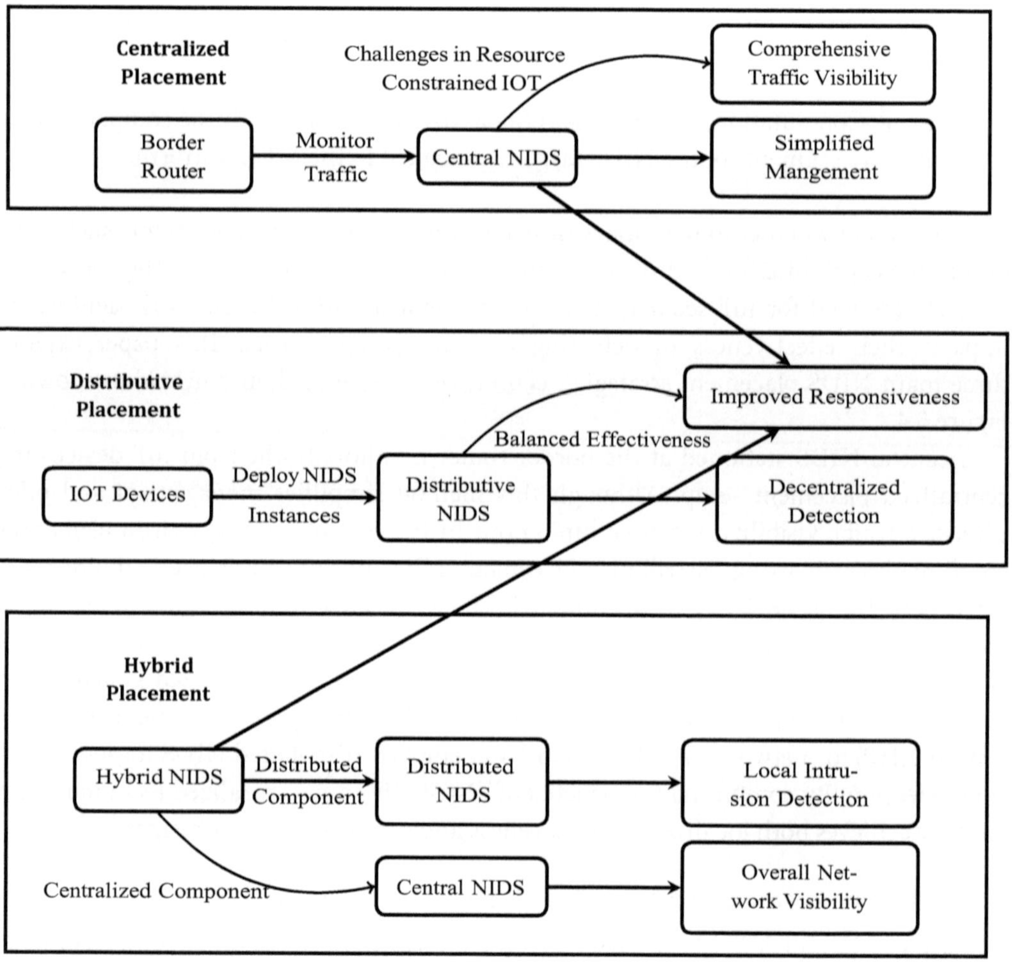

FIGURE 5.4 Placement of NIDS.

TABLE 5.6 Confusion Matrix

	Predicting the Anomaly Class				Predicting the Normal Class		
		Attack	Normal			Attack	Normal
Actual Class	Attack	α_A	β_A	Actual Class	Attack	α_N	β_N
	Normal	γ_A	δ_A		Normal	γ_N	x_N

The performance of IDS is evaluated using metrics based on true positives (correctly identified attacks), true negatives (correctly identified normal traffic), false positives (incorrect alarms), and false negatives (missed attacks). These metrics are then used to calculate key statistics like True Positive Rate (TPR), False Positive Rate (FPR), and Recall (R).

$$\mathrm{TPR} = \frac{\alpha A}{\alpha A + \beta A} \qquad \mathrm{FPR} = \frac{\gamma A}{\gamma A + \delta A} \qquad \mathrm{P} = \frac{\alpha A}{\alpha A + \gamma A}$$
$$\mathrm{F} = \frac{2 \times \mathrm{P} \times \mathrm{R}}{\mathrm{P} + \mathrm{R}} \qquad \text{Success Rate} = \frac{\alpha A + \delta A}{\alpha A + \delta A + \beta A + \gamma A} \tag{5.1}$$
$$\text{Error Rate} = 1 - \text{Success Rate}$$

These metrics apply identically when evaluating normal traffic classification (using parameters α_N, β_N, γ_N, and δ_N).

It is clear from reviewing several studies on IDS in the context of MEC and IoT that there are notable improvements and drawbacks to the various approaches. The dynamic and resource-constrained nature of IoT environments poses a challenge for traditional IDS, such as signature-based and anomaly-based detection, which have been proven effective [13]. The comparison of research emphasizes the need for more effective and adaptable IDS that can function well in the resource-constrained and dispersed environments of managed energy centers (MEC).

This study shows that although signature-based intrusion detection systems (IDSs) are effective at detecting known threats by matching patterns, they are vulnerable to zero-day assaults and need to be updated often to stay effective [16]. On the other hand, by creating baselines of typical activity and spotting deviations, anomaly-based intrusion detection systems (IDSs) provide superior protection against new threats. However, their high false positive rate might cause problems in real-world scenarios [14]. Hybrid intrusion detection systems (IDSs) aim to integrate the advantages of both methods, improving detection efficiency and decreasing false positives. However, they pose challenges in IoT environments due to their added complexity and resource requirements [5].

IDS systems are becoming more and more equipped with ML approaches to enhance detection precision and flexibility. Massive data sets can be analyzed by ML-based IDSs to find trends and abnormalities that point to malicious activity. However, IoT device heterogeneity and resource limits present serious problems for machine learning models, requiring compact and effective algorithms that can work within these constraints.

5.5 CONCLUSION

This study makes a significant contribution to the understanding of IDS within the realms of IoT and IIoT, highlighting the essential functions of MEC and machine learning. By delivering an extensive review and proposing a MEC-based NIDS framework, we tackle the intricate security issues arising from the swift expansion of IoT devices. Our research underscores the urgent need for tailored IDS in dynamic smart environments and provides valuable insights into the incorporation of machine learning to improve the efficiency and precision of IDS. Additionally, we conduct a thorough evaluation of the security mechanisms currently employed in IIoT, pinpointing deficiencies and suggesting directions for future research. This work not only consolidates the existing knowledge of IDS but also propels the field forward by delineating both practical and theoretical advancements necessary for securing the forthcoming generation of IoT networks. The in-depth analysis of IDS methodologies, challenges associated with edge computing, and the role of machine learning emphasizes the critical need for developing flexible, scalable, and resilient security solutions. Our results serve as a vital reference for researchers and practitioners dedicated to strengthening IoT and IIoT systems against emerging cyber threats.

The continuous advancement of IoT and MEC technologies offers numerous opportunities for additional research to tackle existing challenges in IDS development. Subsequent studies should concentrate on designing lightweight machine learning algorithms specifically for resource-limited IoT environments to improve detection accuracy without overburdening the devices' limited computational capabilities. Improving real-time detection is essential for enhancing the responsiveness and precision of IDS in real-time scenarios, particularly in light of zero-day attacks and rapidly changing threats. Enhancing interoperability guarantees that IDS solutions are adaptable to a wide array of IoT devices and communication protocols, which is critical given the diverse nature of IoT ecosystems. Privacy-preserving methods must be devised to safeguard the privacy of processed data, considering the sensitive nature of IoT data. Furthermore, the creation of energy-efficient solutions reduces energy consumption, prolonging the operational lifespan of battery-powered IoT devices. By addressing these areas, future research can further boost the effectiveness and efficiency of IDS in safeguarding IoT ecosystems, ensuring strong protection against evolving cyber threats.

REFERENCES

1. Munirathinam, Sathyan. "Industry 4.0: Industrial internet of things (IIOT)." *Advances in Computers* 117. 1 (2020): 129–164.
2. Mouha, Radouan Ait. "Internet of things (IoT)." *Journal of Data Analysis and Information Processing* 9.2 (2021): 77.
3. Shah, Yash, and Shamik Sengupta. "A survey on classification of cyber-attacks on IoT and IIoT devices." 2020 11th IEEE Annual Ubiquitous Computing, Electronics Mobile Communication Conference (UEMCON). IEEE, 2020.
4. Bharati, Manisha, and Sharvaree Tamane. "Intrusion detection systems (IDS) & future challenges in cloud based environment." 2017 1st International Conference on intelligent Systems and Information Management (ICISIM). IEEE, 2017.
5. Gyamfi, Eric, and Anca Jurcut. "Intrusion detection in internet of things systems: A review on design approaches leveraging multi-access edge computing, machine learning, and datasets." *Sensors* 22.10 (2022): 3744
6. Thakkar, Ankit, and Ritika Lohiya. "A review on machine learning and deep learning perspectives of IDS for IoT: Recent updates, security issues, and challenges." *Archives of Computational Methods in Engineering* 28.4 (2021): 3211–3243.
7. Stefan, A. Intrusion detection systems: A survey and taxonomy. Technical report, Chalmers University of Technology Göteborg, Sweden, 2000.

8. Arrington, B., L. Barnett, R. Rufus, and A. Esterline. "Behavioral modeling intrusion detection system (BMIDS) using internet of things (IoT) behavior-based anomaly detection via immunity-inspired algorithms." 2016 25th International Conference on Computer Communication and Networks (ICCCN), 1–6, Waikoloa, 2016.
9. Khraisat, Ansam et al. "Survey of intrusion detection systems: Techniques, datasets and challenges." *Cybersecurity* 2.1 (2019): 1–22.
10. Okoli, Ugochukwu Ikechukwu et al. "Machine learning in cybersecurity: A review of threat detection and defense mechanisms." *World Journal of Advanced Research and Reviews* 21.1 (2024): 2286–2295.
11. Heartfield, Ryan et al. "Self-configurable cyber-physical intrusion detection for smart homes using reinforcement learning." *IEEE Transactions on Information Forensics and Security* 16 (2020): 1720–1735.
12. Mitchell, R., and I.R. Chen. "A survey of intrusion detection techniques for cyber-physical systems." *ACM Computing Surveys (CSUR)* 46 (2014): 55. doi: 10.1145/2542049.
13. Arnaboldi, Luca, and Charles Morisset. "A review of intrusion detection systems and their evaluation in the IoT." arXiv preprint arXiv:2105.08096 (2021).
14. Mothukuri, V., P. Khare, R.M. Parizi, S. Pouriyeh, A. Dehghantanha, and G. Srivastava. "Federated learning-based anomaly detection for IoT security attacks." *IEEE Internet of Things (IOT) Journal* 9 (2021): 2545–2554. doi: 10.1109/JIOT.2021.3077803.
15. Saheed, Yakub Kayode, Oluwadamilare Harazeem Abdulganiyu, and Taha Ait Tchakoucht. "Modified genetic algorithm and fine-tuned long short-term memory network for intrusion detection in the internet of things networks with edge capabilities." *Applied Soft Computing* 155 (2024): 111434..
16. Kasinathan, P., C. Pastrone, M.A. Spirito, and M. Vinkovits. "Denial-of-service detection in 6LoWPAN based internet of things." In: 2013 IEEE 9th International Conference on Wireless and Mobile Computing, Networking and Communications (WiMob), IEEE, Lyon, 2013, 600–607.
17. Surendar, M., and A. Umamakeswari. "InDReS: An intrusion detection and response system for internet of things with 6LoWPAN." 2016 International Conference on Wireless Communications, Signal Processing and Networking (WiSPNET), Chennai, 2016, 1903–1908.
18. Shreenivas, Dharmini, Shahid Raza, and Thiemo Voigt. "Intrusion detection in the RPL-connected 6LoWPAN networks." Proceedings of the 3rd ACM International Workshop on IoT Privacy, Trust, and Security, 2017.
19. Zhang, Kuan, Xiaohui Liang, Rongxing Lu, and Xuemin Shen. "Sybil attacks and their defenses in the internet of things." *IEEE Internet of Things Journal* 1.5 (October 2014): 372–383. doi: 10.1109/jiot.2014.2344013.
20. Perera, C., A. Zaslavsky, P. Christen, and D. Georgakopoulos. "Context aware computing for the internet of things: A survey." *IEEE Communications Surveys & Tutorials* 16 (2013): 414–454. doi: 10.1109/SURV.2013.042313.00197.
21. Duque, S., and M.N. bin Omar. "Using data mining algorithms for developing a model for intrusion detection system (IDS)." *Procedia Comput Science* 61 (2015): 46–51.
22. Mei, Lin, Chungen Xu, and Lin Li. "Check for updates efficient forward and backward private searchable symmetric encryption for multiple data sources." Advances in Artificial Intelligence and Security: 7th International Conference, ICAIS 2021, Dublin, Ireland, July 19–23, 2021, Proceedings, Part III. Vol. 1424. Springer Nature, 2021.
23. Sheikh, Zakir Ahmad, and Yashwant Singh. "Review of cyber-physical system-based security datasets for learning-based intrusion detection dystems." The International Conference on Recent Innovations in Computing. Singapore: Springer Nature Singapore, 2023.
24. Canedo, J., and A. Skjellum. "Using machine learning to secure IoT systems." Proceedings of the 2016 14th Annual Conference on Privacy, Security and Trust, PST; Auckland, New Zealand. 12–14 December 2016, 219–222.

25. Alsoufi, M.A., S. Razak, M.M. Siraj, I. Nafea, F.A. Ghaleb, F. Saeed, and M. Nasser. "Anomaly-based intrusion detection systems in IoT using deep learning: A systematic literature review." *Applied Sciences* 11 (2021): 8383. doi: 10.3390/app11188383.
26. Bostani, H., and M. Sheikhan. "Hybrid of anomaly-based and specification-based IDS for internet of things using unsupervised OPF based on MapReduce approach." *Computer Communications* 98 (2017):52–71.
27. Garcia-Font, V., C. Garrigues, and H. Rifà-Pous. "Attack classification schema for smart city WSNs." *Sensors* 17.4 (2017): 1–24.
28. Oh, D., D. Kim, and W.W. Ro. "A malicious pattern detection engine for embedded security systems in the internet of things." *Sensors* 14.12 (2014): 24188–24211.
29. Khan, Z.A., and P. Herrmann. "A trust based distributed intrusion detection mechanism for internet of things." 2017 IEEE 31st International Conference on Advanced Information Networking and Applications (AINA), IEEE, Taipei, 2017, 1169–1176.

CHAPTER 6

The Legal and Ethical Crossroads of Artificial Intelligence in Cybersecurity and Digital Forensics

Gyanendra Tiwari, Khushi Pandey, Manali Desai, Vinayak Musale, Dhanashri Wategaonkar, and Mangesh Bedekar

6.1 INTRODUCTION

Artificial intelligence (AI) plays a noteworthy role in developing solutions for cybersecurity along with improving the security of areas like the Internet of Things (IoT), automotive networks, and critical infrastructure. The rate of change in the capabilities of AI is accelerating and is increasingly impacting every sector of society. As AI systems' transformative impact is evident in everyday life, the potential for criminal use is rising. While harnessing AI to protect our valuable assets, such as sensitive personal information, digital and physical infrastructure we come across a multitude of discrepancies. Algorithmic bias culminates into discriminatory results if the data used in training the model is biased. Fairness-aware modeling and disparate impact analysis prove to be two substantial approaches in mitigating any algorithmic bias to facilitate fairness and equality.

Transparency is a foundational aspect of building trust in AI technologies. It provides a look into the operational processes of AI in its decision-making capabilities. While taking into consideration the importance of transparency with respect to the ethical and legal landscape, we encounter a conflict when organizations are hesitant toward providing proprietary details. Aligning the motive of protecting proprietary information whilst simultaneously ensuring transparency is a challenging task.

DOI: 10.1201/9781032714813-6

Furthermore, we come across concerns regarding data privacy. AI utilizes extensive data over which it is trained for better performance purposes. This data might include personal information which if exploited can account to extreme financial, reputational or security damages. On one side of the coin, AI can be utilized to enhance cybersecurity capabilities in cyber threat intelligence, malware analysis, and crime detection but on the flip side, the compliance to data protection regulations namely General Data Protection Regulation (GDPR) and the Information Technology (Reasonable Security Practices and Procedures and Sensitive Personal Data or Information) Rules under the IT Act is just as crucial. The use and control of AI in India have been open to debate, with reports such as the Responsible AI Report identifying principles for responsible development of AI. Instead of breeding in specific AI laws, the Indian government adopts governance using legislation made for privacy protection law, data omission statute, intellectual property right, and cybersecurity. This method is in line with the ICT policies and principles of "Digital India" initiative.

Ultimately, we arrive at the concept of liability. When pervasive threats strike, the primary question arising is, "Who needs to be held accountable for the actions taken by an AI?." AI made decisions are highly controversial in connection with ethical boundaries and need to be reviewed with utmost precaution to maintain a responsible cyberspace. This chapter acknowledges the lack of a comprehensive ethical and legal framework and aids in policymaking to help resolution of existing enforcement gaps as well as provide legal solutions to the question of protecting data and privacy in the rapidly evolving landscape of AI technology in the Cybersecurity domain.

This chapter emphasizes the ethical and legal issues of deploying AI in cybersecurity and then discusses the role of AI in maintaining critical infrastructure that could be vulnerable to cyberattacks. The authors then argue that AI is better than conventional cybersecurity solutions. This chapter suggests the need for an ethical framework and global regulations for issues created by such deployments like algorithmic bias and possibility of job threats to human employees because of AI. It dives into AI's interaction with both the law and ethics, such as the Citizenship via Investment program, revealing the possible bias supporting its indirect use by revealing the false positives preventing the approval of citizenship, as well as the privacy implications and proposes possible fixes by instilling mechanisms such as data minimization and encryption. This chapter highlights the malicious utilization of AI and how sophisticated the attacks are and suggests that we need frameworks of cooperation among the different stakeholders. Another paper speaks of incorporating accountability and ethics into legal structures to form responsible AI governance. One of the papers on the IoT calls for a holistic legal framework. Also in this slot, a piece compares data-protection laws across the globe and notes that we need a new ethical framework for AI regulation, expressed through a holistic AI regulation.

The purpose of compiling this document is to analyze and add the ethical, legal, and regulatory implications posed by AI. Privacy concerns, inadequate International regulatory framework, algorithmic bias, lack of transparency, and other multifaceted issues are the perspectives of the literature survey. It aims to harmonize the ethical and effective use of AI under a global regulatory framework.

The core concept of artificial intelligence digital forensics involves the utilization of AI algorithms to carry out automated analysis of cyber-physical and digital systems for legal reviews. With the aid of AI, forensic teams are able to accurately detect, classify, and comprehend patterns and irregularities within extensive data sets that encompass digital evidence. Through the integration of machine learning and predictive analysis, AI has the capability to provide indispensable insights that can greatly contribute to digital investigations and the combat against cybercrimes.

6.2 LITERATURE SURVEY

The author S. Zeadally et al. explored various AI techniques such as deep learning, machine learning (ML), natural language processing and ML algorithms for developing solutions for cybersecurity. The research highlighted the very important concerns of privacy of the data that is collected by Internet-connected devices like smart watches, and smart home devices. A large amount of data is collected by these devices, which could be misused by the threat actors. Privacy protection of data being gathered and processed is one of the major concerns about artificial intelligence integration into cybersecurity. Much as these are important frameworks for this purpose, GDPR and IT Act's provisions on data privacy. The legislation imposes stringent guidelines on data collection, processing, and retention to ensure that individuals' right to privacy is respected. Nonetheless, Zeadally et al. observed that these legal frameworks are often outrun by the fast-pacing IoT and AI technologies resulting in enforcement gaps and accountability shortfalls. When deploying AI in cybersecurity ethical considerations including algorithmic bias, transparency, and accountability must be considered. The focus then shifts toward the use of AI in protecting critical infrastructure of oil, gas, defense, electricity, and nuclear sectors that are crucial for social and national security. Conventional cybersecurity solutions are inadequate in keeping up with the complexities of modern infrastructure; this has led to the emergence of new solutions that use artificial intelligence techniques for the prediction of faults, classification of anomalies, dynamic access control, logic-based authorization, and self-healing mechanisms (Zeadally et al., 2020).

The authors Mansoori et al. urged the creation and adherence to an ethical framework for conducting AI and ML research in the cybersecurity realm, as well as established guidelines and frameworks for data privacy and protection. Algorithmic bias is pointed out as a problem that can lead to discriminatory procedures in cybersecurity systems. Dyson advocated for two possible corrective actions: fairness-aware modeling (so that the sample-space is less likely to be unwittingly biased), and disparate impact analysis. One of the concerns with AI and ML is ethics, whose automation capabilities may lead to job threat. Liability issues such as who is responsible for decisions taken autonomously by machines these are just some of the complicated legal and regulatory problems raised by the rapid development of AI and ML. The lack of a coherent global set of regulations for AI and ML technologies is viewed as a major problem. The text urged "multi-stakeholder work to develop universal standards and regulatory guidelines" to ensure the safety, reliability, and ethical soundness of AI technologies worldwide (Al-Mansoori et al., 2023).

The authors Joseph et al. investigated the intersection of AI with the law and ethics and the program called Citizenship via Investment (CBI), an issue prompting discussions of bias, profiling, and false positives where: when bias in an AI algorithm leads to discrimination but does not constitute a civil rights violation, correlation between the decision making of AI applications and discrimination is absent. For instance, the Dutch AI scandal identified approximately 26,000 households as frauding the government, resulting in good citizens being alleged when AI detection strategies were improperly applied. It grabbed attention to the dangerousness approach adopted by the European Union's (EU), to finally emphasize the importance of clearly defining high-risk AI systems. The evaluation concludes that AI applications ought to take a very similar pragmatic danger-based tactic: be governed by clean criminal legislation and ethical tips (Joseph and Turksen, 2022).

This increasing literature emphasized the ethical concerns surrounding the potential of AI in healthcare. Four overarching ethical issues found in the literature are: (1) the need for informed consent in the use of patient data; (2) safety and transparency in AI systems; (3) the issues of algorithmic fairness and biases; and (4) the defense against a breach in data privacy. It politely glossed over the fact that the topic of whether AI systems are proper legal persons is currently a highly contested issue in legal theory and practice. According to literature, algorithmic transparency is troubled by limited possibilities. Among considerable ethical concerns argued in the literature is the difficulty of identifying liability in AI decision-making. AI systems are "opaque," and not only do these present obstacles to thoughtful review but raises questions about responsibility (Nithesh et al., 2022).

The review identified two key ethical issues arising from the unprecedented quantities of personal information analyzed by machine learning and AI in cybersecurity: (1) The potential neglect or unconscious perpetuation of privacy, especially if the algorithms behind cybersecurity tools are trained on datasets with known forms of bias or demographically underrepresented groups; and (2) new forms of personal data being collected (e.g., behavioral biometrics) that people might not be aware about, and whose collection raises transparency and accountability issues. Following strict security protocols (e.g., long, complex passwords, and multi-factor authentication) on every access point can make a system safer, but your users may tire or be frustrated by the interference, which in turn will reduce productivity and user experience. One approach is data minimization, which places limits on the amount of personal data that can be collected and processed in support of a particular purpose. This is aligned with data protection regulations such as the European Union's GDPR and its successor in the Californian market, the California Consumer Privacy Act (CCPA). Encryption is another important security feature and an essential element of a layered defense against cyber threats by protecting sensitive data in both transmission and at rest. A pragmatic measure can be to appoint a data protection officer to monitor compliance with privacy (Allahrakha, 2023).

The literature's major goal was to help us systematically think about the malicious use and abuse of AI. A key part of this literature review was the level of sophistication that exists in both AI-enabled and AI-aided attacks—from nefarious actors strategically gaming the output of algorithms to nation-states launching highly sophisticated attacks on systems. This section followed the call by exploring existing frameworks and possible avenues for improvement or development of policies that are likely to minimize risks and mitigate harms. Lastly, the review highlighted the need for greater cooperation among governments, industries, and civil society actors to increase overall preparedness and resilience to malicious use and abuse of AI (Blauth et al., 2022).

The authors Kamaruddin et al. have studied the legal ramifications of AI-based technologies in the country of Malaysia. They mentioned that the post-pandemic period was an onset for AI-based tools to be brought into action to safeguard private data and personal sensitive information alike. The use of AI technology relies on processing of personal data of EU citizens, thereby enforcing compliance to GDPR in order to fine-tune the legal framework surrounding AI. A combination of both GDPR and Malaysia's Personal Data Protection Act becomes a holistic approach to ensure that the risk is minimized for organizations, not only for litigation and the accompanying penalties but also for organizational reputation, ensuring that stakeholders have trust in them. The authors called for a thorough review of existing legislative mechanisms following the lack of stronger suits and proposing comprehensive work that can aid in policymaking to resolve any enforcement gaps within the AI ecosystem (Kamaruddin et al., 2023).

The authors V. Poonia et al. explored the laws governing the role of AI in diverse landscapes through this chapter. While there are no such specific laws catering to AI exclusively, the author has established that the legal framework applicable aligns with the cybersecurity regulations namely GDPR and the Information Technology (Reasonable Security Practices and Procedures and Sensitive Personal Data or Information) Rules under the IT Act. The need for a strong legal infrastructure is highlighted while addressing issues such as transparency, algorithmic bias, and ethical dilemma to prevent any mistakes or unseen consequences. Within the field of AI governance, fulfillment is played out by incorporating accountability, transparency, and ethics into legal structures thereby promoting responsible development of AI (Poonia, 2022).

The next research paper presented the need for an integrated legal framework for the IoT using AI to enhance user experience in all spheres of daily life. This chapter addressed issues of statutes by exploring when statutory requirements should apply for lack of self-regulation or market solutions to address risks, and discussed issues of privacy in IoT devices and the need for statutory standardization of privacy requirements, considering that the US lacks certain necessary standards for privacy needs across industries. The literature review explored the issue of discrimination with the IoT, and concluded that legally protected interests should be narrowly construed. The restrictions on solicitation and use of sensitive personal information should be a part of this effort to curb potential harms and protect the rights of consumers. Additionally, the review explained that some interests relating to transparency in algorithmic decision-making should be balanced against the market interests and consumer fairness interests (Tschider, 2018).

The authors Alic explored the legislative issues of data protection and cybersecurity in AI across the European Union (EU), United States (US), and China. It discusses how individual regions approach cyber policy in relation to AI, and seeks to identify similarities and differences to establish an ethical, global framework to regulate AI. While the GDPR is praised as an example of the Euros considering that AI should serve humanity's interests. It seems to be a response to the criticism that the bloc should invest more to stay competitive with innovators. This chapter outlined the effect of the USA Patriot Act on records control, and emphasized national protection and customer safety as pinnacle priorities. The review commended China for implementing strong educational measures in cybersecurity and adopting the Cybersecurity Law of the People's Republic of China (CSL), it criticized China for not explicitly providing for a right to data protection as part of its law-making instruments (read: explicitly part of the CSL). It pointed out that there are difficulties in the legal and policy frameworks keeping up with AI innovation, that individual countries tend to emphasize national frameworks, and the need for global AI governance to be more thoroughly clarified (Alic, 2021).

The authors F. Casino et al. suggested that unraveling malicious activities can be quite challenging especially when dealing with the vulnerabilities in contracts. Identifying and preventing actions adds another layer of complexity. The field of forensics faces difficulties in handling datasets requiring advanced techniques for effective analysis. Retrieving evidence from devices within distributed file systems and databases proves to be a significant undertaking. Security concerns and anti-forensic methods further compound these challenges. With the rise of IoT, a new frontier emerges, bringing along a set of security challenges that necessitate standardized forensics procedures and real-time investigations due to enhanced security features. Addressing these intricacies requires collaboration and interdisciplinary research in forensics emphasizing the importance of approaches, for adaptable tool utilization (Casino et al., 2022).

The authors A. Jarrett et al. underlined that digital investigation encircles huge amounts of data and time constraints; hence the importance of AI and automation in digital forensics is crucial. They stressed on impacts and challenges that emerge with the involvement of Al in digital forensics, benefits of advanced technological solutions for digital forensics in coping with the evolving challenges of cybercrimes, challenges of applying the appropriate technology to digital forensics, importance of equilibrium between advanced technology and digital forensics for reaching efficient and accurate digital forensic outcomes (Jarrett et al., 2021).

The deepfake impersonation scam targeting the Hong Kong company acts as a pointer to the fast-growing menace from advanced AI technology. Scammers convinced an employee to allow a huge $25 million financial transfer with a very realistic digital avatar of the CFO. This is how deepfakes are giving new life to social engineering attacks against organizations. The incident can only be taken to full comprehension by drilling down to the technical details of deepfaked video creation, the company's security measures and employee training, and the greater implications for society from this type of technology (Sankaran, 2024).

The case also throws up some important legal loopholes, since current laws may not be prepared to deal with crimes related to deepfakes. The admissibility of the evidence, jurisdiction, and definition of identity in this digital age are a few of the broad concerns. Most importantly, this case raises the need for international cooperation in prosecuting trans border cybercrimes. With the rapid evolution of the technology of deepfakes, the legal infrastructure will have to evolve to protect citizens and organizations from exploitation. (Incode Technologies, 2024).

Many new and great advancements have come out with the increasing sophistication of artificial intelligence, but so have new challenges related to cybersecurity and forensics. A very relevant case study, one that will prove it, is the AI-driven voice cloning scam in Delhi-NCR, India. One such case was that of a resident of Noida. She received a distress call from a boy whom she thought was her son, asking for Rs. 60,000 in an urgent tone. Though so convincing, the voice was an artificially intelligent-aided cloned imitation. The case exemplifies exactly AI's dual-use dilemma: while it can power innovation and convenience, it can equally well facilitate very sophisticated frauds (Zoya et al., 2022).

The application of AI in voice cloning for cybercrime purposes is a great leap into the modus operandi of the criminals. As per the data received from NCRB, there has been a manifold rise in the cases of cybercrime in the national capital, and all of them were online financial frauds. The sophistication of AI allows scammers to copy a person's voice with high accuracy by using only a short audio sample. According to the Machine Learning Engineer at UC Berkeley, Romit Barua, the voice cloning technology uses advanced developments in audio signal processing and neural networks that manage to closely imitate unique voice characteristics. This technology, though useful in so many domains in its legitimate applications, proves to be detrimental when used for creating fraud (Zoya et al., 2024).

Morally, AI voice cloning without consent is a serious concern, especially considering how easily any person could become a victim of this type of scam, according to the results of a survey conducted by McAfee. This is further compounded by how often people post their voices online. Another ethical dimension to this concern is the emotional and psychological impact on the victim of being manipulated into states of fear and urgency. This case of AI voice cloning fraud shows that, from a legal perspective, there is a dire need for revised cybercrime laws and strong regulatory frameworks at the very earliest. In this context, awareness and education would also be required to share information regarding these new threats with the general public and to facilitate institutes in implementing basic safeguards like checking unexpected calls through another channel and creating family code words. (Zoya et al., 2022).

The potential for AI in cybersecurity is very huge, although certain areas are relatively unexplored. Some of the key emerging areas involve automated retrieval of risk indicators—unpatched systems and attempted security breaches—information that can be used to build an early warning system. A further highly challenging task is detecting zero-day attacks, since such threats are new and hence unknown, requiring full visibility across IT environments. Predictive intelligence can, therefore, automate several routine tasks in cybersecurity; however, with current techniques, high false-positive rates prevail and AI-based advanced techniques remain to be achieved in order to refine the predictions. In addition, advanced AI methods are required for multilingual threat intelligence to have an appropriate approach to non-English threats and AI-powered cyber defenses to automate security controls for better resilience of the organization (Kaur et al., 2023).

The success of AI methods in cybersecurity depends tremendously on the quality of the data representation. Most classical flattened feature vectors often miss essential linkages existing in the data. In the future, research should turn toward alternative representations,

TABLE 6.1 Various Legal and Ethical Concerns and Solutions

Sr. No.	Title of Paper	Concerns	Solutions
1	Harnessing Artificial Intelligence capabilities, Zeadally et al., *IEEE Access*, 2020	Data privacy in IOT devices, cybersecurity of critical infrastructure	Development of AI solutions for prediction, anomaly classification, access control of IoT and critical systems
2	The Role of Artificial Intelligence and Machine Learning in Shaping the Future of Cybersecurity: Trends, Applications, and Ethical Considerations, Al-Mansoori and Salem, *IJSA*, 2023	Bias in AI algorithm, job displacement, liability, need of regulations for AI	Making ethical AI frameworks, data privacy guidelines, spreading awareness, and education people
3	Harnessing AI for due diligence in CBI Programs. Legal and Ethical Challenges, Joseph and Turksen, *JELT*, 2022	Algorithmic bias, profiling, false positives, risky approach	Clearly defining high-risk AI systems, developing danger-based approach
4	Legal and Ethical Consideration in Artificial Intelligence in Healthcare: Who Takes Responsibility? N. Nithesh et al., *Front. Surg.*, 2022	Informed consent, safety, transparency, fairness, privacy	Enforcing strict security protocols, data minimization, encryption, data protection officers
5	Balancing Cybersecurity and Privacy: Legal and Ethical Considerations in the Digital Age, N. Allahrakha, *LIDA*, 2023	Privacy neglection, new data collection, user fatigue	Data minimization, encryption, employing data protection officers
6	Artificial Intelligence Crime: An Overview of Malicious Use and Abuse of AI, T. F. Blauth et al., *IEEE Access*, 2022	Sophisticated attacks, lack of defense solutions for these attack	Keeping track of malicious activities performed by threat actors, making policy frameworks, cooperation among stakeholders
7	Compliance to GDPR Data Protection and Privacy in Artificial Intelligence Technology: Legal and Ethical Ramifications in Malaysia, S. Kamaruddin et al., *ICDT*, 2023	GDPR readiness, enforcement question	Following frameworks such as GDPR and PDPA, reviewing existing laws, and modifying them according to current context
8	Laws Regulating AI in India: Legal Considerations and Challenges," *Indian Journal of Law and Legal Research*, V. Poonia, 2022	Lack of AI-specific laws and regulations, transparency, ethical dilemmas	Aligning with existing cybersecurity regulations and improving them in context of AI, creating strong legal infrastructure
9	Regulating the Internet of Things: Discrimination, Privacy and Cybersecurity in the Artificial Intelligence Age, C. A. Tschider, *Denver Law Review*, 2018	Proper requirements, privacy, discrimination	Integrated legal framework for AI and cybersecurity, correct standardization of privacy of the users, balancing interests of various parties
10	The Role of Data Protection and Cybersecurity Regulations in Artificial Intelligence Global Governance: A Comparative Analysis of the European Union, the United States, and China Regulatory Framework, D. Alic, 2021	Variation and differences in regulations of different regions, lack of global framework	Creating an Ethical global framework considering specificities of different regions

(Continued)

TABLE 6.1 *(Continued)*

Sr. No.	Title of Paper	Concerns	Solutions
11	Research Trends, Challenges and Emerging Topics in Digital Forensics: A Review of Reviews, F. Casino et al., *IEEE Access*, 2022	Challenges faced in tasks such as data handling and retrieving evidence	Standardized forensic procedures, interdisciplinary research for the use of AI in digital forensics
12	The impact of automation and artificial intelligence on digital forensics, A. Jarret et al., *Wiley Interdisciplinary Reviews Forensic Science*, 2021	Time constraints and huge amount of data in digital forensics	Identification of AI tools and technologies, creating equilibrium between advanced technologies and digital forensics
13	Artificial intelligence for cybersecurity: Literature review and future research directions, R. Kaur et al., *Information Fusion*, 2023	Current AI techniques in cybersecurity face challenges such as high false-positive rates, difficulty in detecting zero-day attacks, etc. limiting their effectiveness and accuracy	Research should focus on alternative data representations, context awareness, incremental learning, multi-source data integration, explainable AI, and the development of real-time threat intelligence platforms

such as trees, graphs, and tensors, that better represent the phenomena in cybersecurity. Context awareness is also a very relevant issue: the inclusion of broader context information can allow dramatically better detection of suspicious activities. Further, incremental learning and recency mining are important in the development of adaptive security models that learn from changing user and adversary behaviors and help keep AI models relevant and effective over time (Kaur et al., 2023).

Sophisticated AI techniques are needed to harness the power of these different data sources for improved cybersecurity outcomes. Integration of multiple data source sets through multi-source data analysis can provide a holistic assessment. Transparency of AI-driven decisions and explainable AI form a critical mass for gaining the trust and acceptance of stakeholders. Augmented intelligence refers to a balanced approach toward decision-making in cybersecurity, where human expertise is combined with AI. Furthermore, AI application in cybersecurity requires the development of new infrastructures, such as real-time threat intelligence platforms and updated datasets. Current datasets are significantly outdated and require new and real-time datasets that can characterize the latest cyber threats (Kaur et al., 2023).

Table 6.1 highlights proposed solutions for the various legal and ethical concerns.

6.3 PROBLEM STATEMENT

To review the existing legal and ethical challenges of AI in the cybersecurity sector, necessitating a comprehensive, globally coordinated effort to address the multifaceted issues and highlighting frameworks that ensure responsible and ethical AI development and deployment in cybersecurity.

The rapid advancement of AI in cybersecurity has presented numerous legal and ethical challenges that necessitate a comprehensive, globally coordinated effort to address. One of the primary issues is the lack of a robust legal infrastructure capable of validating the actions of AI systems in this critical field. As AI becomes increasingly integrated into cybersecurity measures, the potential for misuse and unintended consequences grows, underscoring the urgent need for effective governance frameworks. Without such frameworks, the deployment of AI in cybersecurity can lead to significant risks, including violations of privacy, biases in threat detection, and accountability gaps when AI systems malfunction or are exploited by malicious actors.

Currently, the legal landscape governing AI in cybersecurity is fragmented and insufficient to address the complex ethical dilemmas that arise. There is a clear absence of uniform regulations and standards that can guide the responsible development and deployment of AI technologies across different jurisdictions. This lack of harmonization not only hampers international cooperation but also creates loopholes that can be exploited by cybercriminals. For instance, AI algorithms used in cybersecurity can inadvertently discriminate against certain groups or perpetuate existing biases, leading to unjust outcomes. Moreover, the opacity of AI decision-making processes makes it challenging to attribute responsibility when things go wrong, complicating legal recourse, and accountability.

To mitigate these challenges, it is imperative to establish comprehensive legal frameworks that ensure AI systems in cybersecurity are developed and deployed ethically and responsibly. Such frameworks should incorporate principles of transparency, fairness, and accountability, providing clear guidelines for AI developers, policymakers, and cybersecurity professionals. International cooperation is crucial in this endeavor, as cyber threats are inherently global and require a unified response. This chapter aims to explore the current gaps in legal infrastructure, propose potential solutions, and highlight existing frameworks that can serve as models for responsible AI governance in the cybersecurity sector.

6.4 SOCIETAL IMPACT AND HUMAN RIGHTS IN AI

AI can play a role in cybersecurity and digital forensics in ways that create a challenging blend of legal, ethical, and technical issues; those considerations have implications for how we develop AI and its incorporation into society. On the one hand, the ever-increasing use of AI in cybersecurity has the promise of improving cyber threat detection and response capabilities. However, this shift also faces important legal challenges, most importantly in terms of liability in autonomous cybersecurity systems. AI in cybersecurity legal frameworks is changing and the tension between the need for AI to improve security and the need for accountability within existing legal frameworks is important. Recent legal developments such as the EU's GDPR are a step toward understanding and developing new legal frameworks for the ethical issues of AI in cybersecurity. DF, Privacy, and Graphics: Larks and Owls. AI-powered tools do a better job of analyzing digital evidence than humans. Issues of privacy and data protection will become central—problems associated with opaque, unaccountable algorithmic decision-making are likely to come to the fore as AI is woven deeper and deeper into forensic practice. The key to finding the right ethical balance lies in clear rules regarding how AIs must be used.

The integration of AI into the fields of cybersecurity and digital forensics will spill over into social contexts as well. Scholars caution against blurring the line between counterterrorism and human rights, since the use of AI for surveillance, threat assessments, and law enforcement has troubling implications for freedom and security. The International Covenant on Civil and Political Rights (ICCPR), the International Economic, Social and Cultural Rights (ICESCR), and the Universal Declaration on Human Rights (UDHR) create ambiguity in AI development because they pit maintaining human rights against creating AI. This raises the important question of how to have a legal framework that is both sensitive and nimble enough to balance the needs of innovation alongside the unknowable consequences of AI in the future.

6.5 ETHICAL AND LEGAL CONSIDERATIONS OF AI IN CYBERSECURITY

As the world moves into realms such as cybersecurity, healthcare, and governance, the applications of AI are astounding and transformative. And the future looks no less breath-taking. But as AI technologies are increasingly applied in areas that have an effect on the public interest or infringe people's rights, ethical questions, and legal issues keep cropping up and will have to be addressed. What are the implications of using AI algorithms for personalized policing? How should the design, implementation, and use of AI fit into data-privacy frameworks and human rights norms? Can automated reasoning supplement or replace state regulation, and how will we deal with situations where the public relies on

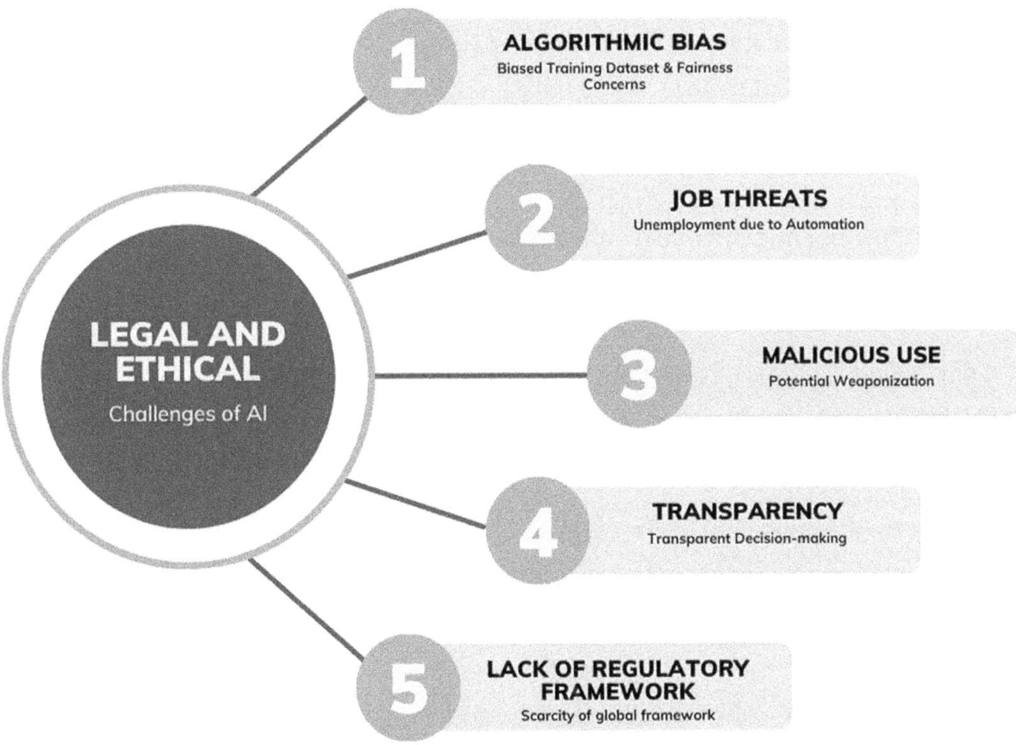

FIGURE 6.1 Ethical and legal challenges of AI.

algorithmic and AI-based decisions? What guarantees can be given in areas where algorithms lack an explanation or are "black boxed"? The ethics surrounding data-collection and processing, algorithmic bias, the influence of AI on democratic norms and what constitutes transparent AI are only some of the issues that are addressed in a large literature on the ethics of AI. Figure 6.1 depicts various ethical and legal challenges of AI.

6.5.1 Privacy Concerns in IoT and Personal Devices

Intense data collection by Internet-connected things poses severe risks to privacy. Threat actors could misuse this data. Traditional security methods, including encryption, prove inadequate in the face of evolving digital infrastructure.

6.5.2 Ethical Considerations in Cybersecurity and AI Implementation

All AI and ML research should be guided by an ethical framework, one that incorporates ideas such as informed consent, transparency, and conflict of interest. Algorithmic bias introduces discriminatory procedures, requiring fairness-aware modeling and disparate impact analysis.

6.5.3 Job Threat through Automation in AI

The core capability of the AI is "automation" which presents threats to cybersecurity professionals for the process of digitalization, reskilling, and upskilling. There are complex legal and regulatory challenges for liability responsibility for autonomous decisions through AI.

6.5.4 Legal and Ethical Issues Related to CBI Programs

The application of AI and the legal and ethical issues for CBI programs reveal the number of problems such as bias and profiling as well as false positives on discrimination hinders the inclusion of vulnerable groups, as it could be possible for AI applications used by states. Particularly, given the lack of distinct discrimination categories for visible as well as invisible minorities and migrants, states already lack precision in identifying such groups. The risk from AI application errors is further amplified by the infamous Dutch AI scandal and discrimination case.

6.5.5 Ethical Issues Relative to Implementation of AI in Healthcare

Ethical issues relative to the implementation of AI in health care include informed consent, algorithmic fairness, discrimination practices, as well as data-privacy breaches.

6.5.6 Using AI Application Technology to Shape the Future of Cybersecurity

Artificial intelligence is seen as the key technology to enhance the efficiency of cybersecurity work. Thus, norm setting ahead of time is vital, as the legal frameworks for AI remain ill-defined.

6.5.7 Strategic Trade-Offs for Cybersecurity and Privacy

Weighing cybersecurity against the right to privacy is a perennial issue as strategic trade-offs, for instance, data minimization combined with data encryption is imperative.

6.5.8 Building a Culture of Privacy for Cyber Resilience

It is vital to build a culture of privacy by undertaking privacy impact assessments and appointing data protection officers (DPOs) as well as cybersecurity officials.

6.5.9 Malicious Use and Abuse of AI in Criminal Activities

As AI technology may be abused to enhance criminal activities, new dimensions of threats require governance and global policy approaches to combat the misuse of AI. In this regard, governments, industries, and civil society need to strengthen their coordination to become more resilient to attacks launched by AI-enabled bot-based threats.

6.5.10 Compliance with GDPR in AI System in India

AI systems need to comply with the GDPR, which, besides being the legal requirement for maintaining the integrity of personal data, is also the right ethical approach to the development of AI. Transparency, for example, dictates that organizations dealing with personal data must inform data subjects about the purposes and means of processing through AI systems. Together with the principle of data minimization, which states that data processed should be no more than necessary, GDPR presents two ethical AI milestones. The right of individuals to access the data collected about themselves and, when necessary, to correct or delete related data—functions thoroughly embedded in AI ecosystems—is also safeguarded by European legislation.

In basic terms, GDPR compliance in AI entails the adoption of strong data protection measures (e.g., encryption and pseudo randomization), a clear consent to gather and use sensitive data for AI purposes, as well as algorithmic or AI-specific technical and organizational measures, all based on the GDPR requirements. AI development is successful because of technical resource pooling, organizational transparency, and sufficient protection of sensitive data gathered and misused for purely selfish ends. Consequently, having DPOs seems like a technical and organizational necessity given the growing hybridities of AI and its growing entanglements with ethics and law. With future techno-legal developments, GDPR-compliance mandates will become even more important, not just for the sake of holding AI accountable but also for trusting it, rendering it transparent and protecting privacy-related concerns.

As there is a massive use of AI in this country in government as well as private-sector operations, GDPR compliance presents some of the biggest challenges. However, clear merits of balancing legal, ethical, and privacy issues in AI technology practices are required in Malaysia. Reviewing the Existing Enforcement Mechanisms in the Legal Framework in Malaysia, an urgent and immediate need is to re-analyze existing enforcement mechanisms and address potential legal loopholes in addressing data protection and privacy.

6.5.11 Legal Framework for IoT Using AI

The potential risks and threats from IoT using AI technology, driven by the market, illustrate the absence of a legal framework for IoT security to protect people from autocratic attacks. Moreover, privacy requirements, transparency in algorithmic decision-making, as well as clear consumer rights, need to be standardized by statutory regulations in practice.

6.6 ACTS AND FRAMEWORKS FOR AI AND CYBERSECURITY

The importance of needing to safeguard informational assets as well as all digital assets was recognized globally considering the rapidly evolving nature of digital landscape. As better technological advancements were made, there was a directly proportional leap in the exploitations of these advancements. To ensure that these exploitations were minimized and if any, rightly punished, different statutory frameworks were brought into action all across the globe.

6.6.1 Personal Data Protection Act, 2023

India has an ever-growing cyberspace as well as a burgeoning digital economy. With the rise of different technologies and connectivity, one of which is AI, the need for a coherent legislature to protect its cybercitizens is also emphasized upon. Amongst the recent advancements, a notable one is the passing of Personal Data Protection Act in 2023. This Act is a revolutionary step toward securing India's digital assets by focusing on data protection. Some of its key features include "Consent" meaning approval before collection of personal data and creating regulations and limitations that require due diligence for maintaining the security posture of organizations.

It also focuses on handling complaints, grievances, and issuing penalties for non-compliance. While previously the Information Technology Act, 2000 provided legal recognition for electronic usage and communication, only a quarter of its legislation pertained to privacy. The Personal Data Protection Act is a positive factor for businesses subject to the law. It exclusively does not have any regulations based on AI decision-making and it's ethical and legal considerations but can be extended to incorporate them in the future.

6.6.2 General Data Protection Regulations, European Union

Ideated and implemented by the European Union, the General Data Protection Regulation is one of the most fundamental legislations that concentrates on giving control to citizens over their personal data. The European Data Protection Regulation is applicable as of May 25, 2018 in all member states to harmonize data privacy laws across Europe. The focal point of GDPR is to safeguard sensitive information and personal sensitive information belonging to any particular crime, victim, suspect, or weakness. It also mentions that data collected must be optimally used for legitimate purposes and any misuse shall be punishable under the enforcement.

6.6.3 Personal Data Protection Act, Singapore

Very similar to the Data Protection Act in India, this particular regulation is a commendable framework applicable in Singapore for the protection of citizen's personal and sensitive data. The government has also deployed a Personal Data Protection Commission along with a comprehensive website wherein digital citizens are notified of the latest amendments and ways in which the framework can aid in strengthening the security posture for organizations or businesses and safeguard individuals.

6.6.4 California Consumer Privacy Act, California

The California Consumer Privacy Act amended in 2018 is an effective framework that focuses on giving consumers higher authority over the data they provide to business organizations.

It remarks the consumer's authority over controlling what data they want to share and what they can keep concealed. If any consumer wishes to retract their data from the organization, they can request the business to do so. Overall, this Act is highly beneficial in protecting sensitive data and minimizing the possibility of it being exploited.

6.6.5 Personal Information Protection and Electronic Documents Act (PIPEDA), Canada

PIPEDA, is applicable to private-sector organizations and is crucial for organizations in recognizing their responsibility toward providing security for their individuals. It promotes organizations to provide authority to individuals over a collection of data.

It mentions that the organization must provide services irrespective of refusal of consent toward sharing data. The individual has rights to know for what purposes their data is being collected and launch grievances if they come across negligence toward compliance.

6.6.6 Cybersecurity Law of People's Republic of China

The CSL or Cybersecurity Law of People's Republic of China was brought into implementation in the year 2017. It brought a revolutionary transformation in China's digital space by formulating regulations with the interest of safeguarding data, data localization, and streamlining cybersecurity measures.

This law is applicable to all digital citizens of the People's Republic of China including business owners and network operators. Failing to abide by the law, there are penalties and punishments that help keep the national security tamed.

AI has emerged powerful as a double-edged sword that acts on both offensive and defensive fronts in the cyber realm. Further, employing state-of-the-art approaches make AI a formidable asset that continues to take the digital landscape by a storm, making it more tedious to tame any cyberattacks and take actions against them following the lack of befitting cyber laws. The case study mentioned in the literature survey above highlights the use of AI to scam netizens by deepfaking audios, videos, images, or text. This involves cloning a certain individuals' voice while also replicating its mannerisms and emotional nuances to make it seem real. AI also uses strong evasion mechanisms to mislead security systems.

On the other side of the coin, AI helps with threat detection by predicting patterns that help in understanding the modus operandi and get to the root of cyberattacks. For example, file carving can be done easily by AI to recover deleted files or fragmented files from memory dumps to process evidence accurately. In digital forensics, evidence may get tampered with if not handled with precautions and analyzed securely. Such evidence gets rejected by the law and may lead to obstacles in discovering who is accountable for the said crime.

TABLE 6.2 Pre-existing Cyberlaws, Frameworks, and Their Distinction

Parameter/Cyberlaws	Personal Data Protection Act, 2023 (India)	General Data Protection Regulations (GDPR), EU	Personal Data Protection Act, Singapore	California Consumer Privacy Act (CCPA), California	Personal Information Protection and Electronic Documents Act (PIPEDA), Canada	Cybersecurity Law (CSL), China
Year of Implementation	2023	2018	N/A	2018	N/A	2017
Scope	Protection of personal data, consent, and security	Control over personal data, data privacy harmonization	Protection of personal and sensitive data	Consumer control over data, data sharing and retraction	Responsibility toward data security, consent refusal	Safeguarding data, data localization, cybersecurity measures
Consent Requirement	Yes, approval before collection	Yes, control over personal data	Yes, approval before collection	Yes, control over what data is shared	Yes, individual authority over data collection	Yes, consent and data localization
Regulatory Body	N/A	European Data Protection Board	Personal Data Protection Commission	N/A	N/A	N/A
Penalty for Noncompliance	Yes	Yes	Yes	Yes	Yes	Yes
Grievance Handling	Yes	Yes	Yes	Yes	Yes	Yes
Focus on AI Regulation	No, but is intended to be extended in the future	No	No, but will be extended in the future	No	No	No

If used judiciously, AI can aid in protecting digital assets by also providing evidence of potential cyberattacks, which could be admissible in law enforcement organizations. This is possible if the pre-existing laws are reviewed to incorporate the prospect of AI being used to infiltrate cyberspace. Table 6.2 explains about various pre-existing cyber-laws, frameworks, and their distinction.

6.7 AWARENESS AND ADVANCEMENTS

The spreading of awareness about the limitless advantages and significance of AI to punch through these legal and ethical crossroads has to be stepped up. This balance can only be achieved if there is collaboration among the actors who have relevance to the general public, the making of the policy, legal experts, technologists as well as the policymakers. For this balance to be struck in an effective manner, it is necessary that ethical guidelines and the regulatory framework provide a way of conclusions, and they are not prescriptive since AI technologies change with time.

6.8 CONCLUSION

This chapter discusses the legal, ethical, technical, and technical considerations necessary for responsible AI development in cybersecurity, digital forensics, and society. Our research enhances existing knowledge through complex balancing needed between innovation promotion and social security on opportunities. By examining the complex interactions of these factors, we highlighted the need for coherent dialogue, international cooperation, and the evolution of the legal system. These systems must not only meet current challenges but also anticipate future issues brought about by the rapidly advancing AI of our digital age. This work contributes to an ongoing discourse by providing comprehensive research that informs policymakers, technologists, and ethicists, thus guiding AI development through ethical standards and social norms.

ACKNOWLEDGMENT

We would like to express our sincere gratitude and heartfelt thanks to the management of Dr. Vishwanath Karad, MIT World Peace University, Pune for their encouragement, support, and making resources available throughout the research work. We hope that our findings will make a meaningful contribution to the field of Cybersecurity and Digital Forensics.

REFERENCES

Allahrakha, N. (2023). Balancing cyber-security and privacy: Legal and ethical considerations in the digital age. *Legal Issues in the Digital Age*, (2), 78–121.

Alic, D. (2021). The role of data protection and cybersecurity regulations in artificial intelligence global governance: A comparative analysis of the European Union, the United States, and China Regulatory Framework. *Search in*.

Al-Mansoori, S., & Salem, M. B. (2023). The role of artificial intelligence and machine learning in shaping the future of cybersecurity: Trends, applications, and ethical considerations. *International Journal of Social Analytics*, *8*(9), 1–16.

Blauth, T. F., Gstrein, O. J., & Zwitter, A. (2022). Artificial intelligence crime: An overview of malicious use and abuse of AI. *IEEE Access*, *10*, 77110–77122.

Casino, F., Dasaklis, T. K., Spathoulas, G. P., Anagnostopoulos, M., Ghosal, A., Borocz, I., ... & Patsakis, C. (2022). Research trends, challenges, and emerging topics in digital forensics: A review of reviews. *IEEE Access, 10*, 25464–25493.

Incode Technologies, $25 Million Deepfake Fraud in Hong Kong: How Incode Protects against AI Scams, July 2024.

Jarrett, A., & Choo, K. K. R. (2021). The impact of automation and artificial intelligence on digital forensics. *Wiley Interdisciplinary Reviews: Forensic Science, 3*(6), e1418.

Jobin, A., Ienca, M., & Vayena, E. (2019). The global landscape of AI ethics guidelines. *Nature Machine Intelligence, 1*(9), 389–399.

Joseph, J. D., & Turksen, U. (2022). Harnessing AI for due diligence in CBI Programmes. Legal and Ethical Challenges. *Journal of Ethics and Legal Technologies (JELT), 4*(2), 3–25.

Kamaruddin, S., Mohammad, A. M., Saufi, N. N. M., Rosli, W. R. W., Othman, M. B., & Hamin, Z. (2023, May). Compliance to GDPR data protection and privacy in artificial intelligence technology: Legal and ethical ramifications in Malaysia. In *2023 International Conference on Disruptive Technologies (ICDT)* (pp. 284–288). IEEE.

Kaur, R., Gabrijelčič, D., & Klobučar, T. (2023). Artificial intelligence for cybersecurity: Literature review and future research directions. *Information Fusion, 97*, 101804.

Kayode-Ajala, O. (2023). Applications of Cyber Threat Intelligence (CTI) in financial institutions and challenges in its adoption. *Applied Research in Artificial Intelligence and Cloud Computing, 6*(8), 1–21.

Manyika, J., Silberg, J., & Presten, B. (2019). What do we do about the biases in AI. *Harvard Business Review.*

Naik, N., Hameed, B. Z., Shetty, D. K., Swain, D., Shah, M., Paul, R., ... & Somani, B. K. (2022). Legal and ethical consideration in artificial intelligence in healthcare: Who takes responsibility?. *Frontiers in Surgery, 9*, 862322.

Tschider, C. A. (2018). Regulating the internet of things: Discrimination, privacy, and cybersecurity in the artificial intelligence age. *Denv. L. Rev., 96*, 87.

Vikas, P., Laws regulating AI in India: Legal considerations and challenges. *Indian Journal of Law and Legal Research*, vol. 5, no. 6, 2022.

Vishwam, S., Fraudsters Use Deepfake Technology to Trick Employee into Paying Millions. *The Independent*, February 5, 2024.

Yavanoglu, O., & Aydos, M. (2017, December). A review on cyber security datasets for machine learning algorithms. In *2017 IEEE International Conference on Big Data (big data)* (pp. 2186–2193). IEEE.

Zeadally, S., Adi, E., Baig, Z., & Khan, I. A. (2020). Harnessing artificial intelligence capabilities to improve cybersecurity. *IEEE Access, 8*, 23817–23837.

Zoya, H., Voice cloning scams: How cybercriminals are leveraging AI. *Medianama*, April 2024.

CHAPTER 7

Multi-Factor Authentication for Smart Internet Transactions

B. Madhu, B.N. Shubhada, and Shubham Kumar Saras

7.1 INTRODUCTION

Authentication is a process that takes place when a person is trying to log into a system resource. The resource request can be for a document like image, video, and audio file. Multi-factor authentication (MFA) is a significant tool for securing the consumer data from issues of identity theft. By adopting this method, an additional layer of protection to the username and password login can be provided.

MFA is crucial for securing smart internet transactions, especially given the increasing sophistication of cyber threats. MFA can be implemented effectively using passwords, Biometric, One-time Passwords (OTP), Hardware Tokens, Geolocation Verification, and behavioral analysis. By implementing a combination of these MFA methods, businesses can significantly enhance the security of smart internet transactions and protect against unauthorized access and fraud. MFA is utilized across various industries and platforms to enhance security by requiring multiple forms of verification before granting access to Online Banking, Email Services, Cloud Services, Workplace Applications, E-commerce Websites, Remote Access, Healthcare Systems, etc. MFA is widespread across various sectors and platforms, serving as an effective method to mitigate the risk of unauthorized access and protect sensitive information from cyber threats.

7.2 RELATED WORK

MFA acts as an additional layer of security to prevent an unauthorized access to the users from accessing the accounts even when the password is stolen. Users can use different

DOI: 10.1201/9781032714813-7

applications of the internet with the help of a graphical authentication system. Image-based authentication was suggested by Shah [1]. The method uses alphanumeric and draw metric patterns to generate the passwords. The method creates its own threat model to check against different types of attacks. Cross image-based authentication method is suggested to choose their password. The difficulty of the proposed method is to remember the password sequence. Our paper is a user friendly application, where the passwords are more memorizable and it aims to provide various layers of image and video graphical password which in turn promotes the secured life to the user. Web based password scheme is proposed by Abhijit [2]. The author addresses the challenges of using third party in password authentication. The authors propose a unique time-based password scheme that enhances security. However, the drawbacks of these approaches include the difficulty in remembering textual passwords with various combinations, the limited two-step authentication process consisting of a basic textual password and an image-based password. Moreover, the research process entails architectural complexity, and the authentication process itself can be time consuming. In our paper time consuming is less and it is more secured where multi-level authentication is provided to user. Lightweight Authentication Scheme for Internet of Things (IoT) domain was suggested by Ashok [3]. They have offered some solutions to assist in constructing a more secure and functional user authentication method that provides security to the next generation of IoT infrastructure. The fuzzy extraction method for biometrics verification is implemented here for more security. Pathik [4] suggested graphical password as one of the important tools for authentication. The method suggests textual and image authentication as two-level password based on color. The password sequence and color should match for the successful authentication. Tay et al. [5] reported an authentication for managing the child storing application. The method authentication for Android application for the kid's data storage. Jiya [6] et al. reported a survey on recognition-based passwords. Zahraa et al. [7] reported authentication using mouse behavior technique. The user will remember the password with ease-of-use in mouse motion, while minimizing the risk of password guessing. Ajmeera Kiran [8] reports three-level security with image grid. The method of password manager with MFA is suggested by Dhanalakshmi [9]. The password manager is responsible for securely storing the data using encryption techniques. The method illustrates using physical security keys and graphical passwords. Naga [10] suggested a method on arbitrary password for web applications.

7.3 EXPERIMENTAL METHOD

Our proposed system works in two phases. In the first phase it uses a text-based password and pixel-matching method in the next phase. The image pixel-matching method uses the frames of the given video data. After the two-level verification user will receive a final acceptance based on the OTP.

7.3.1 Steps for Registration

1. User has to enter the information like first and last names, email addresses, passwords, etc. in the registration page.

2. As a continuation, in the next step a graphical password security page with an image-based password will be shown. It is also an option given to the users to select the image shown in the cart.
3. The final step is the website that asks for a password selection based on the video frames' in the visual sequence.

7.3.2 User Login

When the user is trying to access the homepage, they will get two options: register or log in.

1. The new user has to register first. If he is having username and password already, then the login option can be used.
2. The user can log in successfully if their text-based password and username both are correct.
3. After the login page image base password screen will be seen. The user must select the image checkpoints as the password. The next page was redirected only if the image pixels were matched.
4. After this step screen for the video-based password will appear, a user must choose the image frame number of videos based on passwords. The order of the frame numbers should be matched to move on to the next level.
5. If the user receives a successful OTP, the banking home page will be displayed.

The above technique was implemented to increase memorability with the draw metric process. The security of the suggested system is tested against keystroke/mouse logger attacks, dictionary attacks, shoulder surfing, random guessing, phishing or form-taking, and multiple recording attacks. We also examined the usability and memorability of the password. The client must first visit the website's internet page in order to access the records. Additionally, the customer must sign in by selecting frames in the video that are consistent with their choice for signing into page and picking prompt focuses during such images. They must select the same prompt options that they decided upon earlier in the enrollment process on the login page. If the customer attempts to log in again, they must select the identical image factors; if they do so, the login will be successful otherwise a message stating that the data is "invalid" may appear. If the login is successful, the user receives the privilege of access to the official reports to down stack or transfer for more opportunities.

Figure 7.1 shows the block diagram of system design. The image's focal points should be an image focused on the most important factor. The video selection should be appropriate such that the choice of stretch is obvious and difficult to hack. Here, the combination of sign markings from video and image gives an encoded secret phrase for the client to login. The client no longer receives a verified login if all signers determine that either the image or the video is incorrect.

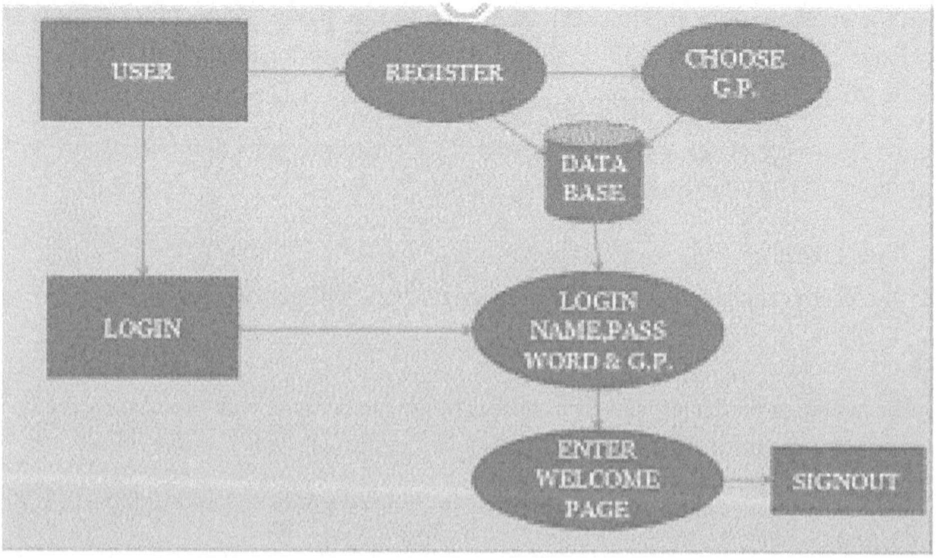

FIGURE 7.1 Block diagram of system design.

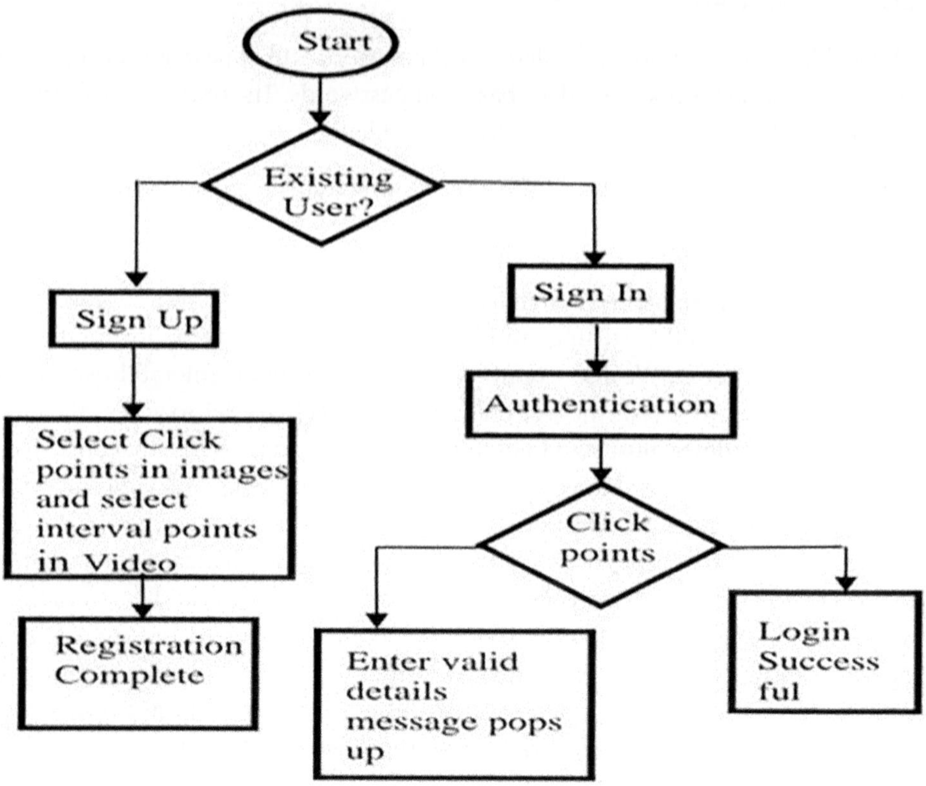

FIGURE 7.2 System flow chart.

Figure 7.2 represents the flowchart of how the user should register and follow the steps to login where he has to select the image as well as frame numbers of a video if he is not the existing user. If he is a registered user the passwords should match for login. After login image and video authentication will be added to the verification process. The stronger security system is built using the reported method.

7.4 RESULT AND DISCUSSION

Our research effort has proven the value of using image and video-based techniques for user authentication by implementing Graphical User Authentication. Overall, our paper produced results that are 80% accurate and efficient.

Image-level password selection is indicated in Figure 7.3. The method introduces a novel approach for secure authentication through the utilization of a collection of images, enabling users to select a password at the image level. This authentication method enhances security and usability by offering an alternative to traditional text-based passwords.

Figure 7.4 illustrates the procedure of configuring a password by providing pixel values based on the client ID. Users are required to input the pixel values corresponding to their chosen password configuration. Additionally, users are provided with the option to reset their password or proceed with login using the provided pixel values.

Figure 7.5 indicates the authentication process at the video level, where users input their ID and select a video for configuring a video-based password. Upon selecting the video, users can click on the 'Register' button to proceed with the authentication process."

The procedure of video presents the video frames where video is converted into image frames user must select any number of the frame numbers and give it as a password (Figure 7.6).

Final authentication level is given in Figure 7.7, as shown above. The OTP will be sent to the registered mobile number.

Figure 7.8 indicates the home page of the bank that is provided by the correct password and OTP by the user. The user can now login to his actual banking website to continue with the transaction.

Figure 7.9 indicates forgot pin page. If a user forgets their password, they can replace it by entering the OTP that was supplied to their cell phone. As seen in Table 7.1, our technique is contrasted with the other ways. It is evident that our approach is superior to others.

Table 7.1 depicts the comparison of state of art and our method. Shah [1] has introduced graphical-based authentication with image pattern and OTP. The method operates in two modes: easy and complex. The limitation of such a method is to switch over two methods. Abhijit [2] also given an algorithm for new web-based authentication system. The main drawback of the method is dependency of platform. Our method uses simple pixel-matching and frame ordering with video authentication method. The method is platform independent and the complete authentication process will take 30 seconds to complete. So our method proves to be good with reference to the reference methods.

FIGURE 7.3 Image-level password selection

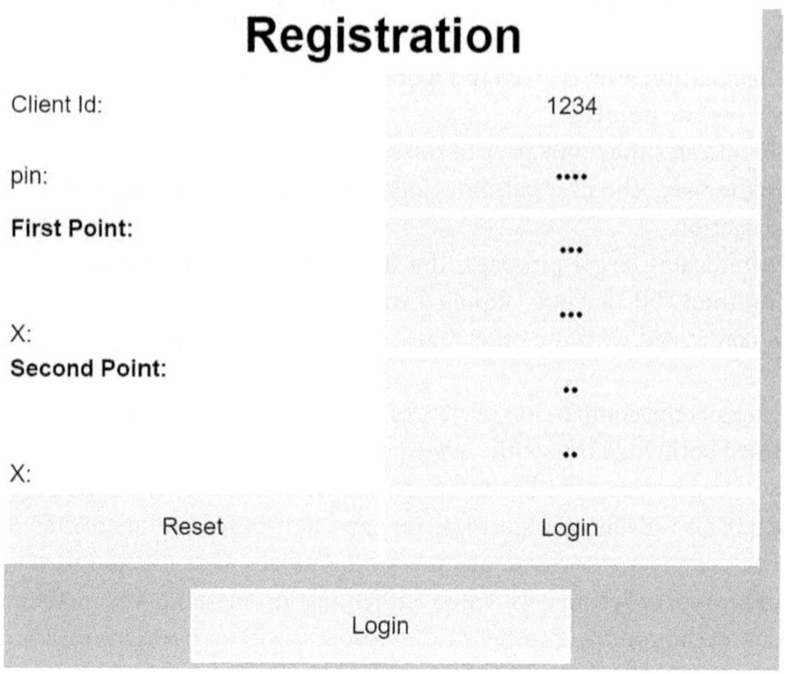

FIGURE 7.4 Image pixel values.

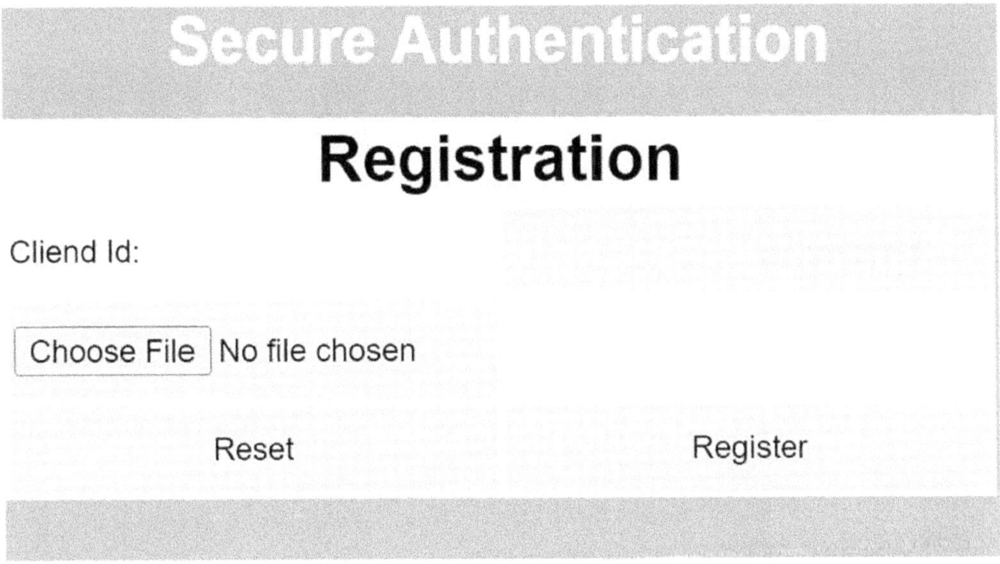

FIGURE 7.5 Updating of video.

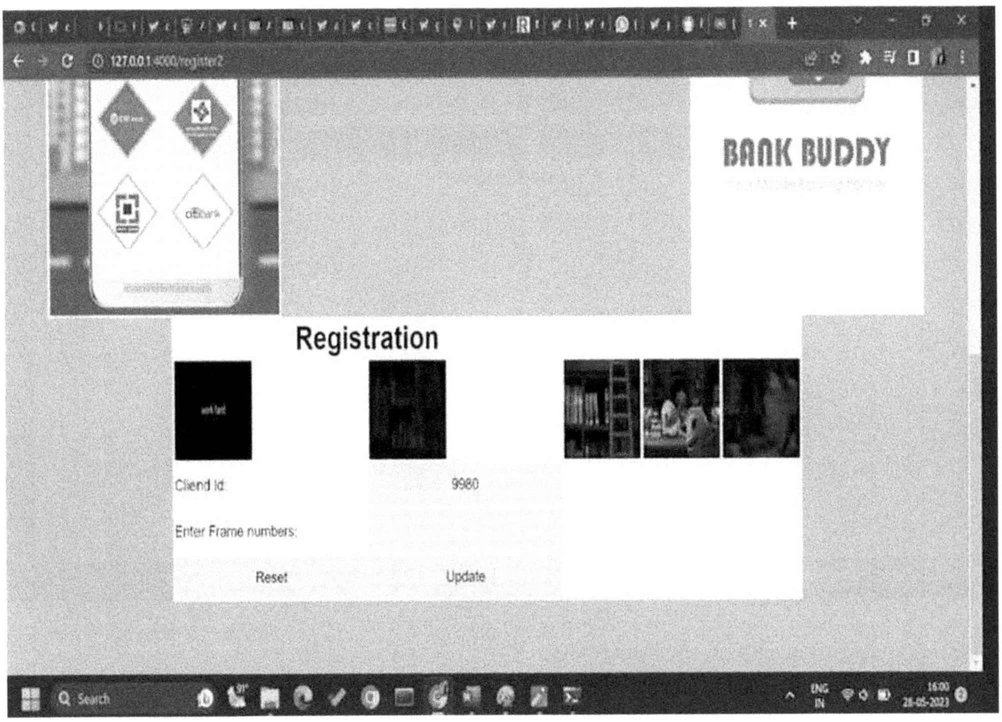

FIGURE 7.6 Video converted to frames of images.

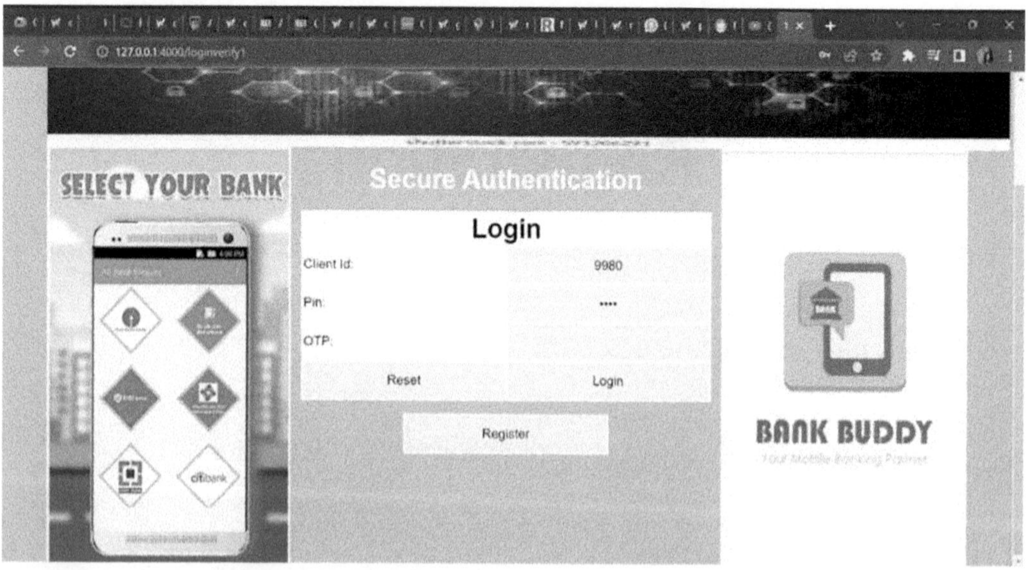

FIGURE 7.7 OTP level authentication.

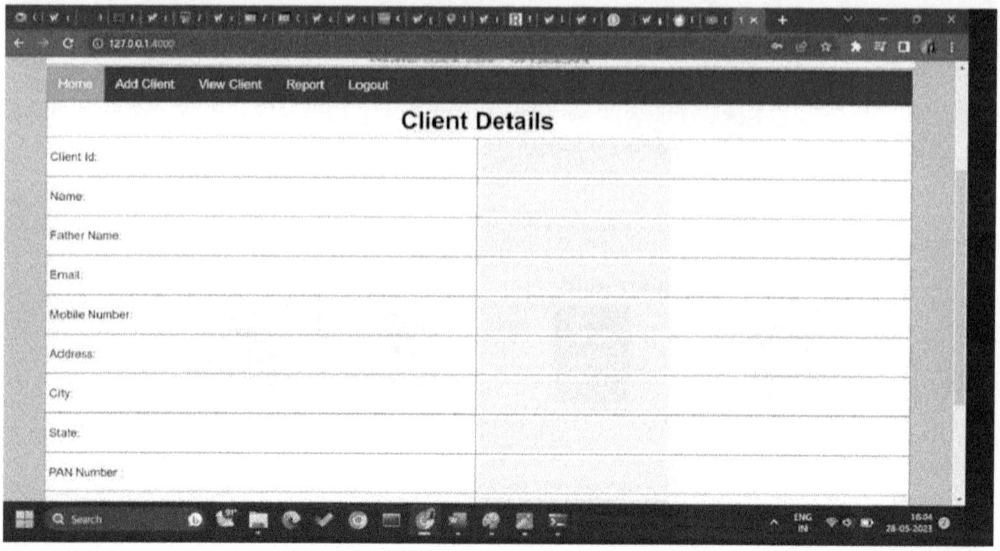

FIGURE 7.8 After logging in, the home page.

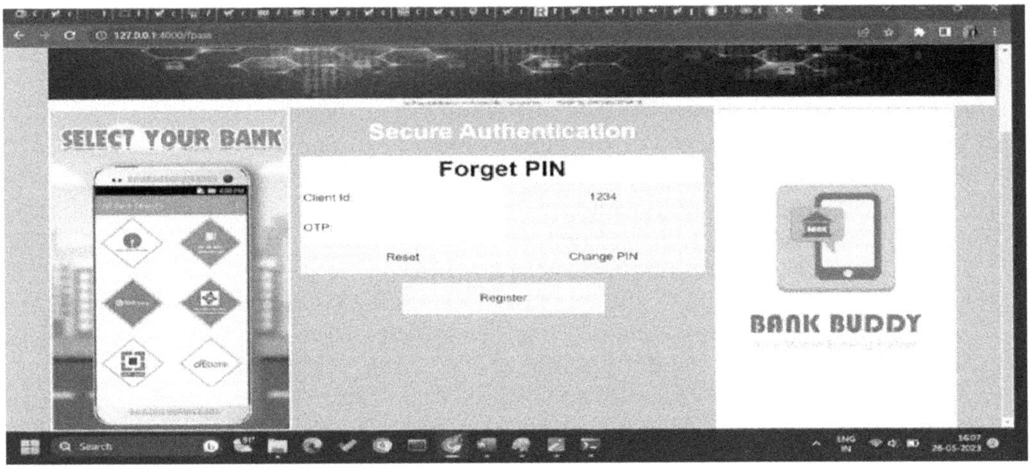

FIGURE 7.9 Forgot password page.

TABLE 7.1 State of Art Comparison

Author	Year	Authentication Type	Technique	Limitations	Time
Shah [1]	2021	Draw Metric	Pattern, OTP	Operate Two Modes and Remembering Pattern	40.16s
Abhijit [2]	2021	Web Based	Pattern, Key	Platform Dependent	Not Mentioned
Proposed work	2023	Pixel-Matching Video Frame	Text, Image, Video, OTP	NA	Less than a minute

7.5 CONCLUSION AND FUTURE SCOPE

The world is rapidly becoming digital as a result of growing technological breakthroughs takes place through online. The customer would like to do online transaction for everything like bill payment, reservations for events, banking transactions, etc. Other online activities include communication through email and messaging applications, document storage, and more. Everything moving online has increased the possibility of cybercrimes and privacy violations. The proposed method comes up with the advanced authentication system using image and video. The initial step login with username and password, followed by image pixel-matching method and finally selecting the frames from the video output. The method will give the security with three layer protection. Thus the user transactions will be kept safe. Thus the algorithm will take less than a minute to complete all the three layer of authentication process. So the proposed work proves to be good.

REFERENCES

[1] S. Z. Nizamani, S. R. Hassan, R. A. Shaikh, E. A. Abozinadah and R. Mehmood, "A Novel Hybrid Textual-Graphical Authentication Scheme with Better Security, Memorability, and Usability," *IEEE Access*, vol. 9, pp. 51294–51312, 2021, doi: 10.1109/ACCESS.2021.3069164.

[2] S. Abhijith, S. Sam, K. U. Sreelekshmi, T. T. Samjeevan and S. Mathew, "Web Based Graphical Password Authentication System," *International Journal of Engineering Research & Technology*, 9(7), 29–32, 2021.

[3] A. K. Das, B. Bera, M. Wazid, S. S. Jamal and Y. Park, "On the Security of a Secure and Lightweight Authentication Scheme for Next Generation IoT Infrastructure," *IEEE Access*, vol. 9, pp. 71856–71867, 2021, doi: 10.1109/ACCESS.2021.3079312.

[4] P. Nandi and Dr. P. Savant, "Graphical Password Authentication System," *International Journal for Research in Applied Science and Engineering Technology*, ISSN: 2321-9653, 2022, doi: https://doi.org/10.22214/ijraset.2022.41621.

[5] T. Y. Yang, P., Shamala, M., Chinniah and C. F. M., Foozy. "Graphical Password Authentication for Child Personal Storage Application," *Journal of Physics: Conference Series*, vol. 1793, February 2021, doi: 10.1088/1742-6596/1793/1/012065.

[6] J. G. Kaka, O. O. Ishaq and J. O. Ojeniyi, "Recognition-Based Graphical Password Algorithms: A Survey," *2020 IEEE 2nd International Conference on Cyberspace (CYBER NIGERIA)*, Abuja, Nigeria, 2021, pp. 44–51, doi: 10.1109/CYBERNIGERIA51635.2021.9428801.

[7] Z. A. Abdalkareem, O. Z. Akif, F. A. Abdulatif, A. Amiza and P. Ehkan, "Graphical Password Based Mouse Behavior Technique," *Journal of Physics: Conference Series*, vol. 1755, IOP Publishing, February 2021, doi: 10.1088/1742-6596/1755/1/012021.

[8] A. Kiran, B. Ben Sujitha, P. Vijayakarthik, M. V. Krishna, S. Nikitha and T. H. Singh, "Implementation of 3-Level Security System Using Image Grid Based Authentication System," *2023 International Conference on Computer Communication and Informatics (ICCCI)*, Coimbatore, India, 2023, pp. 1–5, doi: 10.1109/ICCCI56745.2023.10128606.

[9] R. Dhanalakshmi, N. Vijayaraghavan, S. Narasimhan and S. Basha, "Password Manager with Multi-Factor Authentication," *2023 International Conference on Networking and Communications (ICNWC)*, Chennai, India, 2023, pp. 1–5, doi: 10.1109/ICNWC57852.2023.10127424.

[10] N. S. S. Chaluvadi, L. Chitteti, L. Challa and S. Srithar, "Improved Arbitrary Graphical Password Authentication for Web Application Safety," *2023 5th International Conference on Smart Systems and Inventive Technology (ICSSIT)*, Tirunelveli, India, 2023, pp. 714–720, doi: 10.1109/ICSSIT55814.2023.10060964.

CHAPTER 8

Adaptive Machine Learning Strategies for Next-Generation Botnet Host Detection

Aniket Jhariya, Dhvani Parekh, Anurag Mogal, Joshua Lobo, and Mangal Singh

8.1 INTRODUCTION

The Internet of Things' (IoT) explosive growth has changed the technical landscape by making it possible for a vast range of devices to connect and communicate with each other over the internet. But this rapid expansion has also brought forth serious weaknesses, especially in the area of cybersecurity. The most dangerous of them are botnets, which are hostile actor-controlled networks of infected devices. Large-scale attacks like Distributed Denial of Service (DDoS), data theft, and virus distribution can be carried out by these botnets, jeopardizing the security of individuals and organizations alike. Especially in IoT environments, traditional cybersecurity solutions frequently fail to identify and neutralize these attacks. The diverse and resource-constrained nature of IoT devices, which restricts the applicability of traditional security procedures, is mostly to blame for this deficiency. New research has brought attention to the need for more advanced and flexible detection systems. While [1] highlighted the potential of machine learning (ML) in addressing these challenges through anomaly detection and behavior analysis, [2] illustrated the shortcomings of signature-based detection methods in handling the dynamic and evolving nature of modern botnets.

Despite the potential of ML, current methods frequently have problems with scalability, have high false positive rates, and are difficult to interpret, especially when used with large and varied datasets produced by IoT devices. Puri et al. [3] also point out that there is a significant void in the literature about the standardization of evaluation measures for these

DOI: 10.1201/9781032714813-8

TABLE 8.1 Summary of Related Work for Botnet Host Detection Systems

Authors	Approach	Metrics	Features	Contribution
Hezam et al. [1]	BiLSTM-CNN model for DDoS botnet attack detection in IoT networks	High accuracy (89.79%)	N-BaloT and IoT-23 datasets	Proposes a model for enhancing detection of DDoS botnet attacks using DL, highlights need for realistic datasets and DL's potential in IoT cybersecurity
Moorthy et al. [2]	AI for botnet malware detection from network flows	High accuracy (92%)	CTU-13, ISOT datasets	Focuses on using AI for botnet malware detection, achieves high accuracy using decision tree model
Puri et al. [3]	AI-based botnet attack classification and detection in IoT devices using ML and DL algorithms	Enhanced IoT security	Real-world data from various IoT devices	Explores AI-based botnet attack classification and detection in IoT devices, including API implementation, offers adaptability to evolving IoT devices and enhanced IoT security
Suryotrisongko et al. [4]	Model for detecting malicious botnet DGA traffic using statistical features	Model effectiveness, robustness	Datasets covering 55 DGA families	Investigates malicious botnet DGA traffic, proposes model for detecting DGA-based traffic, discusses expanding cyber threat intelligence and enhancing model explainability through blending XAI and OSINT
Macas et al. [5]	Survey on DL applications in cybersecurity	Comprehensive overview	Applications of DL in cybersecurity, automated attack detection, tackling complex security problems	Explores applications of DL in cybersecurity, identifies limitations, challenges, and outlines future research directions
Senthil et al. [6]	JBiRSA model for IoT botnet attack detection combining Bi-model RNN with Spatial Attention and GAN	High accuracy (98.75%)	N-BaIoT, IoT-23 datasets	Proposes JBiRSA for IoT botnet attack detection, achieves high accuracy, addresses class imbalance, innovative GAN approach, potential for real-world implementation and exploration of scalability and efficiency.
Hezam et al. [7]	DL solution for IoT-based DDoS attacks using RNN, CNN, LSTM-RNN	Addresses IoT-based DDoS attacks	N-BaIoT dataset	Proposes DL solution for IoT-based DDoS attacks, uses RNN, CNN, LSTM-RNN, tested on N-BaIoT dataset, addresses real-world data and DL comparison
Dong et al. [8]	"BotDetector," a botnet detection model based on extreme learning machines for real-time IoT environments	Accurate botnet identification,resource-efficient	Real-time IoT environments	Presents BotDetector, a botnet detection model based on extreme learning machines for real-time IoT environments, demonstrates accurate botnet identification and applicability in IoT scenarios.

detection systems. These difficulties highlight the need for creative methods that improve detection precision while simultaneously guaranteeing that the solutions are interpretable, scalable, and able to function within the resource limitations that are characteristic of IoT contexts. By putting forth a sophisticated ML-based methodology for botnet host detection in IoT networks, this article seeks to close these gaps. Our method combines a balanced dataset to minimize biases in model training with dimensionality reduction approaches to manage high-dimensional data. We show that our strategy is efficient in increasing detection rates while keeping low false positive rates through extensive trials and evaluations. In addition, we investigate how scalable our method is in various network contexts, making a valuable contribution to the field of IoT security by providing a solid, dependable, and easily comprehensible resolution to the botnet identification issue. We aim to provide cybersecurity experts and researchers with the knowledge and tools necessary to counter these threats successfully and effectively, protecting the IoT's future from the specter of botnet attacks through our meticulous analysis and original contributions.

8.2 BACKGROUND WORK

In recent years, the proliferation of botnets in IoT environments has spurred research efforts towards enhancing detection mechanisms. Hezam et al. [1] proposed a deep learning (DL) model, BiLSTMCNN, specifically tailored for detecting DDoS botnet attacks in IoT networks. Their model, trained on the N-BaloT and IoT-23 datasets, achieved an accuracy of 89.79%, outperforming other methods and highlighting the potential of DL in bolstering IoT cybersecurity. Building on this work, Moorthy et al. [2] delved into the application of artificial intelligence (AI) in detecting botnet malware from network flows, achieving a remarkable 92% accuracy using the CTU13 and ISOT datasets. However, they noted challenges in building a real-time alerting system for malware detection. Dong et al. [8] developed "Botdetector," an extreme learning machine-based IoT botnet detection model, focusing on leveraging ML techniques to identify and mitigate botnet threats in IoT environments, providing a complementary perspective to the DL approach proposed by Hezam et al. [1] Puri et al. [3] extended the scope to AI-based botnet attack classification and detection in IoT devices, leveraging ML and DL algorithms. Their study emphasized the significance of real-world data collection from diverse IoT devices to enhance IoT security. Similarly, Suryotrisongko et al. [4] contributed by focusing on the robust detection of malicious botnet domain generation algorithm (DGA) traffic using explainable AI (XAI) and open-source intelligence (OSINT) for cyber threat intelligence sharing. Their model effectively detected DGA-based traffic across 55 DGA families, demonstrating its effectiveness and improved robustness. Additionally, Almuhaideb and Alynanbaawi [9] conducted a survey on the applications of AI to detect Android botnets, addressing the specific challenges posed by mobile devices in botnet detection. Their survey highlighted the diverse range of AI techniques being employed to detect and mitigate botnet threats in the Android ecosystem, offering valuable insights into the evolving landscape of mobile botnet detection. Alongside these efforts, Vormayr, Zseby, and Fabini [10] provided insights into botnet communication patterns, which are crucial for designing effective detection systems. Their study emphasized the complex nature of botnet operations and the need for advanced detection mechanisms. While their work lacked a specific dataset, it identified research gaps and suggested opportunities for further exploration in botnet DGA detection. In parallel, Macas et al. [5] conducted a comprehensive survey on the applications of DL in cybersecurity. Their survey shed light on various DL architectures, emerging trends, and resources in the field. It also highlighted the increasing volume of data and emerging attack strategies, identifying limitations and challenges associated with the implementation of DL in cybersecurity. The integration of AI techniques for botnet detection and the analysis of botnet communication patterns represents a significant advancement in IoT cybersecurity. These efforts contribute to the development of more robust and effective strategies for detecting and mitigating the threat of botnets in IoT environments. Future research in this area could focus on refining AI models for botnet detection, improving the accuracy of communication pattern analysis, and exploring new threats to further enhance the security of IoT networks

8.3 METHODOLOGY

8.3.1 Machine Learning Classification

In this study, the analysis is conducted on the CICIDS2017 dataset, focusing on various network traffic scenarios to enhance botnet host detection techniques. To prepare the dataset for analysis, extensive data preprocessing steps were applied. Initially, a data frame-based architecture was used, and display options were configured to ensure comprehensive visibility of the dataset content. Subsequently, eight distinct divisions representing different network traffic instances were imported into the study. These divisions encompassed diverse attack types, including DDoS attacks, port scans, infiltration attempts, and web attacks, occurring during different days and times of the week. These individual divisions were loaded into separate data frames representing specific attack scenarios. The data frames serve as the foundation for subsequent analysis, allowing for a detailed exploration of network traffic patterns and facilitating the development of advanced botnet host detection mechanisms. To create a comprehensive dataset for analysis, individual data frames representing different attack scenarios were concatenated sequentially, ensuring a unified dataset. Subsequently, redundant data frames were removed. The resulting combined data frame, contained nRow rows and nCol columns, reflecting the consolidated network traffic data for in-depth analysis. The dataset was preprocessed to enable ML analysis. In the initial preprocessing tasks, label encoding was applied using a transformer-based function transforming categorical fields into numerical values. The dataset was then split into features (X) and fields (y). To ensure balanced training data, a stratified train test split was performed (80% training and 20% testing) using a random state articulation. Additionally, the imbalanced class distribution was addressed using the Synthetic Minority Over-sampling Technique (SMOTE) and Random Under Sampler. Specifically, SMOTE was applied to augment minority classes such as "DoS Hulk," "DDoS," and "PortScan," while RandomUnderSampler was used to reduce the majority classes. Sampling strategies were set for each class, ensuring a more equitable representation of classes in the dataset, vital for robust ML model training and evaluation.

The imbalanced dataset was addressed using a combination of over-sampling and under-sampling techniques to improve the training data's class distribution. The under-sampling technique was applied to the majority class "BENIGN" to reduce its instances to 500,000. Simultaneously, the over-sampling method, SMOTE, was employed to augment minority classes according to the specified sampling strategy. A pipeline incorporating SMOTE and Random Under Sampler was constructed and applied to the training data, resulting in a balanced dataset denoted as X train res and y train res. Subsequently, a Bagging Classifier was utilized with 25 estimators and a random state for model training. To evaluate the model's performance, cross-validation was employed to obtain a robust accuracy estimate. The model demonstrated promising results across five folds. The classification report revealed detailed metrics for each class, providing insights into the model's performance on individual categories. Additionally, overall accuracy, classification error, average precision, recall, and F1 score were computed, demonstrating the model's effectiveness in addressing the imbalanced dataset and accurately classifying network traffic instances. The AdaBoost Classifier was trained with 50 estimators and a random state, utilizing the balanced dataset (X train res and y train res). Cross-validation with five folds was employed to obtain a reliable accuracy estimate. Performance evaluation on the test set demonstrated strong classification results, highlighting the model's effectiveness in accurately classifying network traffic instances. The Bernoulli Naive Bayes (NB) Classifier was trained on the balanced. On the test set, the model showcased robust classification performance. Then two NB classifiers were explored in this study. Firstly, the Gaussian NB model was trained and evaluated. And, the study extended to multinomial NB, incorporating MinMax scaling for feature normalization. The model, trained on the scaled dataset, provided a detailed classification report. Continuing the evaluation of different classifiers, a Random Forest Classifier (RFC) was employed, followed by a K-Nearest Neighbors (KNN) Classifier and a Decision Tree Classifier (DTC). For RFC, KNN, and DTC, classification reports were generated, providing detailed insights into precision, recall, and F1 score metrics for each class, contributing significantly to the comprehensive understanding of classifier performance. The RFC, known for its ensemble learning approach, was adept at capturing intricate patterns in the data, reflected in its robust classification results. The KNN Classifier, relying on data proximity for classification, demonstrated competitive performance, indicating its suitability for the task at hand. Meanwhile, the DTC, employing a tree-like model of decisions, showcased its effectiveness in handling complex decision boundaries, ensuring accurate classification of network traffic instances. These analyses elucidate the strengths and weaknesses of each model, aiding in the selection of the most suitable classifier for botnet host detection tasks. Overall, these assessments serve as a crucial foundation for the subsequent discussion and conclusions of this study, providing valuable insights into the efficacy of different machine-learning algorithms in the context of botnet host detection using the CICIDS-2017 dataset.

8.3.2 PCA and TSNE for Detection

In this phase, the preprocessing of the CICIDS-2017 dataset was conducted to ensure data integrity and enhance the quality of features for subsequent analysis. The dataset was initially examined for inconsistencies, such as leading spaces in feature names, which were promptly removed. Following this, features containing negative values were adjusted to be non-negative, preserving the integrity of the dataset. Columns with zero variance, indicating no variability within the dataset, were identified and removed. Additionally, rows containing infinite or missing values were dropped, further refining the dataset. Duplicate rows were identified and subsequently eliminated to prevent data redundancy. Lastly, columns with identical values were detected and removed, reducing redundancy in feature representation (Figure 8.1).

These preprocessing steps culminated in a clean and refined dataset ready for the subsequent stages of analysis. The resulting dataset was of dimensions (2,830,743 × 79) and was utilized for the subsequent analyses in this part of the study. Following the consolidation of the dataset from multiple divisions, an initial exploratory analysis unveiled several trivial columns ('id', 'Flow ID', 'Src IP', 'Src Port', 'Dst IP', 'Dst Port', 'Timestamp') that were deemed redundant and subsequently removed to streamline the dataset. This meticulous data preprocessing strategy was complemented by the elimination of redundant columns, thus optimizing the dataset further. The result was a meticulously curated dataset, purged of extraneous information and ambiguous labels, laying the groundwork for focused analysis and precise model training in the pursuit of advanced botnet host detection.

After dataset subsampling, dimensionality reduction techniques were employed to facilitate effective data visualization. Initially, Principal Component Analysis (PCA) was leveraged to condense the feature space into two dimensions. The resultant PCA projection, presented in the form of a scatter plot, offered a concise representation of the dataset. Each data point depicted on the plot corresponded to a distinct data instance, with color encoding denoting different classes, thereby simplifying the discernment of potential clusters or patterns within the dataset. In the visualization of the PCA projection of CICIDS 2017 in Figure 8.2, the first plot 2a reveals a preponderance of benign detections, characterized by a cohesive clustering pattern with limited variation along the principal components. Conversely, the isolated depiction of bot detection in plot 2b manifests an inadequate degree of linearity and continuity, indicative of pronounced clustering within

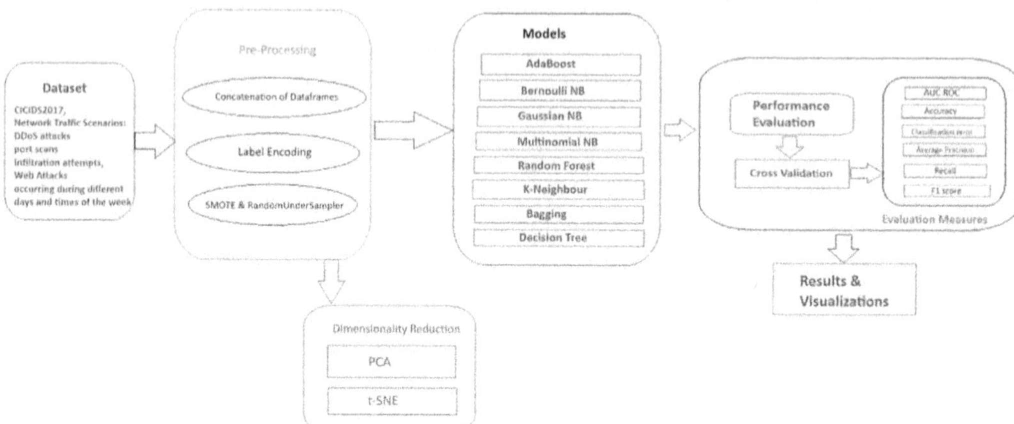

FIGURE 8.1 System architecture for botnet host detection using advanced ML techniques.

the bot detection instances, thereby implying a challenge in extracting discernible feature representations for machine-learning algorithms. In the subsequent Figure 8.3, illustrating PCA projections of the Improvised CICIDS 2017 dataset, the initial plot 3a showcases an accentuation of linearity across the entire dataset, coupled with a sparse occurrence of extraneous outliers. Furthermore, in plot 3b, dedicated to isolated botnet detection, a conspicuous augmentation of linearity and continuity is observed, accompanied by the subsequent dissolution of clustered patterns.

Additionally, t-distributed Stochastic Neighbor Embedding (t-SNE) was employed as a non-linear dimensionality reduction method. This technique aimed to capture complex relationships between features that might not be apparent in higher-dimensional spaces. The t-SNE projection, visualized in another scatter plot, offered a more intricate view of the dataset. Similar to PCA, distinct classes were represented by different colors, enabling a more nuanced understanding of the data distribution.

Similarly, in the representation of the t-SNE projections for the improvised CICIDS 2017 dataset in Figure 8.4, the distribution of the benign detection is predominantly central within however the instances of the same category are bundled up closer in the first plot 4a in comparison to the earlier plots. The second plot 4b again displays that the reduction in dimensions has led to the mitigation of non-linearity and discontinuity, which means that subsampled data points have been brought close to a reduced distance.

Both PCA and t-SNE projections were instrumental in revealing the underlying structure of the subsampled dataset. These visualizations served as a foundation for subsequent analyses, guiding the selection of appropriate machine-learning algorithms and feature engineering techniques.

By transforming the high-dimensional data into two dimensions while preserving essential patterns, these visualizations enhanced the researchers' ability to comprehend the complex relationships within the dataset, ultimately contributing to the refinement of the next-gen botnet host detection model. In the data preparation phase, a balanced dataset was created to ensure unbiased model training and evaluation. All malicious instances were extracted, forming the 'all malicious' subset, while a representative sample of 1,000,000 benign instances was randomly selected from the 'improved df' dataset. This subset, denoted as 'benign 1M', was split into training and testing sets, with 500,000 instances in each. For training, benign instances were labeled as 1, while malicious instances were labeled as −1, facilitating binary classification. To validate the model effectively, a validation set was established using a 15% portion of the combined benign and malicious test data. This validation set, labeled 'X val', 'y val', and 'label val', allowed for fine-tuning the model's hyperparameters and detecting potential overfitting. The remaining 85% of the combined test data formed the final test set, denoted as 'X t', 'y t', and 'label t'. This meticulous partitioning ensured that the training, validation, and test sets were representative of both benign and malicious instances, providing a robust foundation for the subsequent training and evaluation of the next-gen botnet host detection model. The class distribution was carefully examined in each dataset subset, ensuring a balanced representation essential for the effectiveness of the ML algorithms applied.

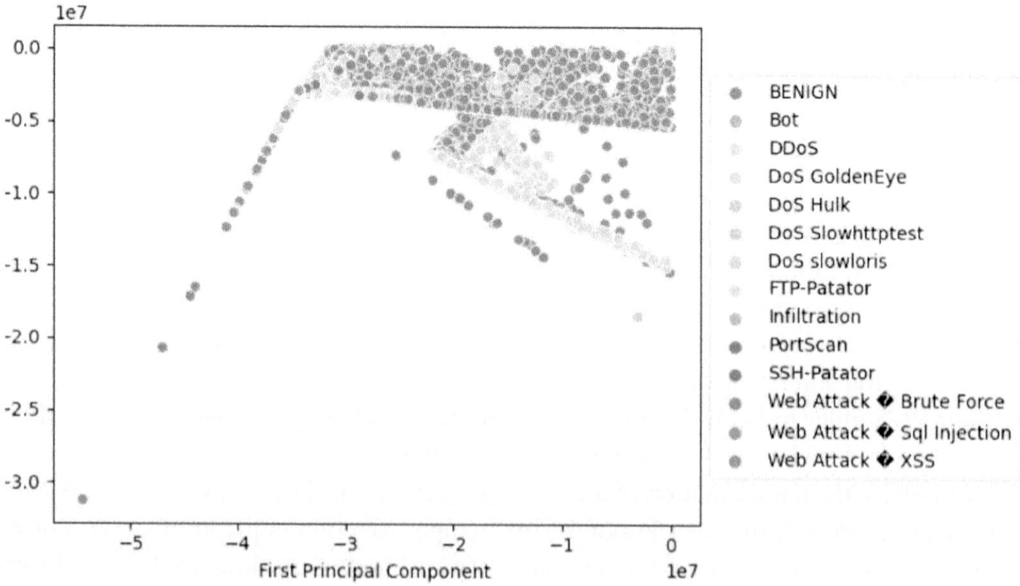

(a) PCA Projection of entire detection

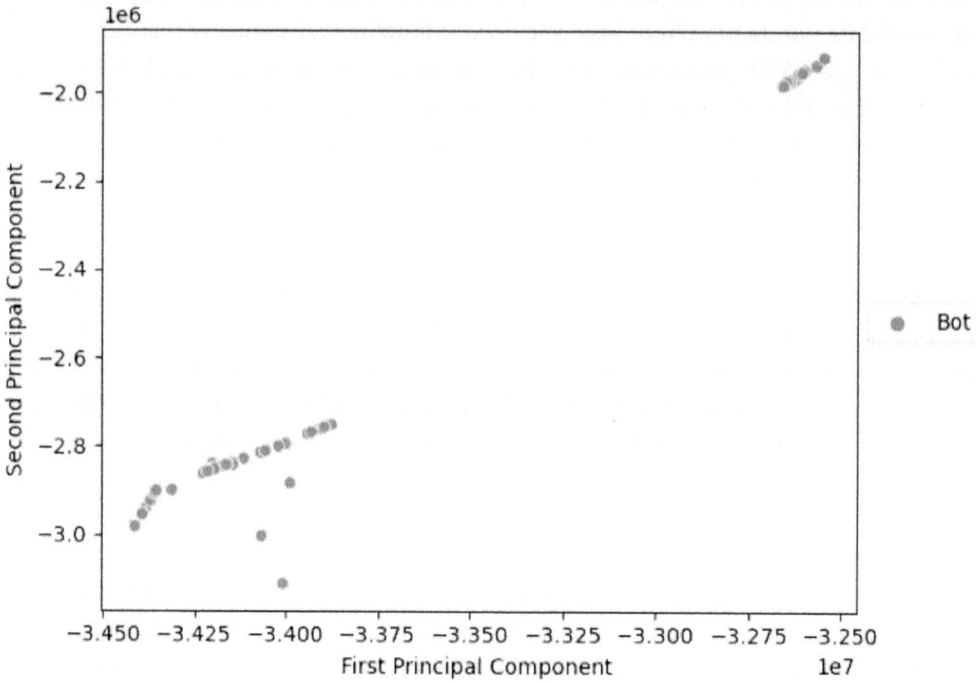

(b) PCA projection of bot defections exclusively

FIGURE 8.2 Plot for principal components analysis (PCA) in two components of CICIDS 2017 dataset: (a) PCA projection of entire detection and (b) PCA projection of bot defections exclusively.

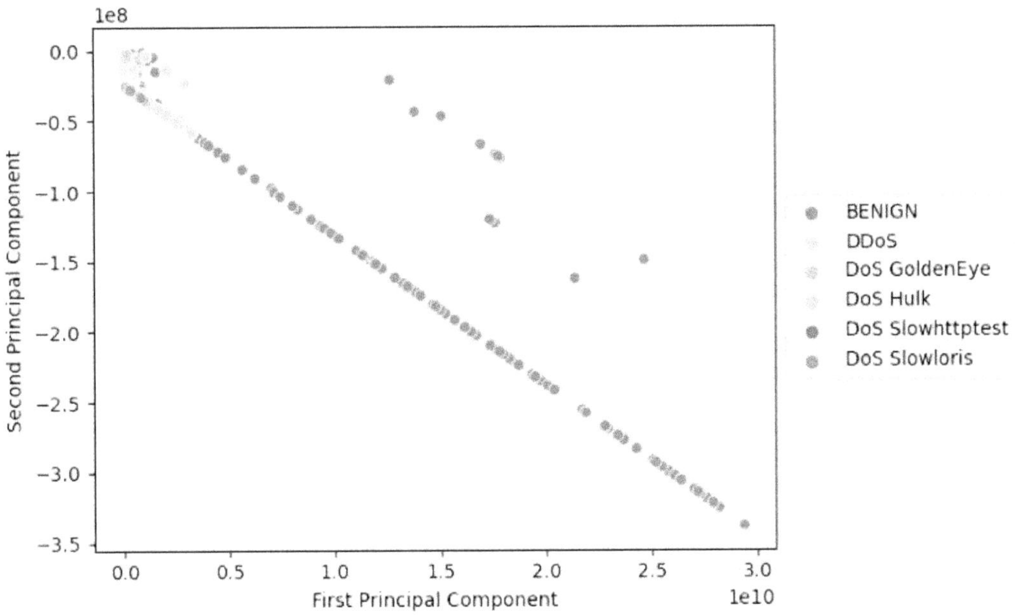

(a) PCA Projection of the entire detection

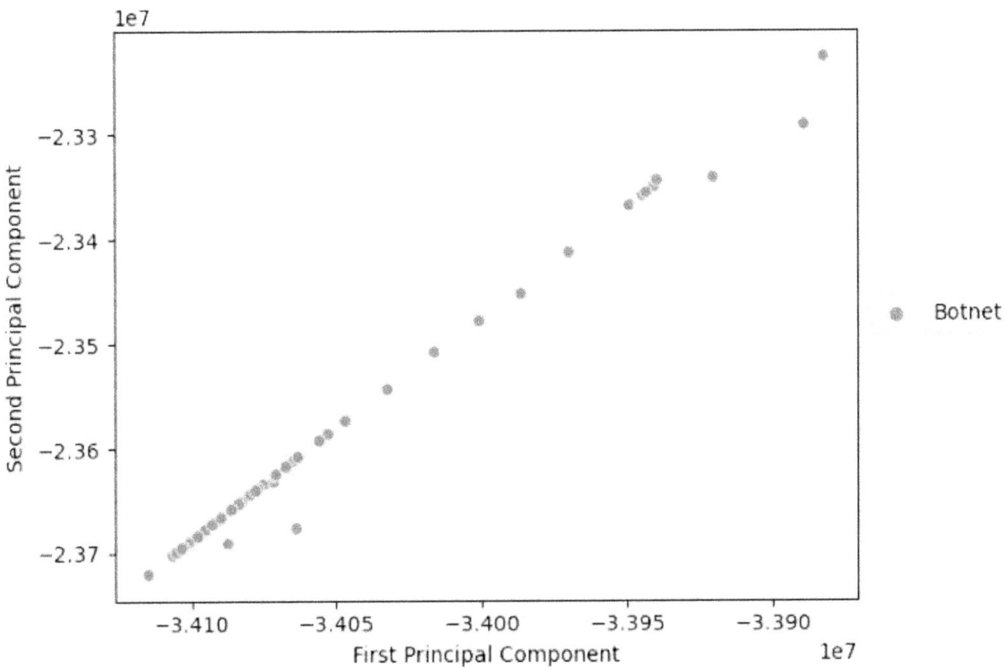

(b) PCA projection of botnet detections exclusively

FIGURE 8.3 Plot for PCA in two components of the improvised CICIDS 2017 dataset: (a) PCA projection of the entire detection and (b) PCA projection of botnet detections exclusively.

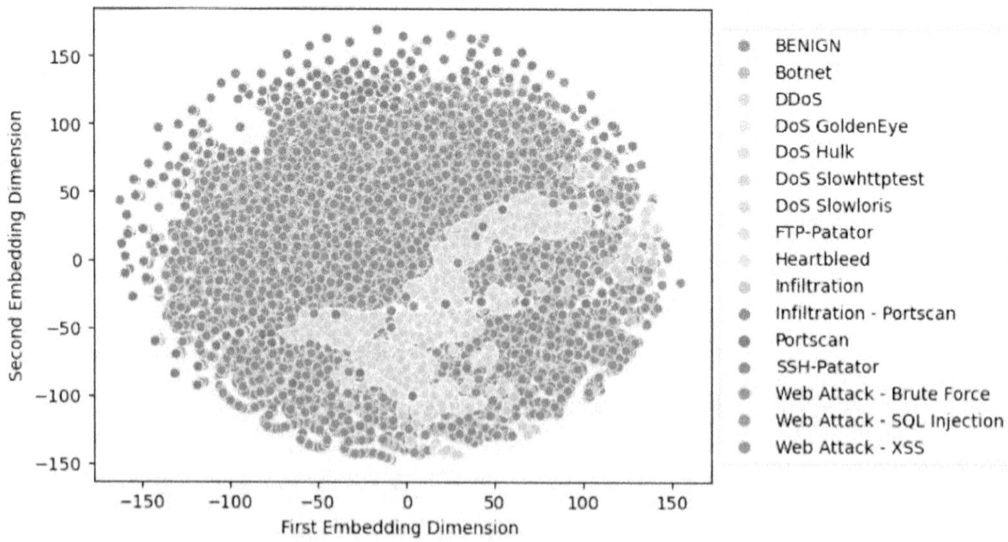

(a) t-SNE visualization of the entire detection

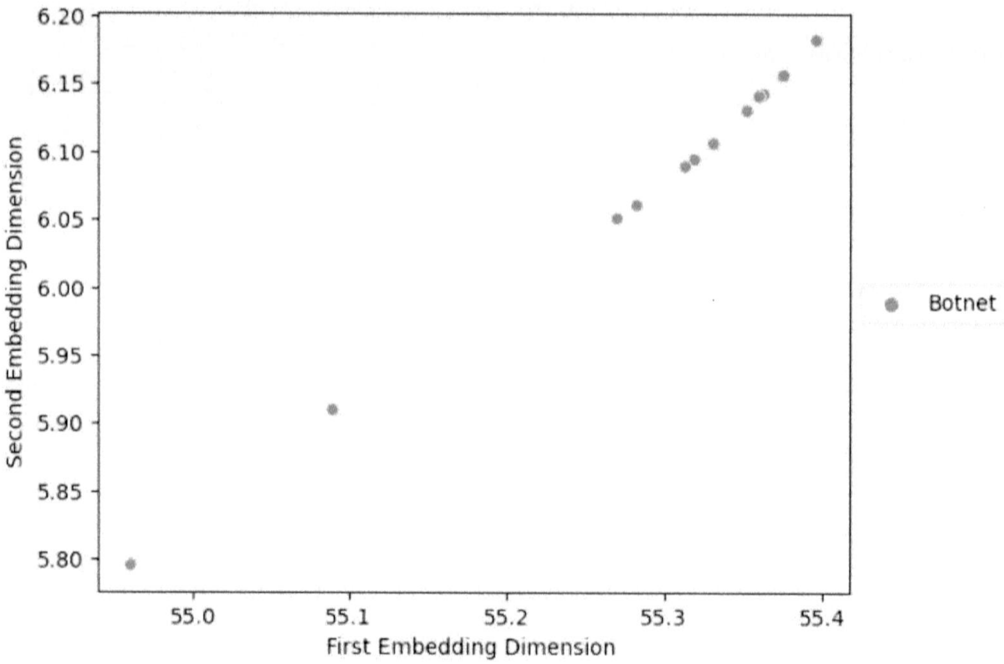

(b) t-SNE visualization of botnet detections exclusively

FIGURE 8.4 Plot for t-SNE in two components of the improvised CICIDS 2017 dataset: (a) t-SNE visualization of the entire detection and (b) t-SNE visualization of botnet detections exclusively.

In the model fine-tuning phase, an extensive grid search was conducted to optimize hyperparameters, specifically focusing on various scalers and the number of principal components (n components) for PCA. The performance of each combination was evaluated using the validation set, measuring key metrics like area under the receiver operating characteristic curve (AUROC). The objective was to identify the best scaler and PCA configuration that maximized anomaly detection accuracy.

Following the grid search, the top-performing combination of scaler and PCA was selected based on the highest AUROC score. This best configuration was then applied to test data containing different malicious labels and benign instances. Each class's performance was evaluated individually, utilizing metrics such as precision, recall, and F1-score to assess the model's ability to accurately distinguish between benign and specific malicious activities. This comprehensive evaluation strategy ensured a robust assessment of the model's effectiveness across various classes, contributing crucial insights into its real-world applicability for next-gen botnet host detection.

In the interpretability phase, the model's predictions were examined using SHapley Additive exPlanations (SHAP) to gain insights into the features' impact on the classification decisions. A subsample of the test data was selected to enhance computational efficiency while retaining the dataset's representativity. SHAP values were computed for this subsampled data using an explainer, shedding light on the significance of each feature in the model's predictions.

The SHAP waterfall plot for the first prediction illustrated the step-by-step contribution of each feature towards the final classification outcome. This visualization provided a clear understanding of which features played pivotal roles in distinguishing between benign and malicious instances. Additionally, to provide context, a scatter plot was generated as shown in Figure 8.5, displaying the relationship between 'Bwd Packet Length Mean' and 'Packet Length Mean,' two features crucial for the classification process. The plot was annotated with labels denoting different classes, aiding in the interpretation of the data distribution concerning the model's decisions. Through these visualization, the researchers gained valuable insights into the model's inner workings, facilitating a deeper understanding of its decision-making process and enhancing the overall transparency of the next-gen botnet host detection system.

8.4 RESULTS AND DISCUSSION

8.4.1 Dataset Description

The CICIDS 2017 dataset is a widely used cyber security dataset that contains network traffic data for intrusion detection system (IDS) research. It includes various types of network traffic, both benign and malicious, captured in a controlled environment. The dataset comprises different attack scenarios, such as denial-of-service (DoS), distributed denial-of-service (DDoS), and intrusion attempts, allowing researchers to analyze and develop effective intrusion detection techniques.

8.4.2 Machine Learning Classification

8.4.2.1 Performance Metrics of Different Classifiers

Classifier	CV Accuracy	Overall Accuracy	Benign Detection Precision	Bot Detection Precision
Bagging	1.00	1.00	1.00	0.71
AdaBoost	0.69	0.89	0.92	0.00
Bernoulli NB	0.61	0.57	0.99	0.01
Gaussian NB	0.36	0.16	1.00	0.00
Multimodal NB	0.80	0.88	0.96	1.00
Random Forest	1.00	1.00	1.00	0.71
K-Neighbor	0.99	0.99	1.00	0.39
Decision Tree	0.87	0.94	0.96	1.00

8.4.3 Dimensionality Reduction

8.4.3.1 PCA Intrusion Detection

Intrusion	AUROC	F1 Score	Precision	Recall
All Attacks	0.92	0.85	0.81	0.90
BotNet	0.97	0.63	0.47	0.99

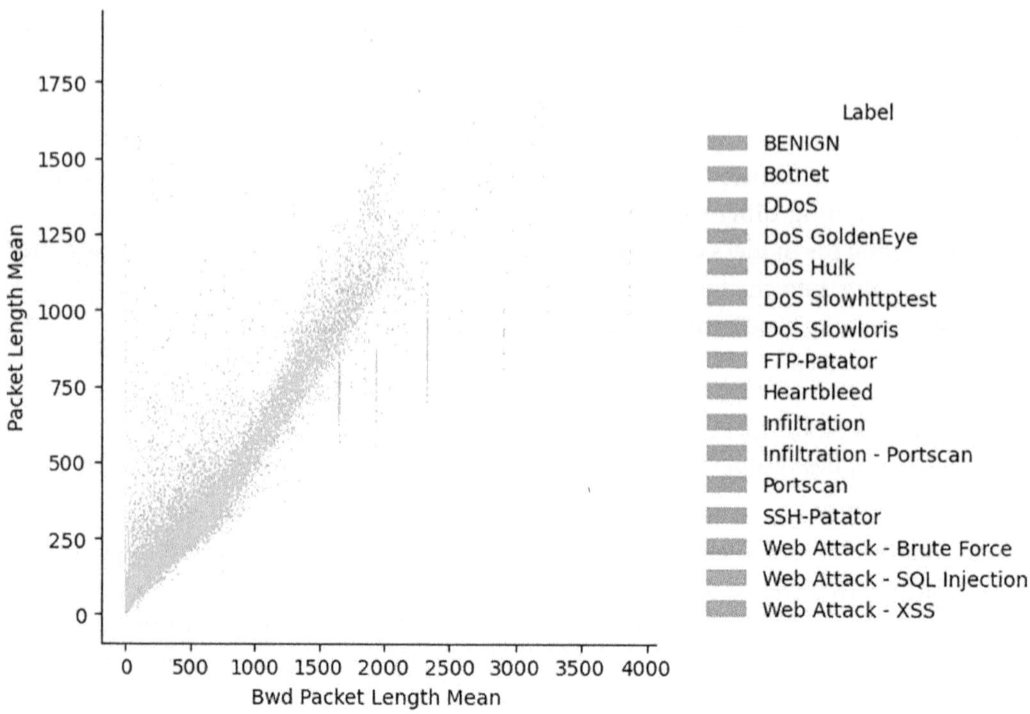

FIGURE 8.5 Scatter plot showing "Bwd Packet Length Mean" vs. "Packet Length Mean" with labeled benign and botnet instances, guided by SHAP explainability.

In our collective pursuit of advancing botnet host detection, several research gaps have emerged, demanding our immediate attention and innovative solutions. Firstly, the lack of standardized evaluation metrics poses a significant challenge. While accuracy, precision, recall, and F1 score are essential, a comprehensive evaluation framework encompassing diverse network environments and attack scenarios is imperative. Additionally, the scalability of ML models in handling large-scale network traffic data remains an unresolved issue. As our datasets grow, optimizing algorithms to operate efficiently on vast and dynamic data sets becomes crucial. Moreover, the interpretability of sophisticated models such as DL architectures is a persistent concern. Transparent and interpretable AI-driven solutions are essential for cybersecurity professionals to comprehend and trust the decisions made by these advanced systems. Furthermore, the integration of real time, adaptive learning mechanisms is a research frontier that demands exploration. Building systems capable of adapting to evolving botnet strategies and tactics in real time can significantly enhance our detection capabilities. Lastly, there exists a gap in understanding the contextual relevance of features within network traffic data. Investigating the contextual significance of specific features and their interdependencies in different attack scenarios can lead to more nuanced and accurate detection methods. Addressing these gaps collectively will enable us to construct more robust, scalable, and interpretable botnet detection systems, ensuring the resilience of our digital infrastructures against ever-evolving cyber threats.

8.5 FUTURE SCOPE

In the realm of botnet host detection, our collective efforts have laid a robust foundation, yet the future promises exciting avenues for exploration and innovation. As a research community, we must continually push the boundaries of ML and data analysis techniques to enhance the accuracy and efficiency of botnet detection systems. DL architectures, especially convolutional neural networks (CNNs) and recurrent neural networks (RNNs), hold tremendous potential in capturing intricate temporal and spatial patterns within network traffic data, making them compelling candidates for future research. Furthermore, the integration of anomaly detection techniques, like autoencoders and one-class Support Vector Machines (SVMs), can augment traditional classification models by identifying subtle deviations from normal network behavior. Embracing real-time processing and analysis is paramount, enabling the development of proactive botnet detection systems that can respond swiftly to emerging threats. Collaboration with cybersecurity experts and industry professionals is essential, facilitating the integration of domain knowledge into ML algorithms. Additionally, exploring the feasibility of deploying blockchain technology to secure the integrity of datasets and model outcomes could revolutionize the trustworthiness of botnet detection frameworks. By staying at the forefront of technological advancements and fostering interdisciplinary collaborations, we, as a research community, can fortify our arsenal against evolving botnet threats, ensuring a safer digital landscape for all.

8.6 CONCLUSION

In conclusion, this study on botnet host detection has delineated both significant advancements and persistent challenges within the cybersecurity domain. We systematically evaluated a spectrum of ML algorithms—including ensemble methods like Random Forests and Gradient Boosting Machines, support vector machines, and deep neural network architectures—effectively addressing class imbalance through techniques such as Synthetic Minority Over-sampling Technique (SMOTE) and cost-sensitive learning approaches. Robust model evaluation was ensured via cross-validation schemes and the application of comprehensive performance metrics, beyond simple accuracy measures. The comparative analysis of these classifiers has yielded critical insights into their respective strengths, weaknesses, and suitability for different detection scenarios. However, our investigation has also identified several technical gaps: the necessity for standardized evaluation metrics to enable consistent benchmarking; the development of scalable algorithms capable of handling large-scale, high-dimensional network traffic data; the creation of interpretable models to facilitate transparency and trust in decision-making processes; the implementation of real-time adaptive learning mechanisms to counteract evolving botnet behaviors; and the incorporation of contextual feature analysis to enhance detection accuracy and robustness. Recognizing these challenges positions us at the threshold of a transformative phase in botnet detection research. By fostering interdisciplinary collaboration among ML experts, network security professionals, and data scientists; embracing emerging technologies such as federated learning and adversarial detection frameworks; and refining our methodological approaches to incorporate advanced feature engineering and model optimization techniques, we can bridge these gaps. This will pave the way for more effective, adaptive, and resilient botnet detection systems. Our collective efforts will continue to advance the cybersecurity landscape, contributing to a safer and more secure digital ecosystem for users worldwide.

REFERENCES

[1] A. A. Hezam, S. A. Mostafa, Z. Baharum, A. Alanda, and M. Z. Salikon, "Combining deep learning models for enhancing the detection of botnet attacks in multiple sensors internet of things networks," *JOIV: International Journal on Informatics Visualization*, vol. 5, no. 4, pp. 380–387, 2021. doi:10.30630/joiv.5.4.733.

[2] R. S. Moorthy and N. Nathiya, "Botnet detection using artificial intelligence," *Procedia Computer Science*, vol. 218, pp. 1405–1413, 2023. doi:10.1016/j.procs.2023.01.119.

[3] V. Puri, A. Kataria, V. K. Solanki, and S. Rani, "AI-based botnet attack classification and detection in IOT devices," *2022 IEEE International Conference on Machine Learning and Applied Network Technologies (ICMLANT)*, 2022. doi:10.1109/icmlant56191.2022.9996464.

[4] H. Suryotrisongko, Y. Musashi, A. Tsuneda, and K. Sugitani, "Robust botnet DGA detection: Blending XAI and OSINT for Cyber Threat Intelligence Sharing," *IEEE Access*, vol. 10, pp. 34613–34624, 2022. doi:10.1109/access.2022.3162588.

[5] M. Macas, C. Wu, and W. Fuertes, "A survey on Deep Learning for Cybersecurity: Progress, challenges, and opportunities," *Computer Networks*, vol. 212, p. 109032, 2022. doi:10.1016/j.comnet.2022.109032.

[6] S. Senthil and N. Muthukumaran, "Joined bi-model RNN with spatial attention and Gan based IOT botnet attacks detection," *Sādhanā*, vol. 48, no. 3, p. 141, 2023. doi:10.1007/s12046-023-02188-y.

[7] A. A. Hezam, S. A. Mostafa, A. A. Ramli, H. Mahdin, and B. A. Khalaf, "Deep Learning Approach for detecting botnet attacks in IOT environment of multiple and heterogeneous sensors," In *International Conference on Advances in Cyber Security* (pp. 317-328). Singapore: Springer Singapore.

[8] X. Dong, C. Dong, Z. Chen, Y. Cheng, and B. Chen, "Botdetector: An extreme learning machine-based internet of things botnet detection model," *Transactions on Emerging Telecommunications Technologies*, vol. 32, no. 5, e3999, 2020. doi:10.1002/ett.3999.

[9] A. M. Almuhaideb and D. Y. Alynanbaawi, "Applications of artificial intelligence to detect Android botnets: A survey," *IEEE Access*, vol. 10, pp. 71737–71748, 2022. doi:10.1109/access.2022.3187094.

[10] G. Vormayr, T. Zseby, and J. Fabini, "Botnet communication patterns," *IEEE Communications Surveys & Tutorials*, vol. 19, no. 4, pp. 2768–2796, 2017. doi:10.1109/comst.2017.2749442.

CHAPTER 9

Artificial Intelligence-Based Cybercrime Prevention and Data Security

Srinivasa Rao Gundu, Panem Charanarur, and J. Vijaylaxmi

9.1 INTRODUCTION

When referring to unlawful activities carried out over digital networks, the word "cybercrime" is often used to refer to the internet. Malware, phishing, and hacking are all examples of methods that fall under the umbrella of cybercrime, which is a broad category of criminal activity that includes a wide range of offenses. In order to disrupt, damage, or gain unauthorized access to computer systems, malicious software is used throughout the process. Attempting to get sensitive information by impersonating a trustworthy organization is an example of phishing, which is a fraudulent practice. The use of cyber tools to carry out terrorist acts, particularly assaults on key infrastructure, is what is meant by the term "cyberterrorism." Identity theft, cyberstalking and harassment, online fraud and scams, theft of intellectual property, denial-of-service attacks, and theft of intellectual property are some of the other kinds of cybercrime. Businesses have the potential to gain money by stealing the personal information of other people. The fact that cybercrime hinders commerce via assaults such as distributed denial-of-service (DDoS) and ransomware, as well as the fact that it costs people, organizations, and governments money, is a negative aspect (Rukavitsyn et al., 2017).

It also has severe personal impacts, such as identity theft causing financial losses and emotional distress, and privacy violations exposing sensitive information to misuse. Security threats include targeting national infrastructure and corporate espionage, undermining national security and economic stability. Social impacts are seen in the spread of misinformation influencing public opinion and cyberbullying causing psychological

DOI: 10.1201/9781032714813-9

harm. Technological advancements, like the proliferation of Internet of Things (IoT) devices and artificial intelligence (AI) exploitation, introduce new vulnerabilities and sophisticated attack methods. Mitigating these threats requires enhanced cybersecurity measures, updated legislation and regulation, increased awareness and education, and well-developed incident response plans. In summary, cybercrime poses significant and multifaceted threats in the modern digital age, affecting economic stability, personal security, and national safety, necessitating proactive measures in cybersecurity, legislation, and public awareness to combat and mitigate these evolving threats (Ugale et al., 2011).

9.2 CYBERCRIME HISTORICAL PERSPECTIVE

Cybercrime, the use of technology to commit crimes or harm others, has evolved significantly over the past few decades. In the 1960s and 1970s, early computer misuse in academic and military settings and phone phreaking marked the beginning of technological exploitation. The 1980s saw the rise of personal computers and hacking culture, leading to legislative responses such as the U.S. Computer Fraud and Abuse Act of 1986, highlighted by notable cases like the "414s" hackers. The 1990s, characterized by widespread internet adoption, saw the emergence of cybercrime syndicates exploiting the internet for financial gain, with incidents like the 1994 arrest of Russian hacker Vladimir Levin. The 2000s brought more sophisticated cyberattacks, targeting government and corporate entities, prompting stronger laws and international cooperation, exemplified by the Council of Europe's Convention on Cybercrime. The 2010s experienced major data breaches and cyberwarfare, including the Stuxnet worm and Russian interference in the 2016 U.S. election, along with a ransomware epidemic. In the 2020s, advanced technologies such as AI, IoT, and blockchain have introduced new vulnerabilities, with the COVID-19 pandemic further accelerating cybercrime. As cyber threats continue to evolve, ongoing efforts in cybersecurity, legislation, and international cooperation remain essential to protect against emerging threats (Deebak & Al-Turjman, 2021).

It can be depicted in a comprehensive view using Table 9.1.

Cybercrime has evolved from simple acts of unauthorized access in the early days of computing to sophisticated, organized, and global threats. As technology continues to advance, the nature of cybercrime will likely continue to change, necessitating ongoing efforts in cybersecurity, legislation, and international cooperation to protect against emerging threats (Tan et al., 2018).

TABLE 9.1 Historical Perspective of Cybercrimes World Wide

Decade	Perspective
1960s–1970s	The Early Days – Early Computer Misuse and Phone Phreaking
1970s–1980s	Hacking – Legislative Responses – Notable Cases
1980s–1990s	Internet Expansion and Cybercrime – Cybercrime Syndicates and Notable Incidents
1990s–2000s	Sophistication and International Threats – Government and Corporate Targets -Sophisticated Attacks – Legislations
2000s–2010s	Cyberwarfare and Data Breaches – Espionage and Ransomware
2010s–2020s	Pandemic-Driven Cybercrime and Defensive Measures

9.3 INCREASE IN CYBERCRIME

Figure 9.1 illustrates the increase in cybercrime incidents from the 1960s to the 2020s. It shows a significant rise over the decades, reflecting the growing complexity and frequency of cybercrimes as technology has advanced. This trend underscores the importance of robust cybersecurity measures and international cooperation to combat the evolving threats posed by cybercrime.

The increase in cybercrime from the 1960s to the 2020s can be attributed to several key factors, each contributing to the rise in both the frequency and sophistication of cyber-attacks. The factors such as Proliferation of Technology, Advancements in Technology, Economic Incentives, Insufficient Security Measures, Globalization, Social Engineering and Human Factors, Pandemic-Driven Changes and Political and Economic Factors contributed to the growth of increase in cybercrime (Amaral et al., 2019).

The rapid expansion of the internet has exponentially increased the number of potential targets. From a few interconnected academic and military computers in the 1960s, the internet now connects billions of devices worldwide. The advent of affordable personal computers in the 1980s democratized access to technology, creating more opportunities for cybercriminals to exploit vulnerabilities. The proliferation of smartphones, tablets, and IoT devices in recent decades has expanded the attack surface for cybercriminals. Many of these devices have inadequate security measures, making them easy targets.

Cybercriminals now have access to advanced tools and techniques, including automated hacking tools, ransomware, and sophisticated phishing schemes. The rise of the dark web has facilitated the distribution of these tools and services. Additionally, AI and machine

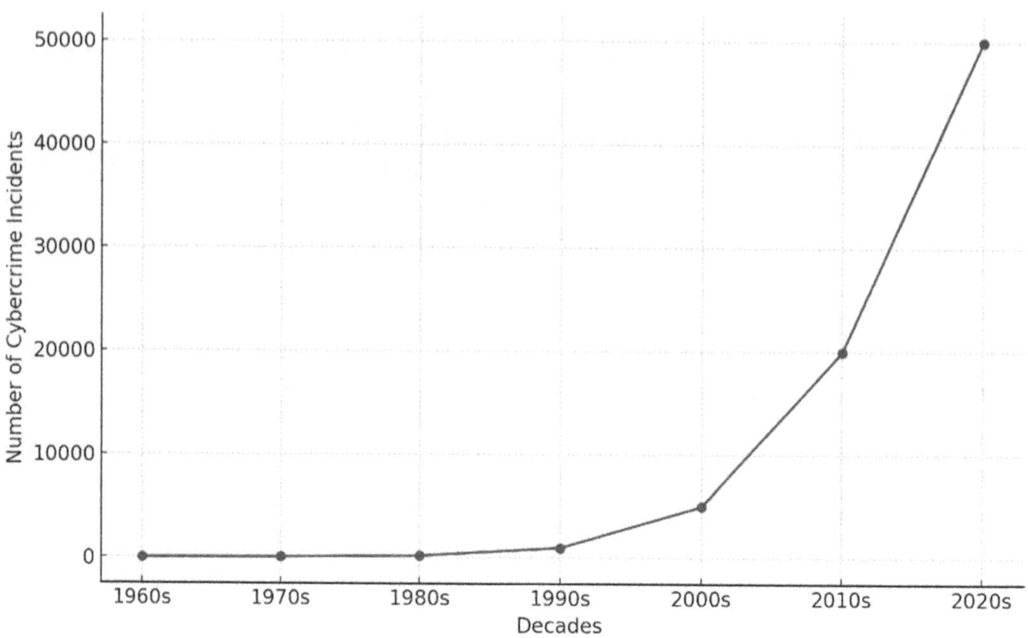

FIGURE 9.1 Increase in cybercrime since 1960s to 2020s.

learning technologies have been leveraged to create more effective and harder-to-detect attacks, such as deepfake videos and adaptive phishing schemes.

The financial gains from cybercrime have driven its increase. Ransomware attacks, online fraud, and the sale of stolen data are lucrative ventures. Cryptocurrencies like Bitcoin have made it easier to conduct transactions anonymously. Organized crime groups have recognized the profitability of cybercrime and have developed sophisticated operations to carry out large-scale attacks and fraud.

As technology has advanced, security measures have often lagged behind. Many individuals and organizations do not prioritize cybersecurity, leaving systems vulnerable to attack. The complexity and interconnectedness of modern systems make it difficult to secure them adequately. Vulnerabilities in one system can often be exploited to gain access to others.

The internet's global nature allows cybercriminals to operate across borders, complicating law enforcement efforts. Jurisdictional challenges and differing legal frameworks make it difficult to pursue and prosecute cybercriminals internationally. Global trade and communication mean that more entities are online, increasing the number of potential targets for cybercriminals.

Cybercriminals have become adept at exploiting human psychology through social engineering techniques. Phishing attacks, for instance, prey on individuals' trust and lack of awareness. Many users are not sufficiently aware of the risks and best practices in cybersecurity, making them easy targets for cybercriminals.

The COVID-19 pandemic accelerated the shift to remote work, often without adequate security measures in place. This has provided new opportunities for cybercriminals to exploit vulnerabilities in home networks and remote access systems. The pandemic also increased overall online activity, including e-commerce and online services, creating more opportunities for cybercrime.

Nation-states engage in cyber espionage and cyberwarfare, targeting other countries' infrastructure, government systems, and private sector assets. These activities have contributed to the overall increase in cybercrime incidents. In some regions, economic hardship drives individuals towards cybercrime as a means of financial gain.

The increase in cybercrime from the 1960s to the 2020s is a multifaceted issue driven by technological advancements, economic incentives, globalization, insufficient security measures, social engineering, pandemic-driven changes, and political factors. Addressing these challenges requires a comprehensive approach involving improved cybersecurity practices, international cooperation, public awareness campaigns, and robust legislative frameworks.

9.4 REDUCING THE CYBER CRIME

It is essential to use a multi-pronged strategy in order to bring about a reduction in the amount of cybercrime. The implementation of this strategy ought to incorporate technological approaches, legal frameworks, educational activities, and international cooperation. By applying a few strategies, such as ensuring that software is frequently updated and patched, enforcing strong password restrictions, installing firewalls and antivirus software, and utilizing encryption to secure essential data, we could prevent ourselves from being victims of cybercrime.

It is important that both employers and members of the general public receive frequent training on the best practices for cybersecurity. Additionally, awareness campaigns should be conducted to educate people about the hazards of cybercrime and how they can protect themselves when using the internet.

It is imperative that comprehensive cybercrime laws be developed and maintained up-to-date, and that data protection mechanisms be put into place and enforced, in order to guarantee that personal information is handled in a responsible manner. Victims should be encouraged to report incidents in order to aid law enforcement in tracking down and combating cybercrime. Plans for responding to events should be made and maintained, clear ways should be established for reporting cybercrime, and victims should be encouraged to report incidents (Qiao et al., 2021).

In addition to demonstrating support for and involvement in international treaties and agreements that combat cybercrime, it is important to foster collaboration across international borders, as well as the exchange of knowledge and best practices among governments. Making investments in research on cybersecurity, collaborating with academic institutions to foster innovation, and offering training to individuals working in the field of cybersecurity are all important responsibilities.

It is important to foster the creation of industry standards and best practices for cybersecurity, as well as to encourage collaboration between government agencies and businesses in the private sector working together. In order to detect irregularities and

TABLE 9.2 Comprehensive View of Different Approaches to Reduce the Cybercrime

Aspect	Description
Strategy Components	The plan must include technology, law, education, and international collaboration.
Technological Measures	Data security requires software updates, patching, strong passwords, firewalls, antivirus software, and encryption.
Education and Awareness	Awareness campaigns on cybercrime hazards and defense, as well as employer and public cybersecurity training.
Legislation and Regulation	Develop and enforce comprehensive cybercrime legislation and data protection procedures to appropriately manage personal information
Incident Response and Reporting	Victim reporting incentives, incident response strategies, clear reporting procedures, and event response plans.
International Cooperation	Supporting international cybercrime treaties, government cooperation, and information exchange across boundaries.
Research and Development	Innovation via cybersecurity research, academic cooperation, and cybersecurity training.
Public-Private Partnerships	Encourage industry best practices, government-private sector collaboration, threat intelligence, and resource sharing.
Technological Advancements	AI and machine learning for real-time danger detection, blockchain for secure data and transactions.
Vulnerability Management	Regular security audits, vulnerability assessments, bug bounty programs, and user behavior monitoring for abnormalities.

possible dangers in real time, it is necessary to make use of AI and machine learning. It is also important to explore whether or not blockchain technology has the capacity to adequately secure data and transactions.

Frequent security audits and vulnerability assessments are essential in order to encourage ethical hackers to find and report security issues. This can be accomplished by conducting these activities. In addition to that, bug reward schemes ought to be implemented. Monitoring the activities of users through the use of behavior analytics and putting in place tight access control methods are both strongly recommended.

It is possible for individuals, organizations, and governments to achieve a more robust cybersecurity posture by implementing these strategies, which will result in a reduction in the frequency and severity of cybercrime. This will be accomplished by creating a more robust cybersecurity posture. Table 9.2 provides a comprehensive view.

9.5 SOFTWARE SUPPORT TO AVOID CYBER CRIME

Currently, there is a plethora of programs accessible to assist in the prevention of cybercrime. Malicious software, such as spyware, viruses, Trojan horses, and worms, are examples of harmful programs that antivirus software is specifically designed to protect computers from. Cybersecurity depends on information technology. Firewalls utilize pre-established security standards to oversee and control every data packet that passes across a company's network. Firewalls efficiently impede unauthorized access by bad actors, such as hackers, by creating a physical barrier between reliable internal networks and the external world. Data packets are encrypted using virtual private networks (VPNs) before being transmitted over the internet. While accessing sensitive data remotely, they use security measures to encrypt it so that only authorized individuals can decipher it.

Intrusion detection systems (IDSs) and intrusion prevention systems (IPSs) are examples of security software that monitor data transfers across networks in order to detect and assess both typical and unusual threats. Security administrators are notified by IDSs anytime they identify what seems like an attempt at unauthorized access, in contrast to IPSs. The endpoint protection systems ensure the safety of all endpoint devices, including computers, laptops, cellphones, and more. Security measures include things like antivirus programs, firewalls, and IPSs. Data loss prevention (DLP) systems aim to prevent unauthorized access by monitoring, detecting, and restricting the flow of sensitive data from computers, storage devices, and networks (Gupta et al., 2021).

System for information and event management (SIEM) systematically searches many logs for indicators of intrusion, policy violations, and other potential threats. In times of crisis, they are second to none when it comes to gathering intelligence on potential threats and keeping a close eye on things. Technologies that encrypt data make it impossible for unauthorized individuals to access or intercept it. Their comprehensive protection extends to every step of the data lifecycle, including generation, transfer, and storage across several devices, channels, and files. Identity and access management (IAM) systems safeguard critical information by keeping tabs on user identities, roles, and permissions. The method they've developed for protecting against internal threats, identity fraud, and unauthorized access is second to none.

TABLE 9.3 Different Software Tools and Their Description

Software Tool	Description
Antivirus Software	Cybersecurity relies on antivirus software to block viruses, Trojans, worms, ransomware, and spyware.
Firewalls	Firewalls control network traffic for security. Protecting trusted internal networks from untrusted external networks prevents data breaches.
Virtual Private Networks	VPNs protect public network data by encrypting internet connections. They prevent eavesdropping, data interception, and other cyberattacks, especially while accessing sensitive data remotely.
Intrusion Detection Systems (IDSs)	IDS and IPS technologies detect abnormal network traffic and attack patterns. IPS blocks or mitigates attacks in real time, whereas IDS notifies administrators to security breaches.
Endpoint Protection	Desktops, laptops, cellphones, and other endpoints are protected by endpoint protection solutions. They usually include antivirus, firewall, intrusion prevention, and other sophisticated functions to guard against attacks.
Data Loss Prevention (DLP)	DLP solutions monitor, identify, and block sensitive data transit across networks, endpoints, and storage systems to avoid unauthorized disclosure.
Security Information and Event Management (SIEM)	By analyzing log data from many sources, SIEM systems are able to detect security events, policy breaches, and threats. They provide services such as real-time monitoring, incident response, and threat intelligence.
Encryption Tools	Data is encrypted to prevent unauthorized access or interception. They protect communication lines, storage devices, files, and sensitive data at rest and in transit.
Identity and Access Management (IAM)	IAM solutions control user identities, roles, and permissions to restrict data and resource access. They guard against identity theft, insider threats, and unauthorized access.
Web Application Firewalls (WAFs)	WAFs filter and monitor HTTP traffic to defend online applications against SQL injection, XSS, and DDoS assaults.

Web application firewalls (WAFs) constantly monitor and filter HTTP traffic to defend networks from typical cyber threats including DDoS, Structured Query Language (SQL) injection, and cross-site scripting (XSS). By reducing the possibility of cybercrime, these software solutions can significantly improve cybersecurity when utilized and maintained effectively. A number of software solutions are described and analyzed in detail in Table 9.3.

9.6 ROLE OF AI IN CYBERCRIME PREVENTION

The significance of AI in combating cybercrime is steadily increasing due to its potential to enhance cybersecurity protocols in various aspects. Systems powered by AI are exceptionally adept at detecting anomalies due to their capability to analyze immense quantities of data pertaining to user activity, system logs, and network traffic in order to identify potentially dangerous patterns that indicate a cyberattack. By employing AI, these devices detect irregularities. Real-time threat perception enables prompt detection and response to such assaults, thereby mitigating the risk of systemic breaches.

Furthermore, AI algorithms consistently extract threat intelligence data from diverse sources, including dark web forums, hacker networks, and security channels. AI enables security personnel to enhance defenses proactively and reduce threats. When vulnerabilities and potential entry points into a system are unknown, AI can detect and classify them. They would be able to take proactive measures to prevent acts of violence.

Moreover, businesses can employ AI algorithms to predict future cyber threats and vulnerabilities by analysing historical data and trends. AI is a critical component of cybersecurity as it fortifies system resilience against malicious actors and prevents security breaches. Moreover, in order to detect unforeseen behavior, technologies fueled by AI and behavioral analytics monitor user interactions and routines with IT systems. By enhancing its existing security protocols, this functionality enhances the organization's capacity to detect insider threats, unauthorized access attempts, and other violations of security.

Additional advantages of employing AI in automated response include prompt containment, cleansing, and issue response. This is made possible by automation and security orchestration systems. By leveraging machine learning and natural language processing, AI mitigates the impact of cyberattacks and improves incident management. Achieving this is the function of AI.

To detect and deter fraudulent activities, the banking and financial industries employ AI algorithms to a significant degree. By analysing transaction data and user activity patterns, AI possesses the capability to detect illicit activities such as unauthorized transactions and identity theft in real time.

Email security solutions that utilize AI-based machine learning techniques can also detect and thwart fraudulent emails. AI protects users from fraudulent email schemes and aids in the detection of phishing attempts through the analysis of email content, sender reputation, and user activity.

Vulnerability assessment systems powered by AI may investigate IT infrastructure, applications, and devices autonomously in order to identify and rank security threats. Organizations have the ability to avert intrusions by automating vulnerability management procedures with the aid of AI. It goes without saying that AI has significantly transformed the field of cybersecurity. As cybercrime increases, organizations are able to strengthen their defenses, detect attacks earlier, refine their responses, and maintain their resilience (Ahsan et al., 2020).

9.7 PREVENTING THE CYBER CRIMINALS WITH STRATEGICALLY

AI-guided cybersecurity measures are essential for safeguarding against cybercrime. These strategies identify, evaluate, and minimize the impacts of these hazards by utilizing sophisticated algorithms and technological innovations. Examine the provided depiction of how AI contributes to combating cybercrime:

Algorithms driven by AI continuously examine system data, human interaction, and network traffic in order to detect anomalies. We do this procedure to detect any discrepancies. AI-based solutions have the potential to identify and alert security personnel about unauthorized access attempts or abnormal data transfers before they become actual cybercrimes.

Automated threat intelligence systems sift vast amounts of data supplied from dark web forums, hacker networks, and security channels. AI can enhance the ability of security teams to identify new attack methods and risks, so strengthening their defense against cybercriminals.

BYOB-driven behavioral analytics solutions analyze humans' utilization of IT systems and their behavior to detect problems. Organizations can successfully prevent or reduce the impact of cybercrime by using AI to identify abnormal behavior that could be caused by internal or external threats. Considering the fact that AI has the capability to identify deviations from the norm, this statement is accurate and specific.

AI-powered automation and orchestration systems enable automatic responses to security threats and breaches. The ability of AI to quickly respond, control, and rectify is enabled by its machine learning and natural language processing (NLP) capabilities. These actions reduce the influence of cybercriminals.

Automated vulnerability assessment systems, driven by AI, can detect security vulnerabilities in IT infrastructure, applications, and devices and determine the order of importance for fixing them. Implementing AI can enhance an organization's security processes and decrease its vulnerability to threats. This strategy proactively identifies and resolves security vulnerabilities before hackers have the opportunity to possibly exploit them.

The financial services and banking sectors employ AI algorithms to identify and mitigate fraudulent behavior. AI can be used to monitor user behavior patterns and real-time transaction data, allowing for the detection of fraudulent activity. Financial institutions are frequently targeted by malevolent individuals that carry out cyberattacks, stealing sensitive data and engaging in unauthorized financial activities.

Email security systems, enhanced by AI, detect and prevent phishing attacks by employing machine learning algorithms. Applying AI to analyze email content, sender reputation, and user activity can aid in identifying phishing attempts. This security measure decreases the probability of consumers being victims of fraudulent software downloads or the exposure of critical information.

By using cybersecurity solutions powered by AI, organizations may strengthen their ability to withstand cyberattacks and minimize the negative impact on individuals, governments, and enterprises. These systems actively identify, prevent, and resolve cybercriminal actions (Sneps-Sneppe et al., 2019).

9.8 INFORMATION SECURITY AWARENESS FOR WOMEN

Women's information security awareness may be tailored to address specific difficulties and hazards that they may face in the digital environment by using AI-based cybercrime prevention techniques and procedures. This may be done by using the approaches and tactics. The following is a list of essential concerns to address, along with relevant AI-based software and cybersecurity solutions.

It is critical to provide complete internet safety education, which should include tips on how to protect personal information, detect phishing attempts, and secure social media accounts. Personalized learning experiences tailored to individual knowledge levels and learning preferences may be delivered via educational platforms powered by AI.

It is critical to encourage women to utilize threat intelligence systems driven by AI in order to stay informed about emerging cyber threats and vulnerabilities. These services provide women with real-time updates on potential risks by collecting and analyzing threat data from a range of sources, allowing them to make informed decisions about how to protect themselves online.

It should be encouraged to utilize secure communication solutions equipped with encryption and privacy features based on AI. Encrypted email and messaging apps and platforms may keep critical communications from being intercepted and viewed by unauthorized persons, hence preserving women's privacy and confidentiality.

Identity security solutions powered by AI should be made accessible in order to monitor for signs of identity theft and unauthorized access to personal data. The usage of these technologies enables proactive identification of suspicious behavior, such as fraudulent transactions and account takeovers, as well as notification and remedial suggestions, therefore reducing the risk of possible issues.

It is vital to raise awareness about the importance of behavioral analytics in detecting and mitigating the consequences of cyber threats. Women must be made aware of how AI-powered behavioral analytics tools monitor for unusual actions and deviations from conventional behavior, hence aiding in the discovery of insider threats and hostile operations that specifically target them.

Women should be educated on the most efficient ways to ensure the safety of their online identities and social media accounts. AI-powered social media security systems may assess privacy settings, detect suspicious account activity, and recommend ways to improve account security and privacy limitations.

Women should be encouraged to adopt AI-powered personal safety applications that employ machine learning algorithms to assess ambient variables and user behavior patterns in order to detect potential safety hazards. Women may improve their physical and digital safety by using these programs, which provide real-time warnings and assistance in emergency situations.

To address the issue of cyberbullying and online harassment, it is recommended that AI-powered cyberbullying detection systems be promoted. These technologies utilize NLP and sentiment analysis to identify harmful interactions and abusive content. As a consequence, women feel empowered to take preemptive actions to protect themselves against online abuse.

Women may increase their information security awareness and lessen the risks associated with cybercrime in the digital era by embracing AI-based cybersecurity strategies and employing situationally suitable software solutions. Women may traverse the online world with confidence and safety if they use these tailored tactics.

9.9 INFORMATION SECURITY AWARENESS FOR FAMILY

It is crucial that families understand the significance of information security in this digital age, when houses are more connected and reliant on technology. The following should be considered while attempting to increase families' knowledge of information security.

Everyone living there, regardless of age, has to learn the ropes of cybersecurity. This includes things like using strong passwords, being aware of phishing attempts, and being careful while using the internet in general.

Be sure to emphasize how important it is to lock down all electronic devices, including smart home gadgets, tablets, and laptops. Use antivirus software, update software periodically, and use strong passwords to fight against malware infestations and unauthorized access.

Give your loved ones the rundown on how to be safe while they're dealing with sensitive information online. Part of this includes being aware of how various platforms manage privacy settings, being cautious about revealing too much personal information when posting on social media, and so on.

Tell them to be careful while they're online by telling them to only connect to public Wi-Fi at home, not to accept attachments from unknown senders, and to stay away from suspicious sites.

To monitor your children's internet activities, set up parental controls on their devices and routers. These apps make it easy to limit screen time and access to inappropriate content.

Members of the family, especially those who are younger, should exercise caution while using social media because of the risks associated with cyberbullying, online predators, and oversharing. Encourage those using social media to exercise care and thoughtfulness while doing so.

Stress the need of regularly backing up important files and data to the cloud or external hard drives to everyone in the company. As a result, data loss due to virus attacks, hardware failure, or other unforeseen events is less likely to occur.

Get the family talking about their cybersecurity-related problems, current occurrences, and fears. It is critical that all family members understand the need of reporting any suspicious conduct or security breaches promptly in order to address them appropriately. Make a plan for how you and your loved ones would respond in the event of a cyberattack or other security incident. Included in this are methods for reporting vulnerabilities, informing cybersecurity professionals, and isolating affected devices.

Enrolling in awareness and continuing education classes is a great way for cybersecurity professionals to stay educated about current dangers, trends, and best practices. Make sure your loved ones know how important it is to be cautious and take precautions while using the internet.

Knowing the importance of data security and doing all they can to keep themselves and their families safe online may go a long way towards making the internet a better place for everyone. Help those you care about learn how to use technology safely and responsibly by providing them with the resources they need (Eddermoug et al., 2019).

9.10 INFORMATION SECURITY AWARENESS FOR POLICE

It is crucial that families understand the significance of information security in this digital age, when houses are more connected and reliant on technology. The following should be considered while attempting to increase families' knowledge of information security.

It doesn't matter how old they are; all family members should get comprehensive cybersecurity training. This includes things like using strong passwords, being aware of phishing attempts, and being careful while using the internet in general.

Be sure to emphasize how important it is to lock down all electronic devices, including smart home gadgets, tablets, and laptops. Use antivirus software, update software periodically, and use strong passwords to fight against malware infestations and unauthorized access.

Give your loved ones the rundown on how to be safe while they're dealing with sensitive information online. Part of this includes being aware of how various platforms manage privacy settings, being cautious about revealing too much personal information when posting on social media, and so on.

Tell them to be careful while they're online by telling them to only connect to public Wi-Fi at home, not to accept attachments from unknown senders, and to stay away from suspicious sites.

To monitor your children's internet activities, set up parental controls on their devices and routers. These apps make it easy to limit screen time and access to inappropriate content.

Members of the family, especially those who are younger, should exercise caution while using social media because of the risks associated with cyberbullying, online predators, and oversharing. Encourage those using social media to exercise care and thoughtfulness while doing so.

Stress the need of regularly backing up important files and data to the cloud or external hard drives to everyone in the company. As a result, data loss due to virus attacks, hardware failure, or other unforeseen events is less likely to occur.

Initiate open dialogue about recent occurrences, challenges, and worries in the family that pertain to cybersecurity. It is critical to emphasize the importance of family members reporting any suspicious activities or security breaches promptly in order to take the appropriate action.

Make a plan for how your family will respond to cybersecurity incidents, including steps to do in the event of a hack or security breach. This includes procedures for reporting problems, quarantining compromised devices, and getting in touch with cybersecurity professionals (Muzammal et al., 2020).

You may stay up-to-date on the latest cybersecurity threats, trends, and best practices by taking part in awareness and continuing education courses. Make sure your loved ones know how important it is to be cautious and take measures to protect their online selves.

By understanding the importance of information security and implementing practical measures to safeguard themselves online, families can contribute to making the internet a safer and more welcoming environment for all users. Giving loved ones the knowledge and tools they need to use technology responsibly and securely is of the utmost importance.

9.11 INFORMATION SECURITY AWARENESS FOR GOVERNMENT EMPLOYEES AND EMPLOTERS

Government employees and private sector employers alike need personalized approaches to information security training that take into account the unique roles, duties, and risks that each group encounters on the job. Presented below is a comprehensive plan:

Training courses should be tailored to the needs of businesses and government agencies in order to meet their unique responsibilities. Included in this are sessions on cybersecurity regulations, processes, and best practices that are relevant to their specific work responsibilities.

To keep government employees and businesses informed on the latest cybersecurity threats, trends, and mitigation strategies, training sessions should be conducted regularly. These sessions may be conducted in person or via a variety of online platforms to make them as convenient and accessible as possible.

Organizations in the private and public sectors can do well to provide their staff with phishing awareness training via online simulations. The primary goal of these activities is to learn how to recognize and avoid phishing emails.

The public has to be informed about the rules, guidelines, and prerequisites for meeting the government's cybersecurity compliance obligations immediately. In order to keep everyone on the job safe, it is imperative that all employees understand and adhere to these regulations. Companies and workers alike are included in this.

Businesses and government agencies may prepare for cyberattacks by enrolling in a course that teaches incident response policies and techniques. Collaboration with appropriate authorities, containment tactics, and reporting standards are discussed in this section.

Everyone has to be kept informed about cybersecurity warnings, best practices, and improvements, therefore it's crucial to build up lines of communication. Email newsletters, intranet portals, and bulletin boards are just a few of the ways that cybersecurity news and updates may be kept up-to-date.

Implementing role-based access control is necessary to safeguard sensitive government data and systems. Government employees and their employers are given authorization according to their duties using this manner. By making it more difficult for unauthorized users to get access, this strategy reduces the likelihood of data breaches.

In cases when government employees and employers engage in remote work or work from home, it is very crucial to provide instructions on secure remote work practices. When it comes to remote access, this means using secure VPN connections, multi-factor authentication, and encrypted communication tools.

Regularly do security audits and assessments to identify any weak spots and gauge the efficacy of current security solutions. Apply the findings to fortify the security posture and fix any discovered vulnerabilities ahead of time.

It is only fair to acknowledge and compensate government workers and businesses who demonstrate outstanding cybersecurity practices and help keep the workplace safe. In addition to encouraging responsible actions, this highlights the significance of being aware of cybersecurity issues.

These strategies may help government agencies increase cybersecurity awareness and resilience by educating both employees and employers on the need of protecting sensitive data. As a result, the organization's cybersecurity is enhanced and critical government data and systems are better protected from cyber threats.

9.12 CONCLUSIONS

Cybercrime in the present day gives rise to several issues, notably its adverse effects on the economy, society, and individuals. Cybercrime has developed throughout time because of increased global connectivity and developments in technology. Consequently, in response to these advancements, new legal provisions have been established to tackle the emerging risks. The COVID-19 pandemic, the IoT, and AI have all had a role in the rise in cybercrime rates, highlighting the need of intensifying efforts in cybersecurity.

Software upgrades, encryption, awareness campaigns, education, strict legislation, and international collaboration are all part of a complete approach for preventing hostile cyber activities. Some software solutions that have been effective in preventing cybercrime include IDSs and antivirus software.

AI plays a crucial role in combating cybercrime by facilitating automated reactions, efficiently handling vast quantities of data, and enabling instantaneous identification of threats. AI is a transformative force in the world of cybersecurity. It offers firms unparalleled support in detecting, deterring, and addressing the activities of cybercriminals. Organizations may benefit from information security awareness efforts that are tailored for women, families, government personnel, and enterprises. Programs like this one provide information, training, and practices that may be used to reduce the impact of cyber hazards. Effective navigation of the digital environment requires individuals and organizations to use suitable software solutions and cybersecurity measures that are driven by AI. By strengthening the internet's defenses, it enhances its overall security, so ensuring a safer experience for all users.

REFERENCES

Ahsan, M. M., Gupta, K. D., Nag, A. K., Poudyal, S., Kouzani, A. Z., & Mahmud, M. A. P. (2020). Applications and evaluations of bio-inspired approaches in cloud security: A Review. *IEEE Access: Practical Innovations, Open Solutions*, *8*, 180799–180814. doi:10.1109/access.2020.3027841

Amaral, D. M., Gondim, J. J. C., De Oliveira Albuquerque, R., Orozco, A. L. S., & Villalba, L. J. G. (2019). Hy-SAIL: Hyper-scalability, availability and integrity layer for cloud storage systems. *IEEE Access: Practical Innovations, Open Solutions*, *7*, 90082–90093. doi:10.1109/access.2019.2925735

Deebak, B. D., & Al-Turjman, F. (2021). Smart mutual authentication protocol for cloud based medical healthcare systems using internet of medical things. *IEEE Journal on Selected Areas in Communications*, *39*(2), 346–360. doi:10.1109/jsac.2020.3020599

Eddermoug, N., Sadik, M., Sabir, E., Mansour, A., & Azmi, M. (2019, June). PPSA: Profiling and preventing security attacks in cloud computing. *2019 15th International Wireless Communications & Mobile Computing Conference (IWCMC)*. Presented at the 2019 15th International Wireless Communications and Mobile Computing Conference (IWCMC), Tangier, Morocco. doi:10.1109/iwcmc.2019.8766621

Gupta, I., Gupta, R., Singh, A. K., & Buyya, R. (2021). MLPAM: A machine learning and probabilistic analysis based model for preserving security and privacy in cloud environment. *IEEE Systems Journal*, *15*(3), 4248–4259. doi:10.1109/jsyst.2020.3035666

Muzammal, S. M., Murugesan, R. K., Jhanjhi, N. Z., & Jung, L. T. (2020, October 8). SMTrust: Proposing trust-based secure routing protocol for RPL attacks for IoT applications. *2020 International Conference on Computational Intelligence (ICCI).* Presented at the 2020 International Conference on Computational Intelligence (ICCI), Bandar Seri Iskandar, Malaysia. doi:10.1109/icci51257.2020.9247818

Qiao, F., Wu, J., Li, J., Bashir, A. K., Mumtaz, S., & Tariq, U. (2021). Trustworthy edge storage orchestration in intelligent transportation systems using reinforcement learning. *IEEE Transactions on Intelligent Transportation Systems: A Publication of the IEEE Intelligent Transportation Systems Council, 22*(7), 4443–4456. doi:10.1109/tits.2020.3003211

Rukavitsyn, A., Borisenko, K., & Shorov, A. (2017). Self-learning method for DDoS detection model in cloud computing. *2017 IEEE Conference of Russian Young Researchers in Electrical and Electronic Engineering (EIConRus).* Presented at the 2017 IEEE Conference of Russian Young Researchers in Electrical and Electronic Engineering (EIConRus), St. Petersburg and Moscow, Russia. doi:10.1109/eiconrus.2017.7910612

Sneps-Sneppe, M., Sukhomlin, V., & Namiot, D. (2019, October). On enterprise information systems and cyber threats: Some pentagon's shortcomings and newer initiatives. *2019 11th International Congress on Ultra Modern Telecommunications and Control Systems and Workshops (ICUMT).* Presented at the 2019 11th International Congress on Ultra Modern Telecommunications and Control Systems and Workshops (ICUMT), Dublin, Ireland. doi:10.1109/icumt48472.2019.8970991

Tan, C. B., Hijazi, M. H. A., Lim, Y., Park, Y. J., & Nisar, K. (2018, November). Performance efficiency analysis on slepian-wolf based proof of retrievability and its variants for cloud storage. *2018 IEEE International Conference on Artificial Intelligence in Engineering and Technology (IICAIET).* Presented at the 2018 IEEE International Conference on Artificial Intelligence in Engineering and Technology (IICAIET), Kota Kinabalu, Malaysia. doi:10.1109/iicaiet.2018.8638472

Ugale, B. A., Soni, P., Pema, T., & Patil, A. (2011, December). Role of cloud computing for smart grid of India and its cyber security. *2011 Nirma University International Conference on Engineering.* Presented at the 2011 Nirma University International Conference on Engineering (NUiCONE), Ahmedabad, Gujarat, India. doi:10.1109/nuicone.2011.6153298

CHAPTER 10

Insight into How Legal and Ethical Consideration Improve Artificial Intelligence Capabilities to Enhance the Performance of Cyber Forensic Accounting

Pham Quang Huy and M.A. Vu Kien Phuc

10.1 INTRODUCTION

The development of the accounting profession has been significantly influenced by Artificial Intelligence (AI) (Johnson et al., 2021). Companies currently collect and store massive amounts and a wide variety of data due to improvements in data collection technology and a significant decrease in storage costs. The necessity for technology like AI that can conduct successful analysis has been sparked by the growing availability of data. In order to complete particular tasks, AI uses robots to comprehend and learn from data. Nevertheless, the application of AI-based technologies is still in its infancy, little emphasis is given to examining their function, relevance, and influence in accounting (Mancini et al., 2021). A small amount of attention is given to the role and relevance of these technologies in the accounting environment, despite the fact that there are many academic and professional publications on the use of intelligent technologies in various areas, such as commercial and marketing activities, strategic processes, and business models. Therefore, research into how accountants can employ AI to improve performance is still in its early stages (Kommunuri, 2022).

DOI: 10.1201/9781032714813-10

Accounting is very relevant to cybersecurity and safety breaches (Gonçalves et al., 2022). Cybersecurity experts have recently begun to investigate AI methods to enhance cybersecurity. Overall, there are both positive and negative effects of AI on cybersecurity. The advent of AI in cybersecurity can be advantageous, but it can also present difficulties (Taddeo, 2019). The advent of cyber forensic accounting is driven by technological breakthroughs, modifications to corporate processes, regulatory reforms, and changes in the global economic environment (Hossain, 2023). Another new development is cyber forensic accounting, which looks into and guards against online financial fraud crimes like identity theft, hacking, and phishing (Akinbowale et al., 2020). In order to prevent financial crime, academics and professionals are concerned that the development of information technology will make it more difficult to apply the advantages of AI to forensic accounting.

Assuring the morality of decisions made using data provided by AI and other information technologies is one of the difficulties surrounding its usage in accounting (Bocean & Vărzaru, 2022). Due to the fact that digital technologies raise the ethical bar of decision-making, compliance with ethical criteria related to their use in accounting is crucial. Although accounting professionals are aware of the significance of making moral decisions when implementing and using AI, academic research on these ethical challenges has lagged. In reality, the ethical implications of utilizing any technologies in accounting have received little consideration. It is unknown whether ethical issues will arise from the actual use and use of AI in the accounting industry (Zhang et al., 2023). The ethical issues associated with the deployment of AI have recently come to the attention of authorities. Only a small amount of study has been done on the ethical implications of AI in the accounting profession (Zhang et al., 2023), particularly in the area of cyber forensic accounting.

To the best of our knowledge, there is currently no comprehensive framework on how legal and ethical consideration (LEC) can encourage AI capabilities (AICs) to improve and enhance the performance of cyber forensic accounting (PCFA) that can serve as a starting point for future researchers. Given the growing importance of LEC for applications of AI and the important contributions that AI may provide, this paucity of research is remarkable. Additionally, this theoretical gap sparks the fascinating research questions (RQs) as follows:

RQ1. What is the effect of LEC on PCFA?

RQ2. Does AIC mediate the interconnection between LEC and PCFA?

The current work is ground-breaking from a theoretical standpoint in the context of a developing country. By developing a framework that can interpret the impact of LEC on PCFA and, through this, offer specific recommendations, the current research's findings expand the current frontiers of understandings on LEC in AI implementation in accounting practices (i.e., Bocean & Vărzaru, 2022; Zhang et al., 2023). This may be helpful for academics and aspiring professionals who want to employ AI in forensic accounting and cybersecurity. Additionally, the novelty and value come from giving academics and professionals alike a comprehensive view of the mediating role of AIC in the interconnection between LEC and PCFA. AI is one of the digital technologies that is pondered to have the biggest impact on accounting because it enables the identification of patterns in vast amounts of accounting data that can aid in decision-making for businesses and be used by stakeholders to conduct financial analyses. AIC is the capacity of an innovation team to use AI machines to mimic human cognitive capabilities and carry out activities intelligently, such as learning and problem-solving (Syam & Sharma, 2018).

In the practical significance, the empirical findings of this chapter will help practitioners better understand the impact of LEC on PCFA and the necessity to focus on developing and implementing LEC by providing them with useful information. The research's observations provide clear and comprehensive instructions for executives who aspire to become AICs. As a result, the findings of the research may also assist senior managers in small and medium enterprises (SMEs) in better planning their aims and timely resource allocation in the interest of PCFA improvement. This chapter gave policymakers a clear understanding of how to create laws and policies for the use of LEC in AI implementation. It also gave them advice on how to focus their efforts on achieving PCFA through digitalization.

The remainder of this manuscript is scheduled as follows. Section 10.2 provides theoretical insight, and Section 10.3 offers the manuscript's study hypotheses and recommended model. Section 10.4 describes the study's research methodology. The penultimate section delves deeper into the analysis and discussion of the results. The final section discusses the implications and future research directions.

10.2 LITERATURE REVIEW LITERATURE REVIEW AND THEORETICAL BASIS

10.2.1 Theoretical Lenses Adoption

Institutional theory. According to institutional theory, a firm's structures, policies, and practices are shaped through institutional changes. In order to strengthen their positions and legitimacy, organizations must abide by the laws and customs of the institutional environment (Bruton et al., 2010). This theory is used by researchers to examine how institutions, whether inside to an organization or external, affect the design, application, and results of technologies. Because of this, the operations of any corporation also reflect the expectations of its institutional stakeholders as well as the laws and customs of the institutional setting. Institutional pressures are thus created by these expectations, laws, and conventions, compelling businesses to adopt cutting-edge procedures (Jiang et al., 2023). Despite the fact that institutional theory has frequently been studied in the context of bigger organizations (Bruton et al., 2010), institutional theory has emerged as a key theory to explain events in small and entrepreneurial enterprises (Yousafzai et al., 2015).

Resource-based view theory. According to the resource-based view theory, key resources determine how well a company performs (Chatterjee et al., 2021). Within a company, resources can be both material and immaterial assets (Mikalef & Gupta, 2021). This thesis states that precious, uncommon, unique, and irreplaceable resources can develop a competitive advantage by adding value and enhancing business performance. Such a benefit can last for a very long time. Resource-based view theory is commonly used to show how firm capabilities, resources, and performance are related (Chen & Lin, 2021). The resource-based view theory has been employed extensively in earlier studies in the larger information system domain. More specifically, Melville et al. (2004) acknowledge the potential of resource-based view theory to enable empirically testable hypotheses that increase our understanding of the function of information system resources in organizational success. The AIC is becoming an increasingly important and intangible resource for improving corporate performance (Mikalef & Gupta, 2021). According to Chaudhuri et al. (2024), all organizations may benefit from using AI to get a competitive edge. Indeed, businesses may gain access to priceless, uncommon, unique, and irreplaceable resources through AIC (Ghasemaghaei, 2021). The resource-based view theory offers a suitable theoretical foundation since gaining a competitive edge requires an understanding of the specific AI resources that a corporation must manage.

10.2.2 Conceptual Respects

Cyber forensic accounting. According to Rezaee et al. (2016), forensic accounting is the application of science and technology to unearth dishonest accounting, financial, and company practices. This aids in the detection and prevention of financial fraud as well as the reduction of corruption and the prosecution of financial crimes. More specifically, the main responsibility of forensic accountants is to investigate illegal activities such as fraud, white-collar crime, corruption, money laundering, computer fraud, conversion, and theft. Forensic accounting guarantees that financial statements give reliable information to diverse stakeholders so they can protect their interests and make important business decisions. Remarkably, it can be difficult to collect pertinent data and spot trends from the huge amounts of data used in cybercrimes. Hacking, identity theft, cyberstalking, and phishing are only a few of the varied types of cybercrimes that can occur (Hossain, 2023). To locate the sources of cyberattacks and recover stolen funds, it involves a variety of approaches including data analytics, digital forensics, and financial investigations. In this regard, cyber forensic accounting is the application of forensic accounting principles to the investigation and prevention of cybercrimes (Hossain, 2023).

Artificial Intelligence and artificial intelligence capabilities. AI is described as technology that displays elements of human intelligence (Huang & Rust, 2018). As technology advances, it now tries to automatically recognize the complex patterns concealed behind data and make wise decisions based on detected data patterns. AI refers to the use of technology tools to attain goals autonomously while taking into account any potential limits while Mariani et al. (2022) argued that AI is defined as computational entities that operate intelligently in order to perceive, learn, memorize, reason, and solve problems in order to engage in goal-directed action. According to Mikalef and Gupta (2021), the AIC of firms is defined as the capacity of firms to develop, integrate, and use resources based on AI. AIC is the capacity of an innovation team to use AI machines to mimic human cognitive capabilities and carry out activities intelligently, such as learning and problem-solving.

Legal and ethical consideration. Many nations and localities have adopted ethical guidelines after realizing the risks that AI poses to morality. In a declaration published in March 2018, the European Group on Ethics in Science and New Technologies outlined seven fundamental principles. These include upholding human dignity by forbidding the use of discriminatory AI algorithms, guaranteeing human autonomy and transparency in decision-making processes involving AI systems, accepting responsibility for preventing harm caused by AI, promoting justice and fairness by addressing biases and creating mechanisms for equitable distribution, enforcing the rule of law and accountability for damages caused by AI, placing a priority on security and safety in human-machine interactions, and more. The "Artificial Intelligence Governance Principles in the New Generation: Developing Responsible Artificial Intelligence" was published by the Chinese Artificial Intelligence Governance Committee in 2019. These five fundamental ethical standards are included. Harmony and friendliness highlight the importance of upholding human ethics and preventing aAI abuse. The goals of justice and fairness are to uphold the rights and interests of all parties. Transparent, dependable, and interpretable aAI systems are necessary for safety and controllability. Stakeholder accountability for aAI development and use is encouraged via shared responsibility. Respecting privacy stops criminal activity involving aAI-used data. These guidelines offer managers, developers, and regulators direction for reducing the ethical hazards associated with aAI. In addition, Professional associations and regulatory bodies in the accounting industry have developed codes of conduct to regulate the accountability of accounting professionals when employing technologies.

10.3 HYPOTHESIS DEVELOPMENT AND RESEARCH MODEL ESTABLISHMENT

Numerous organizational, national, and international documents outlining ethical principles for the deployment of aAI have been produced as a result of the widespread recognition and discussion of the ethical significance of using aAI. To avoid mass monitoring, human deskilling, and other threats brought on by aAI systems that are not under human control, ethical evaluations are required (Taddeo, 2019). Regulations are required to promote ethical conduct, safeguard the rights of individuals, and identify legitimate actors and targets (Taddeo, 2019). Inevitably, the legal system and forensic accountants as expert witnesses will be impacted by aAI. According to Hossain (2023), forensic accounting research will be significant and germane to the ongoing judicial system's adaption to aAI technology since forensic accountants play a crucial role as expert witnesses. Against this backdrop, the higher attention in LEC in AI implementation will enable firms to improve and enhance PCFA. In light of analysis covered above, the first hypothesis of this study is logically proposed as follows:

Hypothesis 1 (H1). LEC brings forth a significant and positive effect on PCFA.

A digital solution may fail even when it functions accurately if the necessary conditions are not met (Biable et al., 2022). Engineering needs are frequently fulfilled without taking ethical considerations into account, which results in numerous ethical violations. AI solutions' security, safety, secrecy, transparency, and integrity have given rise to ethical concerns when they are used in corporate activities and processes.

Accordingly, authorities have begun to consider the societal and ethical ramifications of AI, as seen in documents like the OECD guidelines (Boza & Evgeniou, 2021) and the European Union's aAI plan (Csernatoni, 2019). In these, governments demand that aAI benefit individuals and the global community, ensure a just society, have transparent and responsible disclosure, be durable, secure, and safe across their lifespan, and hold creators liable for AIs' appropriate operation. In this regard, the higher attention in LEC in aAI implementation will enable firms to develop, integrate, and optimize resources for supplier sourcing and internal and external resource allocation based on aAI. In light of analysis covered above, the second hypothesis of this study is logically proposed as follows:

Hypothesis 2 (H2). *LEC engenders a significant and positive effect on AIC.*

With higher AIC, almost all of the enterprises can devote much more human resources to a variety of organizational activities (Mikalef & Gupta, 2021). Notably, cyberattacks are viewed from the standpoint of AI as hostile patterns that are distinct from legal Internet traffic. Because aAI approaches have the ability to analyze vast amounts of data and adapt to the changing nature of Internet traffic, intrusion-detection systems have been designed to discriminate between malicious and lawful traffic. Intrusion-detection systems are where aAI is most useful in the cybersecurity field. Large quantities of Internet traffic may today be automatically and intelligently analyzed and classified using AI. Cybersecurity solutions based on machine learning technologies are being utilized to automate the detection of assaults and to develop and improve their capabilities over time. Intrusion-detection systems are using machine learning-based solutions because they can manage huge data volumes and a variety of data properties needed for categorization.

Based on the perspectives of Leitner-Hanetseder et al. (2021), AI-based technology will soon be used to prepare relevant reports, value assets and liabilities, and undertake intercompany reconciliation tasks. Full automation of a number of time-consuming procedures, including verifying payment transactions and retrieving supporting data for corroborative evidence in substantive testing for auditors, is made possible by AI. It assists in extracting sales, contracts, expenses, and other crucial decision-making data from complicated electronic documents by scanning keywords and patterns in the text. Additionally, aAI technologies can identify any anomalous amounts reported in transactions, which will result in a significant reduction in routine accounting work over the next few years (Kommunuri, 2022). AI technologies are the most crucial methods for analyzing the massive amounts of data and can be seen as a key to improving procedures and applications in

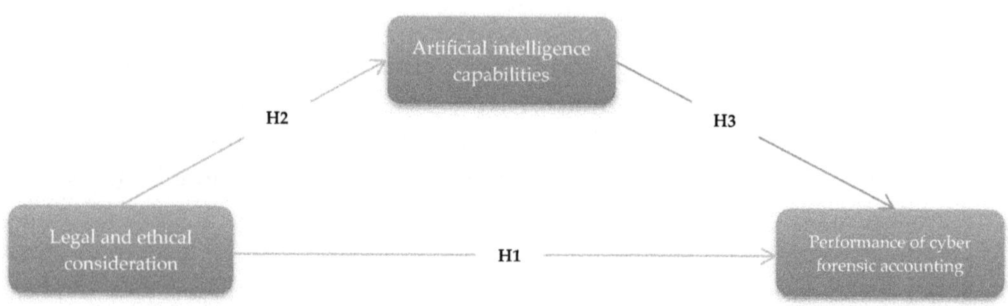

FIGURE 10.1 Hypothesized model.

forensic accounting. In light of analysis covered above, the third hypothesis of this study is logically proposed as follows (Figure 10.1):

Hypothesis 3 (H3). *AIC brings forth a significant and positive effect on PCFA.*

10.4 METHODS AND MATERIALS

10.4.1 Operationalization of Research Variables

A quantitative research deductive design was employed in this study. The research design of this study is illustrated in Figure 10.2. In order to fulfill the objectives of the study, a thorough literature analysis was undertaken to develop the research constructions, and various items from each construct were discovered to be used in the construction of the draft questionnaire. After being created in English initially, the questionnaire was validated by means of a back-translation method (Wilson, 2014). This work is taken on by two bilingual specialists who could speak both English and Vietnamese. A pretest is used to make sure there will not be any unanticipated problems with the questionnaire because it is developed in a variety of cultural and environmental contexts. In order to ensure that all of the measuring items are clear and to get feedback for improvements, the first edition of the survey questionnaire is initially distributed to seven academics and nine managers of SMEs. As a result of their insightful comments, the survey's questionnaire is updated to incorporate a few more significant assessment items.

Legal and ethical consideration. The first-order construct of LEC comprises of five second-order constructs, including cybersecurity, data protection and privacy, Intellectual property law, transparency and effectiveness, algorithmic fairness and biases which are designed from those propounded by Gerke et al. (2020).

Performance of cyber forensic accounting. The first-order construct for assessing the PCFA comprises of four second-order constructs such as cyber anti-fraud policies, IT governance, digital designed forensic procedure, and management control system. More concretely, the criteria employed to evaluate cyber anti-fraud policies in this research are taken as reference

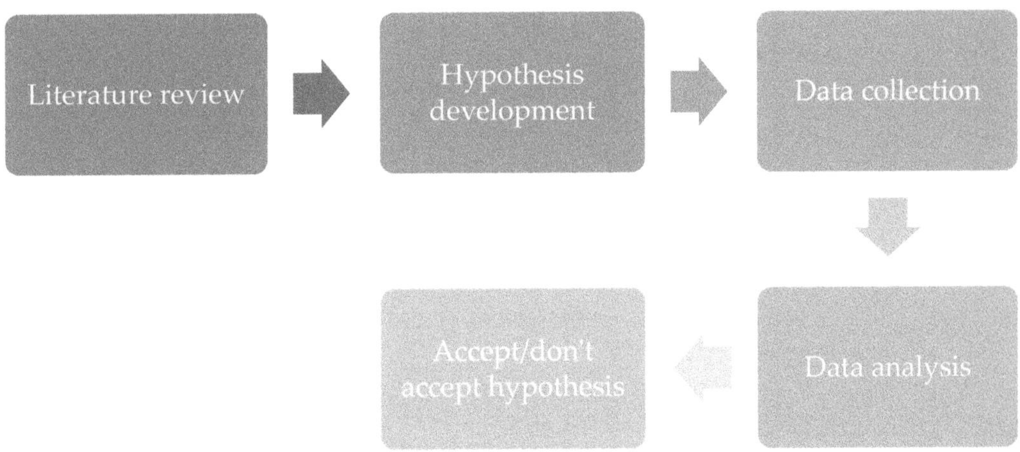

FIGURE 10.2 Research flow chart.

from the contributions of Lloyd Bierstaker (2009), Hossain (2023). The criteria employed to evaluate IT governance in this research are taken as reference from the contributions of Al-Zwyalif (2013), Al-Taee and Flayyih (2023). The criteria employed to evaluate digital designed forensic procedure in this research are taken as reference from the contributions of Ogundele et al. (2023). The criteria employed to evaluate management control system in this research are taken as reference from the contributions of Akinbowale et al. (2021).

Artificial intelligence capabilities. The first-order construct of AIC embodies three second-order constructs including basic, proclivity, and skills which are developed from the contributions of Chatterjee et al. (2021); Mikalef and Gupta (2021).

10.4.2 Target Population and Sampling Procedure

The study's primary data are gathered via a paper-and-pencil questionnaire. SMEs are the subject of the analysis, and one accountant should be able to complete the questionnaire. Non-probability sampling, along with convenient sampling methods and purposeful sampling, is the method used in this study. Hair et al. (2011) suggested that the minimum sample size for Partial Least Square-Structural Equation Modeling (PLS-SEM) should be ten times greater than or equal to the structural path shown in any structural model. Data were collected between the months of August 2022 and March 2023. The responses that had more than 15% of their items missing would be removed from the dataset (Hair et al., 2022). After screening and evaluating the questionnaires, a sample size of 723 cases was left, with a data loss rate of 13.93%. To examine the statistical data for this study, SPSS 29.0 and SmartPLS 4.0.9.2 were used. Table 10.1 provided a thorough breakdown of the demographic information gathered throughout the survey.

TABLE 10.1 Distribution of Participants Based on Demographic Characteristics

Item	Contents	Frequency	Valid (%)
Gender			
	Male	392	54.22
	Female	331	45.78
Age (years)			
	Under 30	22	3.04
	30– Under 40	456	63.07
	40– Under 50	213	29.46
	Above 50	32	4.43
Education			
	Undergraduate	672	92.95
	Postgraduate	51	7.05
Experience (years)			
	Under 10	22	3.04
	10– Under 20	463	64.04
	20– Under 30	206	28.49
	Over 30	32	4.43

10.5 RESULTS AND ELUCIDATION ANALYTICAL OBSERVATIONS

10.5.1 Measurement Model Evaluation

Construct validity and reliability. All variables have values higher than 0.70 when the internal consistency reliability of the measuring items is examined using Cronbach's alpha. To evaluate convergent validity, the convergent validity (CR) and average variance extracted (AVE) were used. All constructs' CR values vary from 0.901 to 0.936, which were well above 0.7 (Hair et al., 2022). The observed AVE values varied from 0.649 to 0.830 which were well above 0.5 (Hair et al., 2022). The values of Dijkstra–Henseler's ρA were reported to be higher than 0.7 (Dijkstra & Henseler, 2015). The construct validity and reliability of the hypothesized model were auspiciously attained, according to the statistical corroboration of these criteria in Table 10.2.

Correlations and discriminant validity. The heterotrait-monotrait (HTMT) correlation ratio was advised for use in assessing discriminant validity (Hair et al., 2022). For the investigation in conceptually comparable constructs, a threshold value of 0.90 was acceptable, but a somewhat lower threshold value of 0.85 was acceptable for conceptually different structures (Henseler et al., 2016). There was sufficient discriminant validity as all observed HTMT values fall below the specified limitations. The obtained values in Table 10.3 demonstrate the discriminant validity test using HTMT ratios.

10.5.2 Structural Model Evaluation

None of the observed VIFs in this investigation were greater than three, showing that there were no collinearity problems (Becker et al., 2015). To determine the significance of the

TABLE 10.2 Results Summary for Convergent Validity

Constructs and Operationalization Factor Loadings		Convergent Validity AVE	Cronbach's Alpha	Construct Reliability Composite Reliability	PA		Result
Legal and Ethical Consideration	**LEC**						
Cybersecurity	CYB	0.822–0.881	0.709	0.863	0.907	0.866	Retained
Data protection and privacy	DPP	0.827–0.952	0.783	0.881	0.915	1.288	Retained
Intellectual property law	IPL	0.806–0.850	0.696	0.854	0.901	0.858	Retained
Transparency and effectiveness	TE	0.887–0.904	0.799	0.874	0.923	0.880	Retained
Algorithmic fairness and biases	AFB	0.898–0.916	0.822	0.892	0.933	0.896	Retained
Performance of Cyber forensic accounting	**PCFA**						
Cyber anti-fraud policies	CAFP	0.780–0.829	0.649	0.865	0.902	0.869	Retained
IT governance	ITG	0.806–0.873	0.704	0.859	0.905	0.860	Retained
Digital designed forensic procedure	DDFP	0.802–0.865	0.715	0.867	0.909	0.870	Retained
Management control system	MCS	0.868–0.895	0.779	0.858	0.913	0.860	Retained
Artificial intelligence capabilities	**AIC**						
Artificial intelligence basic	AIB	0.879–0.904	0.797	0.873	0.922	0.879	Retained
Artificial intelligence skills	AISK	0.898–0.910	0.815	0.886	0.930	0.887	Retained
Artificial intelligence proclivity	AIP	0.902–0.920	0.830	0.897	0.936	0.898	Retained

TABLE 10.3 Results Summary for Discriminant Validity on Heterotrait–Monotrait Ratio

	AFB	AIB	AIP	AISK	CAFP	CYB	DDFP	DPP	IPL	ITG	MCS	TE
AFB												
AIB	0.036											
AIP	0.065	0.138										
AISK	0.081	0.208	0.149									
CAFP	0.147	0.123	0.097	0.318								
CYB	0.050	0.123	0.089	0.116	0.252							
DDFP	0.030	0.058	0.071	0.145	0.071	0.107						
DPP	0.039	0.082	0.071	0.048	0.073	0.155	0.041					
IPL	0.124	0.047	0.019	0.040	0.059	0.060	0.063	0.040				
ITG	0.083	0.072	0.034	0.112	0.141	0.115	0.160	0.036	0.197			
MCS	0.067	0.089	0.045	0.073	0.119	0.135	0.216	0.064	0.086	0.148		
TE	0.186	0.082	0.046	0.083	0.185	0.084	0.043	0.136	0.225	0.034	0.020	

path coefficients, the bootstrapping approach was utilized. This method uses percentile bootstrapping, a two-tailed test, a 0.05 threshold of significance, and 10,000 resamples. The statistical outcomes substantiate that LEC induces significant and positive impact on PCFA (β = 0.226; t-value = 4.534; p-value = 0.000). In the same vein, LEC is authenticated to illustrate a noteworthy and positive impact on AIC (β = 0.136; t-value = 2.893; p-value = 0.004). Additionally, the mathematical analysis underlines that AIC has a significant impact on PCFA (β = 0.215; t-value = 4.925; p-value = 0.000). Thus, H2, H2, H3 are accepted.

The significance of the direct path (LEC → PCFA) and the significance of the indirect or mediated paths (LEC → AIC → PCFA) are shown in Table 10.4. Thus, AIC was verified to partially mediate the effect of LEC on PCFA since both the direct and indirect pathways from LEC to PCFA were relevant.

The R^2 was 0.018 for AIC and 0.111 for PCFA. The analysis reveals that LEC has a small effect size on AIC (0.019) and PCFA (0.056). In the same vein, AIC has a small effect size on PCFA (0.051). The Q^2 was 0.006 for AIC and 0.026 for PCFA.

TABLE 10.4 Results of Hypotheses Testing

Relevant Path	Path Coefficient	SE	95% Confidence Interval	VIF	t-value	p-value	Result
Direct effect							
LEC → PCFA	0.226	0.050	[0.111–0.308]	1.019	4.534	0.000	Accepted
LEC → AIC	0.136	0.047	[0.029–0.214]	1.000	2.893	0.004	Accepted
AIC → PCFA	0.215	0.044	[0.130–0.301]	1.019	4.925	0.000	Accepted
Indirect effect							
LEC → AIC → PCFA	0.029	0.011	[0.006–0.050]	-	2.598	0.009	Accepted
R^2	$R^2_{AIC} = 0.018$; $R^2_{CFAC} = 0.111$						
f^2	$f^2_{LEC => PFAC} = 0.056$; $f^2_{LEC => AIC} = 0.019$; $f^2_{AIC => PFAC} = 0.051$						
Q^2	$Q^2_{AIC} = 0.006$; $Q^2_{CFAC} = 0.026$						

10.6 CONCLUSION

10.6.1 Implication in Practice

Using management viewpoints as a foundation, the study's findings provided a wealth of actionable takeaways. The research's findings suggest that considerably more effort should be put towards developing and improving PCFA within SMEs. In order to guarantee the accuracy and dependability of investigation findings, senior managers in SMEs and policymakers alike should pay greater attention to LEC connected to data analytics, digital forensics, and other digital technologies application in forensic accounting. Therefore, the legal and ethical standards for data analytics, cybersecurity protocols for cyber forensic accounting, and regulatory frameworks for the use of digital technologies in forensic accounting should be developed and published by legislators and governmental influencers. The procedures put in place to combat cyber fraud and other related fraud activities should be strictly followed, according to policymakers and other governmental influences (Ogundele et al., 2023). In order to use new trends in forensic accounting, practitioners and policymakers need to collaborate to produce best practices and guidelines. To lessen the recurrent occurrence of cyber fraud, digitally created forensic procedures should be applied in organizations (Ogundele et al., 2023).

Forensic accountants need to retain professional skepticism, follow ethical norms and procedures, and manage potential conflicts of interest regarding LEC. They also need to safeguard the confidentiality, integrity, and security of digital evidence. It is challenging for forensic accountants to keep up with the most recent methods and tools used by cybercriminals because cyber risks and attack vectors are continually evolving and growing more sophisticated (Wong & Venkatraman, 2015). The accountants must be aware of the limitations of AI, which cannot yet fully mimic human intelligence (Bocean & V ˇVărzaru, 2022). As a result, cyber forensic accountants need specialized technical skills to collect, analyze, and interpret digital evidence from various sources, such as computer systems, networks, and electronic devices (Akinbowale et al., 2020). Forensic accountants should continually update their skills and knowledge to keep up with the emerging trends in the field. This may involve acquiring specialized training in data analytics, cyber forensic accounting, and AI and staying updated with the latest developments and best practices.

The results will make it possible to prioritize the practices and recommend that senior managers in SMEs should focus more on fostering AIC there. As a result, business executives in SMEs should be aware of the benefits of contemporary information technology and look for practical ways to use aAI across organizational borders and in all internal operations. Additionally, executives of SMEs are urged to make every effort to evenly share the resources required for enhancing and strengthening the organization's information technology infrastructure and implementing sound human resource management procedures. The findings of this study also aid in the creation of laws and regulations for the implementation of aAI by policymakers and other responsible entities, which will foster their general acceptance inside SMEs.

10.6.2 Limitation and Future Lines for Up-Coming Research

There are a number of limitations that should be acknowledged in the current research, and these might serve as the starting points of a departure for up-coming studies. Firstly, it is important to use caution when making generalizations because the specifics of the research context can constrain what can be inferred from the data. Since all of the samples originated in Vietnam, more cross-regional research is required to corroborate the results before they can be used generally. In order to obtain more in-depth knowledge, extra data from developed and emerging markets may be gathered. Scholars are advised to conduct comparison studies between emerging and developed nations in order to achieve more fruitful results. Additionally, this study's statistical data primarily depends on a self-report design. As a result, each organization is received survey forms for just one individual. The results from a single participant may be biased because people with better attitudes may be more inclined to complete and return their survey forms. Future research may therefore consider asking other relevant stakeholders about their perspectives in this situation. The third bottleneck, which is brought on by convenience and purposive selection tactics, may have an effect on the study's generalizability. Future research should employ quota sampling to get sample data in order to ensure that the findings are scientific and representative. The study's fourth issue is the relatively small sample size, which necessitated further investigation. Finally, it is suggested that additional constructs should be added to the model in future studies to create a more accurate depiction of the situation.

ACKNOWLEDGMENT

This chapter was funded by the University of Economics Ho Chi Minh City (UEH) in Vietnam.

REFERENCES

Akinbowale, O. E., Klingelhöfer, H. E., & Zerihun, M. F. (2020). An innovative approach in combating economic crime using forensic accounting techniques. *Journal of Financial Crime, 27*(4), 1253–1271. doi: 10.1108/JFC-04-2020-0053.

Akinbowale, O. E., Klingelhöfer, H. E., & Zerihun, M. F. (2021). The integration of forensic accounting and the management control system as tools for combating cyber fraud. *Academy of Accounting and Financial Studies Journal, 25*(2), 1–14.

Al-Taee, S. H. H., & Flayyih, H. H. (2023). Impact of the electronic internal auditing based on it governance to reduce auditing risk. *Corporate Governance and Organizational Behavior Review, 7*(1), 94–100. doi: 10.22495/cgobrv7i1p9.

Al-Zwyalif, I. M. (2013). IT governance and its impact on the usefulness of accounting information reported in financial statements. *International Journal of Business and Social Science, 4*(2), 83–94.

Becker, J.-M., Ringle, C. M., Sarstedt, M., & Völckner, F. (2015). How collinearity affects mixture regression results. *Marketing Letters, 26*(4), 643–659. doi: 10.1007/s11002-014-9299-9.

Biable, S. E., Garcia, N. M., Midekso, D., & Pombo, N. (2022). Ethical issues in software requirements engineering. *Software, 1*, 31–52. doi: 10.3390/software1010003.

Bocean, C. G., & Vărzaru, A. A. (2022). A two-stage SEM–Artificial neural network analysis of integrating ethical and quality requirements in accounting digital technologies. *Systems, 10*(121), 1–17. doi: 10.3390/systems10040121.

Boza, P., & Evgeniou, T. (2021). *Implementing AI Principles: Frameworks, Processes, and Tools.* INSEAD, Fontainbleau, 1–31.

Bruton, G. D., Ahlstrom, D., & Li, H. (2010). Institutional theory and entrepreneurship: Where are we now and where do we need to move in the future? *Entrepreneurship Theory and Practice, 34*(3), 421–440. doi: 10.1111/j.1540-6520.2010.00390.x.

Chatterjee, S., Rana, N. P., Tamilmani, K., & Sharma, A. (2021). The effect of AI-based CRM on organization performance and competitive advantage: An empirical analysis in the B2B context. *Industrial Marketing Management, 97*, 205–219. doi: 10.1016/j.indmarman.2021.07.013.

Chaudhuri, R., Chatterjee, S., Vrontis, D. et al. (2024). Adoption of robust business analytics for product innovation and organizational performance: The mediating role of organizational data-driven culture. *Annals of Operations Research*, 339, 1757–1791. https://doi.org/10.1007/s10479-021-04407-3.

Chen, Y., & Lin, Z. (2021). Business intelligence capabilities and firm performance: A study in China. *International Journal of Information Management, 57*, 1–15. doi: 10.1016/j.ijinfomgt.2020.102232.

Csernatoni, R. (2019). *An Ambitious Agenda or Big Words? Developing a European Approach to AI.* Egmont Royal Institute for International Relations, Brussels.

Dijkstra, T.K., & Henseler, J. (2015). Consistent partial least squares path modeling. *MIS Quarterly, 39*(2), 297–316.

Gerke, S., Minssen, T., & Cohen, G. (2020). Ethical and legal challenges of artificial intelligence-driven healthcare. *Artificial Intelligence in Healthcare*, 295–336. doi: 10.1016/b978-0-12-818438-7.00012-5.

Ghasemaghaei, M. (2021). Understanding the impact of big data on firm performance: The necessity of conceptually differentiating among big data characteristics. *International Journal of Information Management, 57*, 1–13. doi: 10.1016/j.ijinfomgt.2019.102055.

Gonçalves, M. J. A., da Silva, A. C. F., & Ferreira, C. G. (2022). The future of accounting: How will digital transformation impact the sector? *Informatics, 9*(19), 1–19. doi: 10.3390/informatics9010019.

Hair, J. F., Hult, G. T. M., Ringle, C. M., & Sarstedt, M. (2022). *A Primer on Partial Least Squares Structural Equation Modeling* (PLS-SEM) (3rd ed.). Thousand Oaks, CA: Sage.

Hair, J., Ringle, C., & Sarstedt, M. (2011). PLS-SEM: Indeed a silver bullet. *Journal of Marketing Theory and Practice, 19*, 139–151. doi: 10.2753/MTP1069-6679190202.

Henseler, J., Ringle, C. M., & Sarstedt, M. (2016). Testing measurement invariance of composites using partial least squares. *International Marketing Review, 33*(3), 405–431. doi: 10.1108/imr-09-2014-0304.

Hossain, M. Z. (2023). Emerging trends in forensic accounting: Data analytics, cyber forensic accounting, cryptocurrencies, and blockchain technology for fraud investigation and prevention. *SSRN Electronic Journal*, 1–30. http://dx.doi.org/10.2139/ssrn.4450488.

Huang, M.-H., & Rust, R. T. (2018). Artificial intelligence in service. *Journal of Service Research, 21*(2), 155–172. doi: 10.1177/1094670517752459.

Jiang, M., Chen, L., Blome, C., & Jia, F. (2023). Digital technology adoption for modern slavery risk mitigation in supply chains: An institutional perspective. *Technological Forecasting and Social Change, 192*, 1–15. doi: 10.1016/j.techfore.2023.122595.

Johnson, E., Petersen, M., Sloan, J., & Valencia, A. (2021). The interest, knowledge, and usage of artificial intelligence in accounting: Evidence from accounting professionals. *Accounting & Taxation, 13*(1), 45–58.

Kommunuri, J. (2022). Artificial intelligence and the changing landscape of accounting: A viewpoint. *Pacific Accounting Review, 34*(4), 585–594. doi: 10.1108/PAR-06-2021-0107.

Leitner-Hanetseder, S., Lehner, O. M., Eisl, C., & Forstenlechner, C. (2021). A profession in transition: Actors, tasks and roles in AI-based accounting. *Journal of Applied Accounting Research, 22*(3), 539–556.

Lloyd Bierstaker, J. (2009). Differences in attitudes about fraud and corruption across cultures. *Cross Cultural Management: An International Journal, 16*(3), 241–250. doi: 10.1108/13527600910977337.

Mancini, D., Lombardi, R., & Tavana, M. (2021). Four research pathways for understanding the role of smart technologies in accounting. *Meditari Accountancy Research, 29*(5), 1041–1062, doi: 10.1108/MEDAR-03-2021-1258.

Mariani, M. M., Perez-Vega, R., & Wirtz, J. (2022). AI in marketing, consumer research and psychology: A systematic literature review and research agenda. *Psychology & Marketing, 39*(4), 755–776. doi: 10.1002/mar.21619.

Melville, N., Kraemer, K., & Gurbaxani, V. (2004). Information technology and organizational performance: An integrative model of IT business value. *MIS Quarterly, 28*(2), 283–322. doi: 10.2307/25148636.

Mikalef, P., & Gupta, M. (2021). Artificial intelligence capability: Conceptualization, measurement calibration, and empirical study on its impact on organizational creativity and firm performance. *Information & Management, 58*(3), 1–20. doi: 10.1016/j.im.2021.103434.

Ogundele, A. T., Awodiran, M. A., Idem, U. J., Anwana, & Emem, O. (2023). Digitally designed forensic procedure a panacea to cyber fraud control in Nigeria. *2023 International Conference On Cyber Management and Engineering (CyMaEn)*, 1–7. doi: 10.1109/CyMaEn57228.2023.10050964.

Rezaee, Z., Lo, D., Ha, M., & Suen, A. (2016). Forensic accounting education and practice: Insights from China. *Journal of Forensic and Investigative Accounting, 8*(1), 106–119.

Syam, N., & Sharma, A. (2018). Waiting for a sales renaissance in the fourth industrial revolution: Machine learning and artificial intelligence in sales research and practice. *Industrial Marketing Management, 69*, 135–146. doi: 10.1016/j.indmarman.2017.12.019.

Taddeo, M. (2019). Three ethical challenges of applications of artificial intelligence in cybersecurity. *Minds and Machines, 29*(2), 187–191. doi: 10.1007/s11023-019-09504-8.

Taddeo, M., McCutcheon, T., & Floridi, L. (2019). Trusting artificial intelligence in cybersecurity is a double-edged sword. *Nature Machine Intelligence, 1*(12), 557–560. doi: 10.1038/s42256-019-0109-1.

Wilson, V. (2014). Research methods: Triangulation. *Evidence Based Library and Information Practice, 9*, 74–75. doi: 10.18438/B8WW3X.

Wong, S., & Venkatraman, S. (2015). Financial accounting fraud detection using business intelligence. *Asian Economic and Financial Review, 5*(11), 1187–1207. doi: 10.18488/journal.aefr/2015.5.11/102.11.1187.1207.

Yousafzai, S. Y., Saeed, S., & Muffatto, M. (2015). Institutional theory and contextual embeddedness of women's entrepreneurial leadership: Evidence from 92 countries. *Journal of Small Business Management, 53*(3), 587–604. doi: 10.1111/jsbm.12179.

Zhang, C., Zhu, W., Dai, J., Wu, Y., & Chen, X. (2023). Ethical impact of artificial intelligence in managerial accounting. *International Journal of Accounting Information Systems, 49*, 1–19. doi: 10.1016/j.accinf.2023.100619.

Index

Note: **Bold** page numbers refer to tables and *italic* page numbers refer to figures.

For Product Safety Concerns and Information please contact our EU representative GPSR@taylorandfrancis.com
Taylor & Francis Verlag GmbH, Kaufingerstraße 24, 80331 München, Germany

www.ingramcontent.com/pod-product-compliance
Ingram Content Group UK Ltd.
Pitfield, Milton Keynes, MK11 3LW, UK
UKHW050756180926
475701UK00007B/1079
* 9 7 8 1 0 3 2 7 1 4 8 3 7 *